Compiled & edited by

Trudy Toohill

Published by Boolarong Press,
655 Toohey Road
Salisbury Qld 4107
Australia.
www.boolarongpress.com.au

First published 2015

National Library of Australia Cataloguing-in-Publication entry

Creator: Toohill, Trudy, author.

Title: The reporting of Ned Kelly and the Kelly gang / Trudy Toohill.

ISBN: 9781925236262 (paperback)

Subjects: Kelly, Ned, 1855-1880.
Kelly Gang.
Bushrangers--Victoria--Press coverage.
Outlaws--Victoria--Press coverage.
Victims of crimes in mass media.
Police murders--Victoria.

Dewey Number: 364.1509945

Printed and bound by Watson Ferguson & Company, Salisbury, Australia

CONTENTS

To Sean, Connor & James

Legends aren't born,
they are created by the choices we make.

One hundred and thirty-five years have passed since Ned Kelly was hung in Melbourne Gaol and Dan Kelly, Joe Byrne and Steve Hart died at the horrific siege of Glenrowan. I use the term horrific as many lives were lost that day, not just the three bushrangers, but also many innocent victims who were either 'hostages' or there of their 'own volition'. These innocent victims are often forgotten, but they played an integral part in the history of The Kelly Gang and many paid the ultimate price. The aftermath of the siege of Glenrowan saw numerous lives destroyed and many of these innocent victims suffered for years after.

Sergeant Michael Kennedy, Constable Thomas Lonigan and Constable Michael Scanlon, the three police officers killed by The Kelly Gang are also victims of this tragic history. If you ask members of the public who these men are, most would not have heard of them. But ask anyone who Ned Kelly is and they instantly recognise his name. Why is this so? Should not three police officers who were shot and killed in the line of duty be given more respect than The Kelly Gang who killed them? I use the collective term of The Kelly Gang and not Ned Kelly alone as over the years doubt has been cast as to whether Ned Kelly killed all three officers or whether he killed only Constable Thomas Lonigan. Ned Kelly himself had previously stated that if ever he was to 'kill a man', it would be Constable Thomas Lonigan. This hatred came about as a result of a brutal fight between the two men, when previously Constable Lonigan was attempting to arrest Ned Kelly. Ned Kelly had reason to hate Lonigan. Did he shoot and kill him? Judge Sir Redmond Barry believed he did and in late 1880 Ned Kelly was tried and found guilty of murdering Constable Thomas Lonigan and sentenced to be hanged by the neck until dead. However, Ned Kelly was never trialled for the murder of Sergeant Michael Kennedy or Constable Michael Scanlon. This must have been incredibly difficult for Sergeant Kennedy's wife and children and Constable Michael Scanlon's family. Also should not be forgotten are the descendants of the two murdered police officers. As no-one has ever been convicted for these crimes they have had to live without closure. In some respects, the deaths of these two men were forgotten, even over-looked, by the justice system of the time.

Over the years in Australia, Ned Kelly has become a hero to many Australians. You can buy T-shirts, posters, stickers, letterboxes, you name it these days, you can buy pretty much anything with the name or face of Ned Kelly on it. A number of times I have seen men and women with the tattoo 'Such is Life' and I wonder do they really know the true history of Ned Kelly, the murders of the three police officers at Stringybark Creek, the Siege of Glenrowan, the terrible aftermath and great loss of life? Do they ever wonder what and how the relatives of those involved in this tragic history feel when they see a Ned Kelly T-shirt being worn?

I have heard Ned Kelly described as a cold-blooded killer, villain, murderer, ruffian, thief, selfish and a psychopath, just to name a few. I have also heard him described as a man of tremendous courage, fierce loyalty, brave beyond measure, a true hero, a modern-day Robin Hood who stole from the rich and gave to the poor, a man who fought for what he believed in, passionate and tough as nails. Which words best describe Ned Kelly? Perhaps all of them?

To this day, there is still great debate as to the guilt or innocence of Ned Kelly and The Kelly Gang. Were they victims of the cruel, overpowering Victorian Police, forced into bushranging? Had Ned Kelly been successful in his plan to pull up the train tracks, destroying the Police Special train and taking countless lives in the process, would he still be considered a hero of a nation? If Ned Kelly were taken to court and trialled today would he be found guilty of murder, manslaughter or be innocent? 'As bold as Ned Kelly.' Should this commonly used Australian phrase be 'As bold as Kennedy', as Ned Kelly himself said he knew no braver man than Sergeant Michael Kennedy? To this day there are many questions still to be answered, and hopefully this book will give the reader further information on this tragic story and help you to make up your own mind.

Newspapers, back in the day, were the main form of communicating information to the public. Because of this, they had a great deal to do with people's perception of Ned Kelly and The Kelly Gang. Numerous articles were written on the four members of the gang, often daily, not only in Australia, but all over the world. At the time, it was the biggest news story in the country. A clear indication of the ability for the written word to persuade people's perceptions is when Ned Kelly himself tried to have his 'Jerilderie Letter' published. He understood that this was the best means of giving his 'side of the story' to the public. Unfortunately, Ned Kelly never saw this achievement. It was around 50 years after his death before the full 'Jerilderie Letter' was printed.

All of the newspaper articles included in this book have been compiled and edited from The National Library of Australia Trove website.

These newspaper articles, written whilst these tragic events were unfolding, give a great indepth view of the circumstances of the time. There are numerous transcripts from people involved in various aspects of the history. Many articles written offer more of a bias towards the authorities' and victims' viewpoint than that of The Kellys'. Was this how the public perceived the situation at the time or was this simply newspapers' or journalists' bias?

Due to the abundance of articles written on Ned Kelly and The Kelly Gang it is impossible to include them all in this book. I have tried to select articles that will give the reader the best, I believe, sense of what was occurring at the time and how history unfolded.

I have included a number of sketches that appeared in various newspapers. As there are very few photographs of Ned Kelly and The Kelly Gang, these sketches give a wonderful insight into the history.

Due to the great age and condition of the original newspapers some of the articles and words are quite difficult to read. In extreme cases, where it is impossible to read the word, I have had to put a line.

Various newspapers use different spelling for names of the people involved, for consistency and ease of reading I have defaulted to the more common spelling.

Hopefully the following newspaper articles will give you, the reader, a greater insight into Ned Kelly, his Gang and the men who tracked them down, the 'Kelly Hunters'.

These articles also tell the tragic story of the men, women and children who either lost their lives or suffered terribly as the result of being caught up in this tragic part of Australia's bushranging history.

Kelly on Remand

The Benalla Ensign and Farmer's and Squatter's Journal, 19 October 1869

Edward Kelly, on remand, was brought up for robbery on the road between Winton and Greta. The police applied for a further remand till Thursday next, as they could not procure the services of a Chinese interpreter from Beechworth until then. Mr McDonnell, for defence, said "it was a great hardship upon prisoner who was refused bail and his relatives who came from a long distance to attend court, that frequent remands should be made". An interpreter could be found in Benalla and besides, the witnesses in the case, he believed, could understand and speak English. The Bench thought the application reasonable, since the police had made every exertion to have the case proceeded with as speedily as possible. The remand was granted.

A Juvenile Bushranger

The Argus, 22 October 1869

Edward Kelly, aged about 18 years, appeared before the Benalla Police Court on Saturday, charged with highway robbery between Greta and Winton on the evening of the 14th instant. Kelly is the son of a widow residing at the Eleven Mile Creek, near Greta. The particulars of the case are as follows:

On the evening named, a Chinaman, named Ah Fook, who follows the business of a victualler, was travelling from Morse's Creek to Benalla.

Shortly after he passed the Eleven Mile Creek and had entered a lonely part of the bush, he was overtaken by Kelly, who imperatively commanded him to 'stand still,' and deliver up his money. Poor Ah Fook strongly protested that he had no money. Kelly insisted in his demand and finally succeeded in extracting the Chinaman's purse from an inside waist-coat pocket. The purse contained only 10s. Kelly then decamped and Ah Fook pursued his way to Benalla. The celestial pilgrim proved one too many for the amateur highwayman. At the time Ah Fook was 'bailed up', he had the sum of £25 concealed in his boots, which sum he produced at half-past nine o'clock the same evening at the police camp at Benalla, where he gave information of the outrage.

On the following morning, a little before daylight, Sergeant Whelan, in company with the Chinaman, proceeded in the direction of the spot where the alleged robbery had taken place and near to where the widow Kelly resided. On coming in view of the hut, Whelan noticed a woman suddenly enter and immediately afterwards a boy rushed out and took to the bush as fast as his heels could assist him. Whelan, who was well mounted and dressed in civilian's clothes, immediately gave chase, and although the fugitive was fully three quarters of a mile in advance and selected a flight through thickly timbered bush, the sergeant ultimately rode him down and took him into custody. He was subsequently identified by the Chinaman as the person who robbed him.

The Police Bench remanded Kelly until this day (Tuesday). It may be mentioned that while Sergeant Whelan was passing Kelly's hut in pursuit, two ferocious dogs were let loose at him, evidently for the purpose of frightening the horse and thereby gaining time in favour of Kelly. The prompt action taken by Sergeant Whelan is worthy of recognition by the police authorities.

Benalla Police Court

The Benalla Ensign and Farmer's and Squatter's Journal, 22 October 1869

On Saturday, October 16, before Mr Sharpe. Edward Kelly, a youth of about 17, appeared to answer to a charge of highway robbery from a Chinaman. The police applied for a remand for the production of evidence through an interpreter. Mr McDonnell, who appeared for prisoner, consented to the remand provided Kelly was admitted to bail. Sergeant Whelan objected to Mr McDonnell's application, and having in reply to state his objection, explained to his Worship that the offence was of such a serious nature that the law did not allow bail to prisoners of this description. The Bench refused Mr McDonnell's application and remanded Kelly till the following Tuesday.

Benalla Police Court

The Benalla Ensign and Farmer's and Squatter's Journal, 29 October 1869

Edward Kelly, on remand, was placed in the dock on the charge of assaulting and robbing one Ah Fook, a Chinese, on the road between Winton and Greta on the 14th instant. Mr Nicholas appeared to prosecute and Messrs McDonnell and Pow defended the prisoner. William Tze Hing acted as interpreter during the hearing of the case.

Ah Fook, residing at Morse's Creek, examined and stated:

> Remember Thursday the 14th instant I was coming from Morse's Creek to Benalla on that day and passed through Greta. A man robbed me between Greta and Winton. I identify prisoner as the man who robbed me. Besides 10s in a purse in my pocket, I had other money hidden. The purse was in my right-hand-side trousers' pocket. The purse was produced, I identify as mine. When prisoner came up to me, he said, "I'm a bushranger, give me your money, if not I will beat you to death". I proceeded towards prisoner's hut. Prisoner drove me about half a mile and then robbed me. He had a stick in his hand. He ordered me to go and threatened to strike me if I did not. When I saw prisoner he asked where I was going. He took hold of me, put his hand in my pocket and took out the purse. After extracting the 10s, prisoner threw it on the ground. Prisoner assaulted me by hitting me on the right leg and arm with a stick.
>
> I got to Benalla at eight o'clock in the evening and reported the occurrence to the police at the station. Next day, I accompanied the sergeant and a constable to the place where I had been robbed. The sergeant brought the man out and I identified him.

Cross examination by Mr McDonnell:

> The 14th instant was on Thursday. In coming from Morse's Creek to Benalla, I came by the Fifteen Mile Creek. When I was robbed there was only one man. Two other men had gone away. I saw these at first somewhere about Winton. Prisoner was one of the three. Prisoner went with me towards the Fifteen Mile Creek. He did not take me to the hut. I wished to go in

but he prevented me. I saw a girl inside. I did not ask her for a drink of water. I did not threaten to strike her, nor shake my fist at her. I did not threaten to strike the prisoner. I had no stick.

A woman at Winton told me to go to the police. When prisoner took me away to rob me he had a stick two or three fathoms long and thick. (The interpreter here explained that a fathom was in Chinese measurement 6 feet.) Prisoner put his hand into my pocket quickly. The coat I now have on was folded up and on my shoulder. I resisted, but could not get hold of prisoner. I know the purse by the stitch, having made it myself. It took me about six hours and a half to come from the Five Mile Creek to Winton. I was robbed about four o'clock in the afternoon. I was alone when prisoner robbed me.

By Mr Nicholas:

There is a track leading from Greta to Winton and on the way there is the hut which I passed. After I was robbed I came towards Winton. From there I came to Benalla and slept there.

By Mr Wills:

I was travelling on foot and alone. The hut is close to the roadway. The 10s consisted of one half-crown, a sixpence, and seven shillings. Prisoner came out of the hut with the stick. Three other men were with the prisoner. They all came out of the hut together. The other two men went away and prisoner came towards me. The hut is about 12 feet across and is built of slabs, with a bark roof. I live at a Chinese camp at Morse's Creek. The other men could not see what took place, they had gone. There were not many trees about the place.

Sergeant Whelan, on oath, stated:

I arrested prisoner on warrant produced, on the 15th instant. Ah Fook came to the station and said he had been stuck up and robbed between Greta and Winton on the back road. Prosecutor told me that the person who robbed him wounded him with a stick and I saw abrasions on his leg and arms. Ah Fook was taken before a magistrate and an information was sworn. It was sworn through another Chinaman. The description of the interpreter tallied with the prosecutor's, describing prisoner as a boy about 20, five feet, eight inches in height, with no beard nor whiskers and brown hair. He wore moleskin trousers and a straw hat with black band.

On the following morning, I proceeded with a constable and prosecutor. I left Ah Fook concealed behind a brush fence. I saw a woman close to the end of the hut. The woman went into the hut, and the prisoner ran into the bush at full speed. I went in pursuit and kept in sight of him. I was attacked by two dogs when passing the hut. When I caught him I asked him why he ran away. He gave no reason. When we came to the hut, I read the warrant to the prisoner and he said the Chinaman had insulted the woman and struck him with bamboo. He said he did not strike the Chinaman. I asked him why he ran away if he did not do anything wrong. I arrested him and took him to where the two Chinese were. Ah Fook said the prisoner was the man who had robbed him. I then brought him to the watchhouse. I received the purse from Ah Fook on the 15th. He gave it to me out of his pocket.

Cross-examined:

Did not see Ah Fook pick up the purse. Heard the prosecutor's remark about the stick. It might or might not inflict a greater injury than it did. I brought the other Chinaman with me. William Tze Hing gave me the information as interpreter. Did not prompt him to give me a description. I let him tell his own story. He brought a piece of paper with the name of prisoner written upon it. Have not the paper at present. Hing said "prisoner was five feet eight inches". The measurement of the stick was described as fathoms. There is heavy timber in a blind gully near the hut. Could see the hut from the gully. I was dressed in plain-clothes when I went to the hut. I was nearly half a mile away when prisoner ran out of the hut. I kept my eyes on him all the way, until I caught him. I did not caution him.

David McInerney, constable stationed at Benalla, remembered the 15th October. Accompanied Sergeant Whelan to the place where prisoner was arrested. Knew prisoner's hut about four miles this side of Greta, between Greta and Winton. Saw prisoner run away from the hut when we were going to it. After arresting prisoner accompanied him to Benalla. Sergeant Whelan asked him once or twice why he ran away and he said nothing. He said if the fence was a little nearer he would have got away.

Cross-examined by Mr Pow:

Witness was sure it was the prisoner who ran away. They were within half a mile of him. Saw others afterwards, but not at the time. Did not caution the prisoner when they apprehended him. Prosecutor pointed out the place where he picked up the purse.

To the Bench:

Prosecutor said the prisoner took the purse and threw it on the ground.

Sergeant Whelan, recalled:

I produce a small piece of paper I received from Ah Fook on the 15th instant. Ah Fook said he reported the robbery at the first house he came to and the person wrote the name of Kelly, at Greta, on the paper. On the 15th Hing (who was the interpreter) produced £25 which he said he had taken out of prosecutor's boot on the 14th instant. Superintendent Nicholas said he could bring a Chinaman to prove that Ah Fook had the money on the 14th instant. Mr McDonnell said he applied to have the prisoner discharged, as the case had been originally brought under the 110th section of the Police Offences Statute. The objection was overruled.

Mr McDonnell then pointed out what he considered the weak points of the case and called William Gray, a labourer in Mrs Kelly's employ, who said:

I know Edward Kelly was at Mrs Kelly's on the 14th of this month. Saw prosecutor there. Was standing outside the hut when prosecutor came up. He was with Kelly, Mrs Gunn and a Labourer named Skillion. He asked Mrs Gunn to give him water and she did so. I saw the Chinaman raise his fist to strike Mrs Gunn, but she got out of his way. Saw prisoner then push the Chinaman, but not strike him. The Chinaman then struck prisoner two or three times across the shoulder. That was near the hut. It was between one and four o'clock in the afternoon. Prisoner did not put his hand in the Chinaman's pocket. Prisoner ran away when the Chinaman struck him. Heard the Chinaman say he would burn the place down and he then went away. Saw prisoner all the afternoon.

Cross-examined:

Prisoner was with me about the house and not out of my sight during the afternoon.

By the Bench:

Mrs Gunn did not say anything insulting to prosecutor. I did not interfere in any way because it was not my duty to do so.

Anne Gunn, wife of Alexander Gunn, living near Greta, said:

On the 14th of this month I was at Mrs Kelly's all the day. Recollect the Chinaman coming to the hut on that day, having a stick and billycan on his shoulder. Was outside the door, sewing. The Chinaman asked me for a drink of water, which I gave to him. When I gave him the water he spoke angrily in Chinese. He raised his fist to my face and I ran inside. I did not see anything more.

Cross-examined:

I am prisoner's sister.

By the Bench:

Gray, Skillion and Kelly were all standing by when prisoner tried to strike me. Never had words with him previously. Could not understand why he was so violent. William Skillion, of Godfrey's Creek, knew prisoner and prosecutor. Was at prisoner's house on the 14th. The Chinaman was there, Gray and Mrs Gunn were also there. Prisoner was inside. Prosecutor asked Mrs Gunn for a drink of water, which she gave him. He used abusive language to her after getting the water. She went inside. Prisoner then came out and pushed prosecutor away. Prisoner was near the door all the time. Prosecutor struck him several times with a stick. Prisoner ran away. Prosecutor said "I will burn down the place," or words to that effect. The Chinaman went away. Was with Kelly nearly all the day.

By the Bench:

> Did not see the prisoner strike the prosecutor.

Cross-examined:

> I was mining about a month since. I was at Kelly's about a fortnight. Lost my horse or I would not have been at Kelly's. Prisoner never left the hut all the time.

By the Bench:

> I did not strike the Chinaman at all.
>
> The three witnesses for the defence so confirmed each other's evidence, whereas the prosecutor's evidence was unsupported, so there was no option but to discharge the prisoner. The prisoner and his friends then left the court. The hearing of this case occupied over four hours.

Power Recruiting Bushrangers

The Argus, 5 May 1870

A man named Kelly, supposed to be a mate of Power's, was apprehended by the police near Benalla yesterday, at seven in the morning. A party of volunteers has been organised at Trentham, with the view of capturing the man, supposed to be Power the bushranger, who on Thursday last stuck up the Lauriston herdsman. They scoured the bush in all directions, but without result.

A correspondent of the *Kyneton Observer* states:

> The fellow, along with his mate, in the meantime got to the eastern end of the town and entering a hut, drove out the wife of Mr Gregory and his family, and after making a good meal and feeding their horses, made off, shouting at a dog belonging to Gregory, which was rather inclined to be demonstrative. The next morning, about six o'clock, Superintendent Nicholson and Inspector Disney arrived and immediately organised a party

> to go in pursuit. The party consisted of Messrs Nicholson and Disney, Robertson, Hamilton, South, and Constable Quinn, who were shortly reinforced by Constable Tree, of Tylden. The bush was scoured, but no tidings received.

On Monday about 30 police were out, but as yet no capture has been effected. "The bushranger Power," the *Ovens Spectator* says, "Seems to be generating bushrangers all over the eastern part of the colony. A most singular case of highway robbery, after the approved Power fashion, occurred, as we are informed, on Sunday morning, in Bowman's Forest. About a mile and a half from Messrs Taylor's (eleven and a half miles from Beechworth, on the road to Hunt's, in the forest). A tall young man sprang out upon a gentleman who was driving a buggy towards Myrtleford and levelling a revolver at his head, demanded his money. As the amount of cash in his possession at the time was only half-a-crown, the traveller promptly handed it over and though only a 'small contribution' it was 'received thankfully' perhaps, as the charitable subscription-lists have it. Both the traveller and the bushranger parted from one another well pleased with the result of the encounter. The traveller at having experienced all the romance and excitement of being stuck-up for half-a-crown and the bushranger at getting off scot-free, as the latter was evidently rather frightened at the time and his hand shook so much whilst levelling the revolver that he would probably have missed his aim if he had fired." So 'All's well that ends well' and everyone is satisfied, except the police, who have not caught the new highwayman. The gentleman who was stuck up was, we understand, Mr William Moore, of the Buffalo River.

Current Topics

The Geelong Advertiser, 5 May 1870

We are glad to learn that the police of the Melbourne division, detached for the purpose of searching for Power the bushranger succeeded at six o'clock yesterday morning in arresting Edward Kelly, who is supposed to be a mate of Power's, between Greta and Winton. We trust the capture will speedily lead to that of Power himself.

Latest Telegrams

The Geelong Advertiser, 6 May 1870

Edward Kelly, the youngster, who is said to be a mate of Power's, was charged this morning before the local bench with robbery under arms in company, and highway robbery under arms. Superintendent Nicholson asked for a remand for seven days, which was at once granted.

Benalla Police Court Crowded

The Benalla Ensign and Farmer's and Squatter's Journal, 13 May 1870

The Benalla Police Court was crowded yesterday to see the young bushranger Kelly and to hear the result of the charges laid against him. The prisoner has greatly improved under the better and regular diet he has had since his incarceration and has become quite 'flash'. We are told that his language is hideous and if he recovers his liberty at Kyneton and again joins Power – as no doubt he soon would – we are inclined to think he would be far more dangerous than heretofore. He has managed to get out of several ugly scrapes and this success has not only emboldened him, but it has hardened him. Kelly was dismissed on the first two charges, that of robbing Mr McBean in company with Power and of the robbery near Seymour. Mr McBean could not identify him and the man robbed near Seymour could nowhere be found. It will be remembered that Mr McBean did not see the face of the young man who was with Power when he was stuck-up, as he turned his back on Mr McBean all through the ordeal. But the Seymour case looks very like aiding and abetting. We shall see how the young criminal will fare at Kyneton, to which place he has been remanded and where he will be brought up on Friday next, when it will be seen whether Murray can identify him. We regret to learn that there is no word of Power, who is believed to be in ambush in this vicinity.

Edward Kelly on Remand

The Benalla Ensign and Farmer's and Squatter's Journal, 13 May 1870

Edward Kelly was brought up on remand and charged with robbery in company at Kilfera on 16 March. Superintendent Nicholson prosecuted and Mr McDonnell appeared for the prisoner. Superintendent Nicholson said that prisoner could not be identified as having taken part in that robbery and he was discharged. A second charge was then preferred against him for robbery under arms near Seymour on 20 April. Superintendent Nicholson said the police had made every exertion to find the principal witness against prisoner in this case, but he could not be discovered. Without his evidence it was hopeless to proceed against prisoner and he was consequently discharged. Kelly was then charged with robbery under arms at Lauriston, near Kyneton, on 20 April. Mr Nicholson stated that he had that morning received a warrant from Kyneton and that prisoner answered to the description contained in the warrant. He would therefore apply for him to be remanded to that place. After a brief deliberation this was granted and the Court adjourned.

Law Notices

The Argus, 30 May 1870

The Kyneton police state that they are now in possession of information which leaves no doubt that the prisoner Edward Kelly has been concerned with another offender still at large, in the commission of the recent highway robberies in that district. Some strange rumours (*The Guardian* says) are afloat as to the reported robbery of Murray, the herdsman of the Lauriston common, but for the present that journal does not consider it advisable to give additional publicity to them.

Country News

The Argus, 6 June 1870

The youth Kelly, who was brought from Benalla on a charge of being concerned with Power, the bushranger, in sticking-up and robbing Murray, the herdsman of the Lauriston common, was again brought before the Kyneton Bench on Friday morning, when Sergeant Babington applied for his discharge. He was discharged accordingly.

Wangaratta Police Court

The Argus, 14 November 1870

Edward Kelly, who was once known as the mate of Power the bushranger, was brought before the Wangaratta Police Court the other day charged with assaulting and threatening a hawker named McCormack and his wife. Kelly was sent to gaol for three months and was also required to provide sureties to keep the peace for 12 months.

Horse Stealing Charge

The Benalla Ensign and Farmer's and Squatter's Journal, 29 April 1871

Some weeks ago a chestnut horse, the property of Mr Newland, the postmaster of Mansfield, was lost off the run of the Honourable Mr Higben. It has now been found at Greta in the possession of a man named Kelly, who was a mate of the notorious Power's. Kelly has been brought before the bench at Wangaratta on a charge of horse-stealing and remanded until the 29th instant.

The Fight Between Constable Hall & Kelly

The Argus, 2 May 1871

When Edward Kelly, an old accomplice of Power, the bushranger, was taken before the Wangaratta Police Court a few days ago, the evidence showed that a very severe struggle had taken place between him and Constable Hall, who captured him.

The latter stated:

> I saw Kelly at Greta, and told him I wanted him at the camp. I told him I had some receipts. I induced him to come to the camp to sign them, on the ground that the authorities at Beechworth Gaol had forgotten to get him to sign them. He said, "Bring them out!" I said, "No, you can't write here. Come inside". He turned the horse round to go away and I caught hold of him to pull him down from the horse. He jumped down, his clothes gave way and he bolted. I followed him, and took my revolver out of the case and told him three times to stand, or I would shoot him. I presented it and he told me to shoot away and be

damned. He then stood his ground to fight. He turned round sharp and hit me with his fist. My revolver misfired and I then struck him on the head with it five times. It seemed to have very little effect on him. He caught hold of the muzzle of the revolver and turned it round on me and said, "Now I'll let you have it". After a considerable struggle, some people came to my assistance and we got him to the lock-up.

Wangaratta Despatch Country News

The Argus, 8 May 1871

The *Wangaratta Despatch* mentions that information was given to the police at Wangaratta a short time back that the horse which young Kelly was charged with feloniously receiving was actually stolen by a man named Isaiah 'Wild' Wright, living near Greta. A warrant was accordingly taken out against him, but it was only on Tuesday last that Senior Constable Hall and Constable McInerney managed to get sight of the alleged felon. He was splendidly mounted at the time and when challenged to stand and surrender refused to do so, but spurred his horse and made away as hard as he could go, clearing a wire fence four feet and a half high at the time. Finding their summons unheeded, both Hall and McInerney fired, the former once and the latter three times. None of the shots told, however, and Wright managed for the time to escape. Subsequently the news reached Wangaratta that Wright was captured in a shanty kept by Kelly's mother between Winton and Greta. Senior Constable Hall and Constable McInerney entered the house and Wright attempted to conceal himself behind the bed of Kelly's sister, a girl of 18 years of age. Wright had apparently been sleeping in the room. He has been brought before the Wangaratta Police Court, where the case has been adjourned for a week.

Reward for Constable Hall

The Benalla Ensign and Farmer's and Squatter's Journal, 19 August 1871

The following reward has been paid from the police reward fund during the past week to Senior Constable Hall, Greta, Ovens district, £5 for his services in the arrest and prosecution of Edward Kelly, Alexander Gunn and Isaiah 'Wild' Wright, for horse-stealing. The two former sentenced to three years each and the latter to 18 months imprisonment.

Constable Fitzpatrick

The Argus, 17 April 1878

Several members of a notorious family of the name of Kelly and a kindred spirit named William Skillion have committed a serious outrage upon Constable Fitzpatrick at Greta, near Benalla. According to the information which has reached Melbourne, the Constable went to the Kellys' house for the purpose of apprehending one of the sons for horse-stealing. He found the accused at home and placed him under arrest, but allowed him to have something to eat before marching him off to the local watch-house. Whilst the prisoner was regaling himself, a brother, his mother and Skillion entered. The brother fired at the constable with a revolver, but missed and the mother struck the policeman on the helmet with a shovel. Whilst the constable was defending his head with his arm from another blow by the mother with the shovel, the brother again fired and shot him in the wrist. Skillion also presented a revolver at him. Fitzpatrick was then overpowered and disarmed of his own revolver, but eventually made his escape. His injuries are said to be not dangerous. Warrants will be issued for the arrest of the offenders, but it was found yesterday that they had disappeared. The Kellys were intimately connected with Power, the bushranger.

Murderous Attack on a Constable

The Argus, 22 April 1878

The Eleven Mile Creek and its neighbourhood, about midway between Winton and Greta, has long been famed as the resort of notorious characters. It was a well-known occasional trysting place of the bushranger Power, during the committal of his exploits in this neighbourhood some years ago, and ever since that time the place has been looked upon as the nest of some expert horse-stealers, cattle-duffers, and general robbers.

On Monday evening, Mounted Constable Alexander Fitzpatrick, stationed at Benalla, proceeded to arrest a young ruffian named Daniel Kelly, who resides at the Eleven Mile Creek, under a warrant issued from the Chiltern Bench, charged with horse-stealing. The young trooper rode up to the place occupied by Kelly's mother and her family, which consists of a brother named Edward and four young sisters, besides the culprit who was wanted. Daniel Kelly shortly appeared on the scene and was immediately arrested by

Fitzpatrick. At Kelly's urgent request the constable permitted him to enter the hut to get his supper, as he stated he had been riding all day and was very hungry. While standing inside nearby the door, keeping guard over his prisoner, the constable heard another man rush in and a shot fired close to his body. Turning round instantly a second shot was fired, which took effect in the trooper's left arm, about two inches above the wrist. He saw that his assailant was Edward Kelly, an elder brother of the prisoner. In a moment he grasped at the ruffian's pistol, which again went off, the mother simultaneously crashing in the constable's helmet with a heavy iron fire-shovel. Before he could recover himself, two other men, whom he recognised, named Williamson and Skillion, rushed in and presenting revolvers at his head, attacked and bore him down in an insensible condition to the floor. This all occurred in less than two minutes and when Fitzpatrick regained his senses he found himself a prisoner, his revolver and cartridges taken from him and his arm much swollen and very painful. His captors were standing over him and the elder, Edward Kelly, expressed his regret at having wounded him, "as he was about the civilest of the troopers around and had it been any other of the –s he would not have gone away alive". At first, Fitzpatrick thought the bone of his arm was broken, but on feeling and examining the wounded limb he found that the bullet had glanced off the bone and lodged itself just under the skin of the upper side of the forearm, where it could very plainly be felt and its position seen. Upon observing this, Edward Kelly demanded that it should be immediately extracted. "He would not leave the lead there to be evidence against him," he said, and offered to cut it out with his pocketknife. This, however, the trooper refused, preferring to perform that operation himself if it must be done, and on seeing that the other was determined and it would be extremely unsafe to refuse, he gallantly made an incision and squeezed out the bullet, of which Kelly immediately took possession. In the meantime the two men, Skillion and Williamson, had left the place before the constable regained consciousness and it may readily be imagined that he was particularly anxious to get away from such a den before worse befell him, leaving the capture of the villains to a future opportunity, and after being compelled to promise Kelly that he would not inform of the shooting affray, he was allowed to mount his horse and depart, his revolver being returned to him with the charges drawn. After riding about a mile the constable noticed that he was followed by two horsemen through the bush, and fearing further mischief he galloped off, but was pursued nearly to Winton at full speed. These horsemen he states were Williamson and Skillion.

Arriving at Winton he induced a farmer there to accompany him into Benalla, where he arrived shortly before midnight and the services of Dr Nicholson being procured, his wounds were dressed and we are glad to state that he is now progressing favourably. The only danger is of inflammation ensuing.

On Tuesday several constables were despatched from the stations at Benalla, Wangaratta and Greta and they succeeded in arresting the woman Ellen Kelly, Williamson and Skillion the same evening, who were lodged in the Benalla lockup during Wednesday afternoon. A fourth prisoner was also brought in, arrested on warrant for horse-stealing, named John Lloyd, who is also known to be one of the gang.

Yesterday morning the prisoners were brought before Mr F. McDonnell, J. P., at the police court, Ellen Kelly, William Williamson (alias Brickey) and William Skillion being charged with aiding and abetting Edward Kelly in the attempt to murder Mounted Constable Fitzpatrick and were remanded to Friday next, 26th. John Lloyd, on a charge of horse-stealing, was remanded until tomorrow.

Nothing could be seen or heard of the two Kellys by the police party, but it is generally supposed they are hiding amongst the caves and vastnesses of the mountains in the vicinity. Edward Kelly was a mate of the notorious Power and he makes it a boast at times that he accompanied him in some of his most profitable and adventurous expeditions. He has been previously committed for horse-stealing and sentenced to three years imprisonment. He told Mounted Constable Fitzpatrick that it would be no use the police attempting to hunt him down, as he was too well acquainted with the country and could watch the police without himself being seen. He also stated that he would never again be taken alive.

Reward for the Apprehension of Edward Kelly

The Argus, 4 May 1878

The Government has offered a reward of £100 for the apprehension of Edward Kelly, who on 15 April attempted to murder Mounted Constable

Fitzpatrick, while attempting to arrest Daniel Kelly, at Greta, for horse-stealing.

Robbery

The Argus, 7 May 1878

It is reported that Ned Kelly, formerly Power's mate, who shot at the constable at Greta last month and who is yet at large, stuck up a boy named Nolan, near Oxley and robbed him of a horse, saddle and bridle, a watch, and £14 in money.

The Greta Outrage

The Argus, 22 May 1878

At the Benalla Police Court, on the 17th instant, William Williamson, alias 'Brickey', William Skillion and Ellen Kelly on remand, were charged with aiding and abetting at murder. Superintendent Chomley conducted the case on behalf of the Crown.

Alexander Fitzpatrick deposed:

> I am a Mounted Constable, stationed at Benalla. On Monday, the 15th of April last, I was proceeding to Greta on duty. I had to pass the residence of Mrs Kelly, the female prisoner, and called between four and five o'clock. I left after about an hour or more, but seeing two horsemen ride towards Kelly's house I followed them. I saw Dan Kelly come out of a hut and after speaking to him about some stray horses, I told him I would have to arrest him under a warrant out against him for horse-stealing. He said, "Very well, but let me get something to eat, as I have been out riding all day". I consented to this and went after him into the house. It was then getting dusk. Mrs Kelly was in the room and while Dan was getting his supper she said to me, "You won't take Dan out of this tonight." Dan replied, "Shut up, mother, it's all right".
>
> Just afterwards Ned Kelly came in at the door and without a word fired at me with a revolver. I was about a yard and a half inside, rather behind the door, with my back towards it. Mrs Kelly was standing with her back to the fire. The first shot

did not strike me and he immediately fired again, the bullet lodging in my left arm just above the wrist. Mrs Kelly at the same time rushed at me with a shovel, striking a heavy blow on my head and making a large dent in the helmet I wore. (Helmet produced.) I had raised my arm to guard the shovel when he fired the second shot. I knocked the shovel down with my right hand and then turned to draw my revolver, but it had been taken out of my belt. Dan Kelly had it in his hand. I then seized the revolver held in Ned's hand, saying, "You cowardly wretch, do you want to murder me?" We struggled for the pistol, when it went off a third time, the bullet passing through the sleeve of my jumper. Skillion was by the side of Ned Kelly all the time, with a revolver in his hand, but he did not use it. Williamson came out of the bedroom just as the second shot was fired, he was also armed with a revolver or pistol. The pistols were all pointed at me. When I said, "Do you want to kill me?" Ned Kelly called out, "That will do, boys". He turned to Skillion and said, "You –, why didn't you tell me who was here?" Then turning to me, said, "If I had known it was you, Fitzpatrick, I would not have fired, but none of the other – would have left here alive".

The wound in my arm was bleeding all the time and I fainted. When coming round again I heard the men talking. Ned Kelly told Williamson that Bill (meaning Skillion) "would have given that – a pill the other day if he had not prevented him," and Skillion said, "he had a pill in for Sergeant Steele one of these days". Williamson and Skillion soon after left and I got up from the floor, when Ned said he was sorry it had happened, as it was me, he should get into trouble over it. I saw my revolver on the table. I was taken asunder and the charges drawn. I took it up and Ned Kelly took it from my hand, he also took all my ammunition and asked had I more. Examined my wrist, it was swollen and the bullet was seen under the skin. He said he must have it out of that and took a rusty razor to cut it out. I wished to go home and get a medical man to remove it, but he refused. I then said I would operate myself, and taking a sharp penknife I cut it out. It was a small ball. Kelly's sister was present then. Ned

Kelly took the bullet and my arm was bandaged by Mrs Kelly. It was then that I went outside, Ned Kelly following me. He said, "Now, look here, I spared you and you must spare me. How will you manage to say how you were shot?" I replied "I would not mention it." He then said, "You had better say this – that you went to arrest Dan, who was in company with Williamson. That you had your revolver out and in putting the handcuffs on it went off and shot you and that Dan took the ammunition". He afterwards asked me if I knew a man named Whitla and I told him "No". He said, "Look here, this will do better. Say that two men rushed from behind a tree when you arrested Dan, two big men, one like myself. They'll think it was brother Jim and the other was Whitla. Say that one cried out "Oh, Whitla, you've shot him." He gave as a reason for my saying this that both the men were miles away at the time. He also compelled me to make an entry in my notebook. (Book produced and entry read to somewhat similar tale as above.) I wanted to get away then, but Ned would not return my revolver.

He said, "If you go home and say I shot you, you'll get no credit for it. Government won't reward you, but I'll make it right with you. I'll give you, £500 after Baumgarten's affair is over". Mrs Kelly told Ned to say that if I told of it I'd not be alive long, they had plenty of friends about. I went and got my horse from behind the house, where Dan had tied him not to be seen. My hand was very painful. Dan brought my revolver and handcuffs and I went away. Ned showed me out of the panel and I started off for Benalla. After going about two miles and a half, I saw Williamson and Skillion riding after me. I spurred on faster then, until coming to Winton, to Lindsay's. When I dismounted I could not stand and the two Lindsay's helped me in and gave me brandy and David Lindsay accompanied me into Benalla.

Cross-examined by Mr Zincke:

Dan did not refuse to be arrested. Had not a warrant with me, but knew there was one out, saw it in the Police Gazette. Had no instructions to go to Kellys. Was acting perhaps as amateur constable on the occasion. The prisoners reserved their defence and were committed for trial at the Beechworth Assize Court, on 9 October next. Mrs Kelly was admitted to bail in two sureties of £50 each and herself in a like amount.

Bushranging in Victoria, Two Constables Shot and a Sergeant Missing

The Argus, 28 October 1878

A terrible encounter, almost without parallel in Victoria, has taken place near Mansfield, between the police and four bushrangers. The particulars to hand are but meagre owing to the intelligence having only been received at Mansfield yesterday evening, but they are of such a character as to show that four most unscrupulous ruffians are at large in the colony and that no effort must be spared to secure them immediately. As will be seen from the following telegram, received last night from our Mansfield correspondent, two constables have been murdered, a third has had his horse shot under him, while the fate of Sergeant Kennedy is dubious.

MANSFIELD, SUNDAY, SIX P.M.

News has just reached Mansfield that Constables Lonigan and Scanlon have been shot dead by four bushrangers at Stringybark Creek, about 20 miles from here. Constable McIntyre, who escaped, has just arrived with the intelligence. His horse was shot from under him. Sergeant Kennedy is also missing. Sub-Inspector Pewtress, Dr Reynolds, Collopy and others left now on horseback to scour the country and bring home dead bodies. The bushrangers are supposed to be the notorious Kelly party, for whom the constables were in search. The offenders referred to by our correspondent are two brothers named Edward and Daniel Kelly, for the arrest of whom warrants were issued some months ago for various offences, the most serious being a murderous attack made on Constable Fitzpatrick. The Kellys are well known as notorious criminals. Their father died a long time ago and the family remaining consisted of the two brothers, their mother and four young sisters. Edward is 22 years of age, five foot ten inches high, medium build, has a fresh complexion, dark-brown hair and hazel eyes. Whilst Daniel is only 17 years of age, five foot six inches high, medium build, having a fair complexion and blue eyes. The former was arrested in 1870 on suspicion of being the mate of Power, the bushranger, but was discharged owing to the evidence of identification being insufficient. In February, 1874, he was discharged from Pentridge, after serving a term of three years imprisonment for receiving a stolen horse. The younger brother was discharged from the Beechworth gaol in January last, where he had been imprisoned for three months for wilful damage to property. Vague reports as to the Kellys being seen in different parts of the north-eastern area of the colony were received, but the police for a long time could obtain no tangible trace of them.

For some months back the Government have been offering a reward of £100 for the capture of Edward Kelly, on the charge of shooting Constable Fitzpatrick. If the Kellys are concerned in this last affair, as there seems little reason to doubt, they must now be in league with at least two other ruffians as desperate as themselves, and four such characters make a formidable gang of outlaws. Sergeant Kennedy, who is reported as missing, was stationed at Mansfield under Sub-Inspector Pewtress. The two constables who have been shot were both efficient members of the force. Scanlon was well known in Melbourne when stationed here, but that was a good many years ago. At one time he acted as orderly for the Chief Commissioner and was subsequently told off for duty at the Theatre Royal.

Up to an early hour this morning the police authorities in town had received no intelligence of the affair, a circumstance which is perhaps to be accounted for by the probability that Sub-Inspector Pewtress, of Mansfield, on learning of what had taken place from Constable McIntyre, hastened off immediately to the scene of the encounter and was unable for want of time to telegraph to Melbourne.

Atrocious Murders by Bushrangers

The Argus, 29 October 1878

The particulars which we published yesterday in reference to the terrible encounter which had taken place near Mansfield, on Saturday morning last, although meagre, were the general theme of conversation throughout the city yesterday. Further intelligence has come to hand, from which it appears that a premeditated and atrocious crime has been perpetrated by a gang of ruffians. Shortly after noon yesterday three volunteers returned to Mansfield with information confirmatory of the report that Constables Lonigan and

Scanlon had been shot dead by the outlaws. Scanlon had been pierced by a ball through the neck, while Lonigan received a mortal wound in the forehead, which must have caused instantaneous death. No effort will be spared to secure the arrest of the band of desperadoes and for that purpose the Government has offered a reward of £200 for such information as will lead to the apprehension and conviction of each of the offenders. Captain Standish, Chief Commissioner of Police, yesterday afternoon ordered all the available troopers in the Richmond police depot to proceed with their horses by special train to Benalla. The men are all picked troopers and others are being collected from different parts of the colony to follow. During the afternoon Superintendent Nicholson, accompanied by three troopers who are well acquainted with the district, left town for Wangaratta by the train leaving Spencer Street at about three o'clock, and a further detachment of troopers will be sent up to Benalla this morning. Inspector Secretan has telegraphed to Detective Kennedy, who is on official duty at Shepparton, to remain in that district and to render all assistance in his power to the general police.

The following official despatches were received by the Chief Commissioner of Police yesterday:

Benalla, Monday

To the Chief Commissioner of Police:

The postmaster at Mansfield telegraphs that 'Mr Hickson, of Broken River, has just arrived, bringing in Constable Meehan's horse. Meehan is missing between Dinan's and Daw's and nothing has been seen or heard of him.' – S. Maud, Senior Constable for Superintendent.

Mansfield, Monday

Captain Standish:

> There is not a constable here. Cannot you send men up by special train? All the volunteers are in the Wombat Ranges. If I can get more volunteers, may I use police horses that are now in the police paddock? I can get 50 volunteers if I can have a few police to go with them. Before Sub-Inspector Pewtress left last night he despatched Constable Meehan with despatches to Benalla. Meehan's horse was found eight miles from here and

Meehan has not been heard of at Daw's Police Station, which place he had to pass on his way to Benalla. Three volunteers have just returned from Stringybark Creek and report that they found the dead bodies of Constables Scanlon and Lonigan. The camp had been burnt and the pockets of the constables rifled. Scanlon was shot through the throat, while Lonigan was shot in the forehead. Search was made for Sergeant Kennedy, but no traces were found. The horses were tracked towards the King River. The volunteers packed the dead bodies on horseback, where I have sent conveyance to meet them. H. Kitchen, J.P., in absence of Sub-Inspector Pewtress.

Benalla Monday

To the Chief Commissioner of Police:

About half past four pm yesterday (Sunday) Constable McIntyre returned to the station and reported that on Saturday morning early, as they were preparing breakfast at the camp (on Stringybark Creek, about eight miles on the King River side of the Wombat Ranges), they were surrounded by four men who, presenting arms, called upon them to surrender. Lonigan immediately placed his hand behind for his revolver, when he was shot dead, another shot struck Scanlon. McIntyre says he saw him fall, the blood pouring out of his side. McIntyre, being unarmed at the time, jumped on his horse and rode off. Shots were fired after him, hitting his horse, which fell. He then made his way on foot, reaching Matthew Byrnes' farm yesterday afternoon, from whence he was driven in to Mansfield by Ned Byrnes. He states that when he left he thinks Kennedy was all right, but as he rode off he heard shots exchanged. Nothing has been heard of Kennedy yet. The police heard privately that the Kellys, for whom they had been looking for months past, were in the ranges at the head of the King River. The Kelly family live at Greta, 50 miles from here and the brothers were understood to be in concealment where Power once hid himself.

Two parties of police were secretly despatched last week, one from Greta, consisting of five men, with Sergeant Steele in command, and one of four from Mansfield. Though the movements of the Mansfield party were supposed to be dark the object of the expedition leaked out and no doubt was rapidly telegraphed across the bush to Edward Kelly. The ranges are infested with a brotherhood of Kellys, Lloyd's, Quinn's, etc. They occupy land amongst the hills and ostensibly carry on the operations of cattle breeders. From the account given by Constable McIntyre, it appears that the Mansfield party started on Friday, equipped with revolvers, one Spencer rifle and a double-barrelled gun, lent by a resident of the township. They had a tent and a fortnight's provisions. They reached Stringybark Creek, 20 miles from here, on Friday evening and camped on an open space on the Creek. It was the site of some old diggings. They pitched the tent near the ruins of two huts. They were about 15 miles from the head of the King. No special precautions were thought necessary, because the party supposed they were a long way from Kelly's whereabouts. The ranges round about were almost uninhabited and the party were not quite sure whether they were on the watershed of the King or the Broken River, but both Kennedy and Scanlon knew the locality intimately. It was Kennedy's intention to camp for a few days, patrol backwards into the ranges and then shift the camp in.

About six a.m. on Saturday Kennedy and Scanlon went down the creek to explore, and they stayed away nearly all day. It was McIntyre's duty to cook and he attended closely to camp duty. During the forenoon some noise was heard and McIntyre went out to have a look, but found nothing. He fired two shots out of his gun at a pair of parrots. This gunshot, he subsequently learned, was heard by Kelly, who must have been on the lookout for the police for days past. About five p.m., McIntyre was at the fire making the afternoon tea and Lonigan by him, when they were suddenly surprised with the cry, "Bail up, throw up your arms". They looked up, and saw four armed men close to them. Three carried guns and Edward Kelly two rifles. Two of the men they did not know, but the fourth was the younger Kelly. The four were on foot. They had approached up the rises and some flags or rushes had provided them with excellent cover until they got into the camp. McIntyre had left his revolver at the tent door and was totally unarmed. He, therefore, held up his hands as directed and faced round. Lonigan started for shelter behind a tree and at the same time put his hand upon his revolver. But before he had moved two paces, Edward Kelly shot him in the temple. He fell at once and as he lay on the ground said, "Oh Christ, I am shot." He died in a few seconds. Kelly had McIntyre searched and when they found he was unarmed, they let him drop his hands. They got possession of Lonigan's and McIntyre's revolvers. Kelly remarked when he saw Lonigan had been killed, "What a pity, what made the fool run?" The men helped themselves to several articles in the tent. Kelly talked to McIntyre and expressed his wonder that the police should have been so foolhardy as to look for him in the ranges.

He made inquiries about four different men, and said he would roast each of them alive if he caught them. Steele and Flood were two of the four named. He asked McIntyre what he fired at in the forenoon and said they must have been fools not to suppose he was ready for them. It was evident that he knew the exact state of the camp, the number of the men and the description of the horses. He asked where the other two were and said he would put a hole through McIntyre if he told a lie. McIntyre told him who the two absent men were and hoped they would not be shot in cold blood. Kelly replied, "No, I am not a coward. I'll shoot no man if he holds up his hands". He told Mclntyre that the best thing he could do was to advise Kennedy and Scanlon to surrender, for if they showed fight or tried to run away they would be shot. McIntyre asked what they would do if he induced his comrades to surrender. Kelly said he would detain them all night as he wanted a sleep and let them go next morning without their arms or their horses.

McIntyre told Kelly that he would induce his comrades to surrender if he would keep his word, but he would rather be shot a thousand times than sell them. He added that one of the two was father of a large family. Kelly said, "You can depend on us". Kelly stated that Fitzpatrick, the man who tried to arrest his brother in April, was the cause of all this, that his (Kelly's) mother and the rest had been unjustly "lagged" at Beechworth. Kelly then caught sound of the approach of Kennedy and Scanlon and the four men concealed themselves, some behind logs and one in the tent. They made McIntyre sit on a log and Kelly said, "Mind, I have a rifle for you if you give any alarm". Kennedy and Scanlon rode into the camp, McIntyre went forward and said, "Sergeant, I think you had better dismount and surrender, as you are surrounded". Kelly at the same time called out, "Put up your hands". Kennedy appeared to think it was Lonigan who called out and that a jest was intended, for he smiled and put his hand on his revolver case. He was instantly fired at, but not hit, and as Kennedy then realised the hopelessness of his position jumped off his horse and said, "Its all right, stop it, stop it." Scanlon, who carried the Spencer rifle, jumped down and tried to make for a tree, but before he could unsling his rifle he was shot down and never spoke. A number of shots were fired.

McIntyre found that the men intended to shoot the whole of the party, so he jumped on Kennedy's horse and dashed down the creek. Several shots were fired, but none reached him. Apparently the rifles were empty and only the revolvers available, or he must have been hit. He galloped through the scrub for two miles and then his horse became exhausted. It had evidently been wounded. He took off the saddle and bridle and concealed himself in a wombat hole until dark. He then started on foot across country and walked until three p.m. on Sunday, when he reached McColl's place, near Mansfield. Two hours or so after McIntyre reported the murder of the troopers, Sub-Inspector Pewtress set out, accompanied by McIntyre and seven or eight townspeople, for the camp. The police station was so empty of weapons that all the arms they could take were one revolver and one gun. They reached the camp with the assistance of a guide at half-past two this morning. They found the bodies of Scanlon and Lonigan. They searched at daylight for the sergeant, but met with no traces of him. The tent had been burnt and everything taken away or destroyed. There were four bullet wounds on Lonigan and five on Scanlon. Three additional shots had been fired into Lonigan's dead body before the men left the camp. The extra shots were fired so that all might be equally implicated. McIntyre is certain that Kennedy was not hit, but no one here at present ventures to do more than hope that the brave fellow has not been since murdered. It is McIntyre's belief that Kelly meant to spare none, but dispose of them in a way to render their fate a mystery. Now that they know McIntyre has escaped, they may possibly let Kennedy live.

A large party will be despatched tomorrow morning to succour Kennedy if alive and run down the murderers. They will provide themselves with food for several days. Two extra police arrived today and three more will be here in the morning in addition to any who may be sent from town by rail tonight. McIntyre is weak from bruises and from 48 hours' severe exertion. The sorrow felt for the death of Scanlon is universal throughout the district. He seems to have been a brave, cool, amiable, excellent man. Kennedy was an efficient bushman and a resolute officer. He has a wife and five children, and, fortunately for them, should he be killed, his circumstances are good. Scanlon was unmarried and his station was Benalla. Lonigan was from Violet

Town. He has left a widow and four children, badly off. The public ought not to be satisfied until the band of villains by whom the district from here to Greta is kept in a state of terrorism is effectually put down. The wet weather is likely to obliterate all tracks on the ranges and render the pursuit of the Kellys difficult, but an efficient party will be sent out.

The Police Murders

The Argus, 30 October 1878

It was nine o'clock this morning before the last of the search party left the township. There were seven mounted troopers, seven or eight townspeople and Sub-Inspector Pewtress. Most of them were provisioned for three or four days. The police had four or five rifles (two of them excellent weapons, sent by a private individual) and revolvers. McIntyre stated yesterday that for an expedition against men like the Kellys revolvers were comparatively useless and that the police ought to have breechloaders. The main object of the expedition is to find Kennedy, and from the character of the man, his coolness and tact, it is probable that he is still alive, only detained as prisoner. He had not been personally concerned in the pursuit of the Kellys and so they had no special grievance against him.

The scene of the murders lies in the ranges beyond the Wombat Peak, only 16 or 17 miles north-east of Mansfield as the crow flies. The country thence to the head of the King, 12 or 15 miles further on, is described as most difficult to cross. Dense wattle and bogwood scrub prevails everywhere. Not long ago some prospectors lost a horse near Stringybark Creek, but did not find the animal for three weeks, yet all the time it was in hobbles only a mile and a half from camp. The belief generally entertained is that the Kellys can conceal themselves in the ranges for months. They have friends to supply them with food. They have just got eight days provisions from the police, an abundance of ammunition and 10 firearms. For all that, it would not do to let any band of marauders suppose that they can establish themselves in the ranges with impunity. The Government have offered a reward of £200 a head for the men, but they must go a great deal higher than that and send a first-class body of troopers to the ground. It is pretty certain that intelligence of the departure of the police was carried across to Kelly's headquarters last Friday. He came upon the camp on Saturday forenoon, probably alone or with his brother, but did not care to attack the two constables until he had brought up the rest of his party. Hence the delay. They descended on the camp through clumps of saw-edged sword grass between four feet and five feet high. The tent stood in the middle of about three acres of cleared ground and commanded a good view of all approaches except the one through the sword-grass.

No precautions were taken to prevent surprise, because the police never suspected that an attack would be attempted. Edward Kelly must have had full particulars communicated to him, for in his talk with McIntyre he described each of the horses, asked who rode them and who carried the rifle. There were four troopers' horses and two packhorses. The police carried their revolvers buttoned up in cases and so could not get them out in time to fire.

On Monday, two friends of the Kellys came into the township from Benalla, Isaiah 'Wild' Wright and his brother, a deaf and dumb man. He stated in the hotel bars that he meant to go out and join Kelly and somewhat in bravo style warned one or two persons to stay in the township today unless they wanted to get shot. He said he believed Kelly would torture Kennedy and he was only sorry for Scanlon. Though a good many of Wright's remarks only amounted to his customary bluster, yet the police thought it prudent to lock both brothers up. They were about the streets when the party started and had their horses ready, so it was not improbable that one of them meant to ride straight off with news to Kelly. The arrest of Isaiah 'Wild' Wright was made so hurriedly that he had no time to resist.

The post-mortem examination upon the two bodies, by Dr Reynolds, showed that Lonigan had received seven wounds, of which one, through the eyeball, must have caused speedy death. Scanlon's body had four shot-marks upon it and the fatal wound was caused by a rifle ball, which went clean through the lungs. Scanlon was 33, Lonigan 37 years of age. A magisterial inquiry was held by Mr Kitchen, J.P., at the hospital. The principal witness was Constable Thomas McIntyre. Nearly the whole of his evidence was anticipated by yesterday's despatch, but he gave some additional details of the talk with Edward Kelly, which it may be worthwhile to relate. He had not seen Edward or Daniel Kelly before, but recognised them at once from the descriptions given in the Police Gazette. The remark Edward Kelly made when he saw he had shot Lonigan was, "Dear, dear, what a pity that man tried to get away". They then sat down to wait the absentees. One of the two strangers told McIntyre to take some tea and asked for tobacco. He supplied tobacco to two or three of them and had a smoke himself. Daniel Kelly suggested that he should be handcuffed, but Edward pointed to his rifle and said, "I have got something better here. Don't you attempt to go. If you do I'll track you to Mansfield and shoot you at the police station". Edward Kelly said he had never heard of Kennedy, but Scanlon was a flash. McIntyre asked whether he was to be shot. Kelly replied, "No, why should I want to shoot you? Could I not have done it half an hour ago if I had wanted?" He added, "At first I thought you were Constable Flood. If you had been, I would have roasted you in the fire". Kelly asked for news of the Sydney man, the murderer of Sergeant Wallings. McIntyre said the police had shot him. "I suppose you came out to shoot me?" "No," replied McIntyre, "we came to apprehend you." "What," said Kelly, "brings you out here at all? It is a shame to see fine, big, strapping fellows like you in a lazy loafing billet like policemen." He told McIntyre if he was let go he must leave the police, and McIntyre said he would. The best thing McIntyre could do was to get his comrades to surrender, for if they escaped he would be shot. "If you attempt to let them know we are here, you will be shot at once. If you get them to surrender I will allow you all to go in the morning, but you will have to go on foot, for we want your horses. We will handcuff you at night, as we want to sleep." McIntyre asked Kelly if he would promise faithfully not to shoot them if they surrendered, nor let his mates fire. Kelly said, "I won't shoot them, but the rest can please themselves".

Kennedy rode into the camp first and Scanlon followed close behind. They went to the usual dismounting place. McIntyre had advanced to within a yard of Kennedy when the men called out, "Bail up, put up your hands". Sergeant Kennedy grasped the case of his revolver and immediately shots were fired at him. Scanlon was dropped as he made for a tree. McIntyre saw the blood spurt from his right side as he fell. A great many shots were fired, but the police had no time to draw their arms. Though Kennedy surrendered the fire was continued and McIntyre made up his mind that Kelly did not intend to spare any lives. He therefore mounted Kennedy's horse and bolted. As he rode off he heard Daniel Kelly call out, "Shoot that –". More shots were fired, but none struck him. Kennedy was quite close to McIntyre when the latter mounted, but did not say a word. McIntyre got a severe fall as he rode through the scrub, but remounted, and went a long distance further before his horse gave in. He made a brief memorandum of what had occurred as he lay concealed in the wombat hole. It concluded with the words, "the Lord have mercy on me". At dark, he started on foot and walked for an hour with his boots off to make no noise. He took a westerly course to strike the Benalla and Mansfield telegraph line. On Sunday afternoon he reached the latter place.

On Monday morning the search party examined the scrub for a half-mile round the camp, but saw no traces of Kennedy. They gave one "cooee", but received no answer. The account given by McIntyre of the manner of his escape from the camp is not at all clear. Probably the men had emptied all their guns and the two revolvers at the moment he jumped on the horse. They had weapons enough, however, to fire 18 shots one after the other. The post-mortem shows that both troopers were riddled by shots from Edward Kelly's rifle. Two bullets and one slug were extracted from the bodies. Kelly turned with a grin on his face to McIntyre when he shot Scanlon and said, "What a fool he was to run". The police have their suspicions as to who the two strange men are, but do not like to name them. Edward Kelly was the only good shot in the party.

On Sunday, the townspeople were somewhat apprehensive of a visit from the bushrangers. The Kellys can get plenty of assistance in the mountains. They have so many connections round about Mansfield that actually some people are afraid to speak of the recent murders except to assured friends. The deceased constables were buried today, at two o'clock. Father Scanlon, (no relation to Constable Scanlon), of Benalla and Mansfield, has already set to work to get a memorial stone erected over the graves. Mr Tomkins, President of the Shire and one of the members of the search party, has just returned to Mansfield. He reports that they carefully examined the ground all round the camp up and down the creek and went several miles in the direction of the King River, but found no traces of Kennedy. The ranges were very difficult to explore on account of the thickness of the scrub and the steepness of the slopes. The party are confident that the Kellys have gone off to the King River and taken Kennedy with them, but the tracks of the four horses could only be followed a short distance from the camp. The route taken by McIntyre in his flight was crossed and it was plain that he had not been pursued. The police and the other members of the party returned to Monk's Sawmill, about eight miles from here, for the night. Though the party believed the Kellys had gone, they did not like to camp out all night. Tomorrow, when the reinforcements arrive, a fresh start will be made. One of the search party was Father Kennedy, (no relation to Sergeant Michael Kennedy), of Benalla, who drove hither yesterday with Father Scanlon. The two priests started from Benalla on purpose to render help to any wounded men they might fall in with and were provided with medical appliances. Father Scanlon stayed in Mansfield and conducted the funerals. Superintendent John Sadlier arrived from Benalla at 10 o'clock and reported that the troopers from Melbourne were on the road as they missed the train yesterday. The widow of Lonigan came here today in great distress. The family have been left almost helpless. Lonigan, when he took farewell of his friends at Violet Town, said he did not expect to come back alive, but was resolved to go wherever he was ordered. The short exploration made by the search party enabled them to say that McIntyre's escape was miraculous, for he seems to have galloped recklessly down the creek. It is expected that his horse will be found. The wombat hole in which he hid was a mile from the place where he unsaddled the horse.

The Mansfield outrage has excited the greatest alarm and apprehension. The whole district is in a fever of excitement. Senior Constable Irvine started away from Alexandra this morning for Mansfield, having received orders to proceed to the scene of the outrage with all haste. On the news being received in Benalla, there was no hesitation in ascribing the murderous deed to the notorious Kellys, who for some months past have lived in a state of outlawry. At the last Beechworth assizes the mother of the criminals, together with Skillion (a brother-in-law) and Williamson, alias "Brickey", a fellow who was living with the Kellys and was about to marry the second daughter (sister to Ned and Dan Kelly), were tried for being accomplices in the crime of attempting to murder Constable Fitzpatrick. Mrs Kelly, a notoriously bad woman, got three years imprisonment and the other two prisoners six years each and they are now in Pentridge. If the crime which has so shocked the community be the act of the Kellys, it may, in part, be accepted as the revengeful answer of desperate men to the officers of the law for bringing their relations and friends to punishment for their misdeeds.

The Kelly family is notorious in this district and their names are familiar as household words. The father (a man of ill-repute) died some years ago, leaving the widow (now in Pentridge), the two sons, Edward and Daniel, and four girls. The house of the family has been the rendezvous of thieves and criminals for years past and indeed has been the centre of a system of crime that almost surpasses belief. They lived on the Eleven Mile Creek between Winton and Greta and there can be no doubt, made a living by horse-stealing and theft generally. They were surrounded by neighbours of the same bad reputation and it was notorious that to obtain evidence, or arrest the accused, owing to the network of confederates for miles around, was almost impossible. The scoundrels were principally engaged in horse-stealing, a work that, owing to the poor police protection afforded in the district between their haunts and the Murray, could be carried on with impunity. It was the habit of the gang to steal horses wholesale for scores of miles around and cross the Murray with them and there, among the "old hands" and settlers, "swap" or sell them.

This profitable trade was carried on for years, but the outrage upon Constable Fitzpatrick, the outlawry of the brothers Kelly and the consignment of a batch of the horse-stealers to Pentridge, appeared to have broken up the unlawful business and the district began to breathe freely after being relieved of a terrible incubus, when word came of this daring crime, only a score or two miles away. Edward Kelly is notorious as having been arrested in the year 1870 as an accomplice of the notorious Harry Power. Power had the Kellys, Quinns and others of the notorious "Greta mob", as it was termed, for accomplices, if not actually in his pay, and it was they whom he blames for "selling him". In the Vagabond Papers we find him taking "The Vagabond" into his confidence and stating "I always was stuck for want of a mate. There's young Kelly was with me for a time, but he was no good and helped to sell me at last. They say that he or one of the Quinns was dressed up as a blacktracker to deceive me. God will judge them for taking blood-money". And again, the notorious scoundrel Power describes how the Quinns sold him after he had paid the whole family well and how he resisted the temptation to harm their daughter. In the centre of the country where Power carried on his nefarious crimes were the two Kellys, who, not satisfied with highway robbery, have now apparently added to their crimes a double or triple murder. Of course the Kellys had numerous friends who were capable of taking to the road. Daniel, the younger Kelly, not long since served three months in gaol for breaking into a house with the Lloyds, his cousins, and one of the latter was sentenced to three months' imprisonment for indecently assaulting a woman in the house.

The Mansfield Murderers

The Bendigo Advertiser, 30 October 1878

Of course such a crime as that perpetrated on Saturday could not have been anticipated, but nevertheless we think greater vigilance and precaution might have been taken in despatching a party of police after such lawless men as the two young Kellys. Here we find four troopers, armed with the authority of the law, but unfortunately ill equipped otherwise, sent out to apprehend two desperate men, charged with a capital offence, without provision being made to enable them to discharge that duty efficiently. It might have been anticipated that two men of the characters of the Kellys would make a determined resistance. The police, therefore, sent out on that duty should have been armed with the best weapons in the police armory and have been provided with scouts to explore the dens of the reprobates and prevent a surprise. Now it appears that three of the troopers were armed only with revolving pistols, which are inefficient weapons, except at short ranges, and that Scanlon alone had a Spencer rifle. All four certainly should have been provided with similar weapons, but it seems that by some very bad management, though police are stationed at Mansfield and Benalla and elsewhere in the district, the efficiency of the arms placed in their hands was entirely overlooked.

We are told that two hours after Mclntyre reported at Mansfield the murder of his comrades, Sub-Inspector Pewtress, accompanied by seven or eight volunteers, set out for the scene of the outrage, but so imperfectly was the police depot supplied with weapons that there was only one revolver and one gun amongst the eight or nine men. It was a fortunate circumstance that the bushrangers were not made aware of the approach of the volunteers, or other victims would probably have been added to the catalogue of crime. On Friday last, when Sergeant Kennedy's party set out on its disastrous expedition, Constable Mclntyre borrowed a revolver from Constable Meehan, who had consequently to traverse the country between Mansfield and Benalla, with a report of the murders, totally unarmed. But what a state would either of these townships have been in if the bushrangers took it into their heads to attack them. It is too soon yet, perhaps, to express an opinion regarding the ambuscade and its disastrous consequences, but it appears that if secrecy was essential in effecting the capture of the Kellys, that Constable McIntyre acted most injudiciously in amusing himself by firing at parrots. Indeed it now turns out, according to what Edward Kelly told him, that the report of his piece attracted the attention of the bushrangers to the position of the police. The conduct of that constable also in mounting his sergeant's horse and abandoning that officer in the midst of such dangerous men requires explanation. It appears that when Kennedy rode into the camp and ascertained the real state of affairs, he acted differently, by jumping off his horse in order to support his companions. Had his own safety been Kennedy's chief object he might have saved his life by sticking to his horse and galloping away from the murderers. The criminal course of these four ruffians must be quickly stopped at all hazards and at any cost.

We have not the smallest doubt that the Police Department will vigorously do its duty in respect to the hunting down and punishment of these atrocious scoundrels. It is of the most vital importance that this fresh outburst of bushranging in Victoria should be promptly nipped in the bud. We must not have these blood-thirsty miscreants elevated to the position of heroes, as has been the case with some of their predecessors. No chance should be given them of exciting a maudlin sympathy in their behalf by treating them as men with whom anything like fair hostilities may be carried on. They have proved themselves to be treatcherous, sneaking, cold-blooded murderers. They deserve to be shot down like the wild beasts that they resemble wherever or whenever they may be met with. We think, therefore, that the Government would be fully justified in issuing a proclamation of outlawry against them, giving them a reasonable period, say a week or 10 days, to surrender themselves into the hands of justice. Very promptly and properly, rewards have been offered for their capture dead or alive. But these rewards are not high enough. The part of the country in which the ruffians are being pursued is one of the most mountainous and difficult in the whole colony. The scrubby and almost inaccessible nature of the district in many parts renders it possible for them to lay securely in ambush within a few yards of their pursuers and to slaughter them before they could offer any defence. The chance of capturing them is likely, therefore, to be a very long and dangerous one, and considering that Gardiner the bushranger cost the Government of New South Wales no less than half a million and effected his escape to another colony, after all, before he was taken, it would, we believe, be worth the while of our Government to offer at least £1000 a head for the Kelly gang. By this means some of their confederates might be induced to hand them over to the officers of the law. It might be notified also that a 'free' pardon would be granted to anyone of the party who would deliver the rest up to justice. We make these suggestions in the hope of preventing many outrages and much further bloodshed. It is due also to the inhabitants of the district invested by the murderers that they should be relieved as speedily as possible from the terror and the peril which the presence of 'such' a band of utterly unscrupulous villains must necessarily occasion.

The Police Tragedy

The Geelong Advertiser, 30 October 1878

The Police Department has thoroughly roused itself to the necessity which exists for prompt and vigorous action with respect to the Mansfield outrage. Fourteen troopers have been placed at the disposal of Superintendent Nicholson, and numbers of volunteers offer themselves to accompany the police and these are being separated into small bodies in order to thoroughly scour the country. Sufficient reinforcements to protect the most notable of the many scattered townships have also been sent to the district in which the outrage occurred. The whole of the parties now out have a very clear understanding that the desperadoes are to be shot like dogs if they show any resistance, but in spite of the precautions adopted it is extremely likely that their apprehension will prove a tedious task. I happen to be familiar with the country through which they are now ranging, which is wildly mountainous, closely timbered in places and extremely sparsely settled. When we remember also that the pursuing parties must necessarily be constituted stronger than the pursued, that they will have to keep themselves supplied with provisions and with means of frequent communication with the settlements they pass, and that unless the murderers show the direction in which they are travelling by sticking up some of the distant selectors to obtain food, they will be compelled to follow comparatively slowly on a dull trail. It is evident that the task before them, to secure the apprehension of the ruffians who have shocked society, is a difficult and dangerous one, especially in this case, when we remember that the bushrangers may, from their knowledge of the country, separate for days and reunite at rendezvous previously determined upon, that except for flour they are not likely to want for supplies of food and that they probably have a knowledge of the haunts in which Harry Power and other criminals who have taken to the bush found shelter in former times. With a wide range of country, including the main dividing range, over the side of which they may pass into the wild highlands of the Upper Dargo, the Aberfeldy, or the sources of the Mitchell River, and with a choice of those rarely trodden hills of the Buckland and the Buffalo Ranges, a party of four well-mounted men may elude pursuit until enthusiasm is almost exhausted. That they will sooner or later afford a clue to their position by committing some act of violence in the settlements may be confidently predicted, but meantime the public must be warned not to expect too early a success on the part of those who have joined the hunt. The popular idea that a large body of men may draw a cordon round a few and drive them to bay is not applicable to such work as our protectors have to do in these silent and but rarely ridden hills. Up to the present the police have been unable to ascertain who are the Kellys' associates, but it is conjectured that they will probably prove to be men well known in the district, named respectively Quinn and Wright. The two Kellys have been positively recognised by McIntyre, so that there need be no hesitation in at once outlawing them, and the former history of bushranging has amply proved that outlawry has a better practical effect in lessening the numbers of an organisation of miscreants where pardon to accomplices is out of the question than any other device for their capture.

Of Sergeant Kennedy nothing has been heard and in the Assembly attention has been called to the necessity of making still further search for him. In replying, the Honourable the Chief Secretary was understood to say that the steps taken to apprehend the gang would probably result in the discovery of Kennedy's fate. But it must be remembered that the search instituted at the site of the old camp appears to have been a hurried one and that it is still possible that Kennedy might have been left but a short distance off to die of wounds and starvation in the bush. It seems scarcely probable that in their flight a gang like the Kellys' would have encumbered themselves for any considerable distance with a living prisoner, while the fact of his remains not having been found is evidence that he was not slaughtered at the spot.

The following is the text of the reward proclamation, issued as a supplement to the *Government Gazette* on Monday evening: "Attack on Police, King River District Eight Hundred Pounds Reward. Whereas on Saturday morning, the

26th instant, a party of four members of the police force, namely, Sergeant Kennedy, and Constables McIntyre, Scanlon and Lonigan, who were in the King River District, were surrounded by four men who presented arms and called upon the said members of the police force to surrender. And whereas Constables Lonigan and Scanlon were shot dead, McIntyre escaped to Mansfield and Sergeant Kennedy has not been heard of. Notice is hereby given that a Reward of Two Hundred Pounds will be paid by the Government for such information as will lead to the apprehension of each offender". Graham Berry, Chief Secretary, Chief Secretary's Office, Melbourne, 28 October, 1878.

Tuesday Night, two men named Wright have been arrested at Mansfield today charged with threatening the lives of persons who are in search of the bushrangers. A second party has gone out in search of the missing trooper, Kennedy.

A magisterial enquiry has been held on the bodies of the murdered constables. McIntyre gave evidence similar to what has been already reported. Mounted Constables Kissane, of Creswick, and Alexander, of Balmoral, were taken to Melbourne by the mail train from Ballarat last night. They will proceed to Mansfield today to reinforce the police ranks there. Mounted Constable Moore, of Gordon, received notice yesterday to start for Melbourne, enroute for the scene of the tragedy, and he will leave Ballarat today, probably by the midday train. The Geelong troopers have not yet received any orders.

Never Taken Alive

The Argus, 30 October 1878

The local sub-inspector of police, who had the ruffian Edward Kelly, Powers' mate, under remand at Kyneton in 1870, tells me he firmly believes he will never be taken alive, as he is an agile, powerful and determined young man, full of ferocity when only slightly excited. In fact, he told that gentleman plainly at that time that if he ever took to the bush again he would never be taken alive, and my informant says he is quite sure he will keep his word if he can, either by murdering his pursuers, or by destroying himself when he finds all hope of escape cut off.

The Murders

The Gippsland Times, 1 November 1878

Great exertions are being made to track the murderers of the Constables Scanlon and Lonigan. The Government have increased the reward for the apprehension of the Kellys and their two associates in the murders from £200 to £500 for each, and at a special meeting of the Executive Council on Wednesday declared them all outlawed. They may therefore be shot by anyone who is lucky enough to find an opportunity of ridding the world of their presence. This exhibition of sternness by the Government, and the inducement held out in the substantial increase of the reward, will in all probability soon elicit some information of the whereabouts of the villains. The measure they meted out to Power will be meted out to them at last, for the 'friendships' they have formed are not likely to remain proof against the temptation to earn the 'blood-money' which may be won by a word. The New South Wales authorities are on the alert and have made provision for watching the crossing places on the Murray.

The two Wrights were brought up at the Police Court on Tuesday morning for using threatening language towards members of the search party. The dumb brother was discharged, and the elder brother, 'Wild' Wright, remanded for seven days and bail refused.

Four troopers arrived from Melbourne, but they have no knowledge of the country. The search parties, now out, include storekeepers, clerks, clergymen, wardsmen, contractors, labourers and bushmen, headed by the President of the Shire. Business is entirely suspended at Mansfield.

The Police Murders Finding of Sergeant Kennedy's Body

The Argus, 1 November 1878

A general feeling of regret was expressed throughout the city yesterday afternoon when it became known that any hopes which had been entertained with regard to the safety of the missing Sergeant Kennedy had been dispelled by the discovery of the dead body of the unfortunate officer. The melancholy intelligence was brought into Mansfield between one and two o'clock yesterday, by a search party under the direction of Sub-Inspector Pewtress and Mr Tomkins, the President of the Shire. Many conjectures had been made as to the probable fate of the missing sergeant, but while a general impression appeared to gain ground amongst the people in the locality that Edward Kelly and his band of marauders had taken Kennedy with them to the King River, scarcely anybody ventured to do more than hope that the gallant officer, who appears to have been ruthlessly shot, had not been murdered. The worst fears, however, have at length been realised and the desperadoes have added another diabolical deed to their atrocious crimes.

From the particulars telegraphed by our correspondent it appears that the search party, consisting of 10 volunteers and five constables, arrived at Stringybark Creek at half-past seven o'clock on Thursday morning and renewed the search. Shortly afterwards their labours were rewarded by one of the volunteers named Henry Sparrow, an overseer at the Mount Battery station, finding Sergeant Kennedy's body within half a mile of the camp where Constables Scanlon and Lonigan received their death wounds. The body presented a frightful spectacle and from the manner in which it had been mutilated was scarcely recognisable. The unfortunate sergeant had evidently attempted to escape from his murderers by the same track as that taken by Constable McIntyre when he jumped upon Kennedy's horse and rode off, as bullet marks were visible on some of the trees in the line of the track. He had been shot through the side of the head, the bullet coming out in front and carrying away part of the face, while several other bullet wounds were found on his body, one of which had penetrated the lungs. His jacket was singed as if a bullet had been fired into his body from very close quarters, probably after the unfortunate man had fallen. The remains were placed upon horseback and conveyed into the township, where the excitement over the deeds of the outlaws appears to be increasing. Sergeant Kennedy was a vigilant officer and generally well liked, and much sympathy is expressed for his widow and five children, who, however, are believed to be in tolerably good circumstances. If a telegram, which was received yesterday evening from Chiltern, is to be credited, it would appear that Kelly and his gang are endeavouring to make for New South Wales and by this time have probably crossed the border.

The following is the telegram referred to:

> Chiltern, October 31, 3.30 p.m. Kelly and three others stuck up a man named Neil Christian near Baumgarten's place, at

> Bungowannah, before daylight yesterday morning and obtained provisions from him. Kelly threatened to shoot Christian should he give information. Intelligence was not obtained till this afternoon. Assistance required to scour the country in the neighbourhood of Bungowannah. James Lynch, Sergeant.

Bungowannah is a small township situated on the banks of the Murray, on the Victorian side, nearly opposite to Howlong on the New South Wales side, and is believed to be a well-known haunt frequented by the Kellys.

One night in August, 1877, 11 horses were stolen from four farmers residing at Moyhu, near Greta, at which latter place the Kellys then lived. Some time elapsed before information of the offence was given to the police, as it was thought at the time that the horses had only strayed away. Ultimately the police traced the missing horses to the possession of the Baumgartens, who are two farmers living at Bungowannah. The Baumgartens, who were brothers, were tried for receiving the horses, knowing them to have been stolen, the result being that one brother was convicted and sentenced to a term of imprisonment in Pentridge, while the other was discharged. From inquiries made at the time, it was elicited that the Kellys had sold the horses to the Baumgartens and it was whilst endeavouring to arrest Daniel Kelly for horse-stealing in April last that Constable Fitzpatrick was shot in the wrist by Edward Kelly and so narrowly escaped with his life. The distance between Greta and Bungowannah is between 70 and 80 miles, and as the Kellys' had travelled between the two places on several occasions and were evidently well acquainted with the track, it would certainly be within the bounds of possibility that, after having murdered the three constables on Saturday last, they at once made for the residence of Baumgarten, with the intention no doubt of crossing over into New South Wales. The wisdom of such a step on their part may be questioned, as from the wild and almost inaccessible nature of the country near Mansfield, they might have held possession of their secret fastnesses for some time to come, while by passing into New South Wales they will get into comparatively open country. Whether this be the case or not, it now remains for the police to hunt down the maurauders with merciless severity and to leave no stone unturned to effect their capture, dead or alive. The search party in quest of Sergeant Kennedy reached the halting-place about half-past six last evening and camped there for the night. The party numbered in all, including police, 25 persons. An early start was made this morning at half-past five, the party being provided with provisions for the day.

They headed for the vicinity of the scene of the late encounter, when the party formed themselves into an extended line and scoured the country until they reached the place where the murders had been committed. After consultation it was decided to scour for a mile in the direction of McIntyre's escape tracks. Half a mile had scarcely been searched when a "cooee" from Mr Sparrow brought the party together and it was then found that the body of the unfortunate Sergeant Kennedy had been discovered. This was about eight o'clock. The body was stretched out and covered by a uniform cloak. Upon the removal of the cloak the body presented a partially decomposed appearance, particularly where the wounds were visible. The remains were then partially placed in a bag and raised to the back of a horse by Mr Tomkins and Constable Orr. A cart was then sent for to meet the procession and the body was conveyed to the halting place, which it reached at 11 o'clock. The body was found on McIntyre's return tracks. The party reached Mansfield about three o'clock, the news having previously been brought by Messrs Tomkins and Hageman. The body now lies in the morgue awaiting a post-mortem examination and inquiry, which will be held tomorrow morning. The unfortunate man is scarcely recognisable but by general appearance and the clothing. The face is quite blackened, the nose partially gone, and there is one large hole in the breast, as if a rifle had been put close to the body and fired after Kennedy had fallen. His clothes were burnt in the spot and around the wound. The right ear appears to have been cut off as with a knife. There is also a bullet wound under the right arm.

The return party report that they met a party of police from Greta, which was originally organised to act in concert with Kennedy's party. The Greta police reported having come upon the tracks of Kelly's party last evening, by discovering a native bear recently shot by a rifle ball. They are now following up the tracks, but are badly equipped. Volunteers also report that wherever the police are met with they are found inadequately equipped. In one case there was only one rifle between five troopers and that was borrowed on the road. They are disheartened from the fact that they cannot cope with the outlaws of whom they are in pursuit, armed as the latter are with breechloaders. The police generally complain of want of rifles and ammunition. Messrs. P.W. Bromfield and W. Collopy rendered special assistance as guides to the party.

The Police Murders - Supposed Traces of the Kelly Gang

The Argus, 2 November 1878

Another report was circulated yesterday to the effect that the gang had bailed up a puntman and crossed the river. However, some regard this with suspicion and consider that the Kellys are more likely to conceal themselves in the most inaccessible ranges of this colony. Those who think so set down the report that they have made for New South Wales either as a ruse to mislead the police, or as an exaggeration of some incident altogether disconnected with the Kelly gang. This view is substantiated to some extent by some intelligence which reached Benalla yesterday. Particulars received as to the Chiltern case render it highly improbable that the Kellys were the parties. The men were not mounted, it does not appear that they had arms, nor are the descriptions alike. The necessary steps have been taken, however, in case the report should be well founded. The report is evidently believed in Chiltern, where it came from originally. Considerable excitement continues. Four armed troopers reached here by last night's late train and four more by the 1.30 p.m. train today. The first four have gone in the direction of Baumgarten's on the Murray, I hear, while two of the second four have suddenly left again. If the gang have crossed the Murray, it is to be hoped that they will find the New South Wales police on the alert for them.

The *Outlawry Bill* passed by the two Houses of Parliament this week was assented to yesterday by the Governor and the preliminary steps were taken to have the four murderers outlawed. The Governor's proclamation of his assent appears in last night's *Gazette*. An information against the offenders has been sworn by Mr Manwaring, of the detective department, before Mr Call, P.M., and warrants issued. The further steps necessary under the *Act* will be taken today by the Attorney-General.

With regard to the complaints contained in our yesterday's telegrams as to the want of a sufficient number of police and of proper weapons in the Mansfield district, we are assured by Captain Standish that everything possible is being done to meet the requirements of the case. There are several parties of police in the field, whose proceedings are very properly kept secret. The Government have purchased about 30 double barrelled breechloading fowling pieces, which are stated to be a very effective weapon and the most suitable kind for the use of those who are not trained marksmen. The Spencer rifles are certainly superior both with regard to the number of shots they can discharge and the distance they can carry, but although their mechanism is very simple, it is considered that they would not be so useful in the hands of those who are not trained riflemen as the fowling pieces just obtained. The latter are of course being despatched to the field of action.

Today the telegraph wire to Mansfield broke down and communication was cut off. The stationmaster has taken steps to find out where the accident has occurred and effect repairs. To the police, at present, it is of the utmost importance to keep all lines open.

This morning a man came down the road, from Mansfield, with some particulars as to the action of Thursday's search party, of which he was one. Unfortunately he was not present in the camp when the deceased sergeant was found and so could add little to the stock of information already published, but he had some conversation with the police who arrived at the sawmills on Thursday from Greta. They were the men who started from Wangaratta at the same time that Kennedy and his men left Mansfield. They followed up the Fifteen Mile Creek from Greta and passed over some very rough ground, but saw no traces of Kelly and his comrades. The only token that they met with of the presence of men on the ranges was a freshly shot native bear, which they picked up on Tuesday morning, at the head of the Fifteen Mile Creek. Unless Kelly had been trying the Spencer rifle upon it, one can hardly see why he should have fired at the animal. The troopers knew of the murder of the Mansfield police, for they had been followed up by men specially sent out by Superintendent Nicholson.

Both Wright and the Dummy were set at liberty on Wednesday, but probably the fact that the elder brother is at large has not yet been telegraphed. It is difficult to believe that the police would allow Wright to be bailed out after they had once resisted the application and got him remanded for seven days, but a man who knows Wright well and came from Mansfield yesterday, states positively that he met the two brothers in the forenoon on the road to Greta. It appears that one or two warm friends of the unfortunate sergeant privately offered to reward Isaiah Wright handsomely if he would fetch Kennedy in alive, or give information which would lead to his recovery. Though Wright declined to accept any offers of payment, he agreed to perform the duties proposed to him and hence no doubt procurred his liberty. The incarceration had done him a lot of good, for all his bravado had disappeared.

One of the most effective instruments for the capture of the bushrangers will be the new *Act*, and it is fortunate that public opinion has been so actively stimulated as to get it passed promptly. Not only will the measure put some wholesome fears into the hearts of Kellys' friends, but encourage reputable people resident in the ranges to give information without fear, for they have now a guarantee from the Government that the pests will be thoroughly rooted out.

There still exists on the part of many a disinclination to avow the little assistance they have rendered to the police, and one person who was of Thursday's party has specially requested that his name may not be mentioned.

An excellent spirit pervades the police force, and men from all parts of the colony have volunteered for special service. One man on leave of absence has thrown up his leave in order to go out. It will not serve the public interest to mention the details of the plans already carried out, but a considerable number of separate parties are now out. It is the opinion of some people that the reward placed on Kelly's head is still too small, but there are reasons why we should not owe the capture of this marauder entirely or chiefly to the treachery of his acquaintances. The interests of the district require that the police shall absolutely clear the horde out, so that for the future bad characters may not be encouraged to look upon the ranges as a safe retreat. For the next few days every party of strange horsemen will be taken for the Kellys.

At the time that Edward Kelly accompanied Power on the trip that that desperado took via Malmsbury to Little River and back, Superintendent Nicholson, who was then at Kyneton, saw Kelly, and was so taken with his appearance that he had a serious talk with the lad and got him to listen favourably to a proposal to quit the bad company he was in and go to a station in New South Wales. Kelly had not then committed any offence and seemed somewhat eager to go, but one of his relatives got hold of him and took him back to Greta. The opportunity to save him from the career of crime upon which he subsequently entered was thus unhappily lost. It is stated by George Munder that he was stopped by four men on the banks of a lagoon near the Murray. They were armed and they demanded provisions. They threatened to throw him into the river if he did not get what they wanted. He was detained for three hours and warned not to make any report before Sunday. One of the four men appeared to be wounded and lay on the grass all the time the party stayed. This is consistent with the mode of Kennedy's death at the fatal camp. If he ran away immediately after McIntyre, he would have time before he was overtaken to draw his revolver and fire at least one shot. The bullet marks on the trees would show that several shots were fired at him besides those that hit him. Munder was confident that the four men were Kelly's party. The report reached here just before Superintendent Nicholson started by the eight o'clock train for Wodonga tonight. The facts on which this despatch is founded did not reach me in very clear order, but the story has probability.

The weather is very wet and much against the men in the ranges. McIntyre has been moved from Mansfield on account of the state of his health and nerves, which are still considerably shaken. The Mansfield telegraph line is repaired. An inquiry on the body of Sergeant Kennedy has just been held at Mansfield. Constable McIntyre corroborated his previous statements. He believed Kennedy had surrendered, but he heard shots fired while he was escaping. Henry Sparrow deposed to finding the body about half a mile from camp near a tree that had bullet marks in it. The spot was an open space of about 10 yards and the tree was between Kennedy and the camp. Constable Orr said there were no signs of a scuffle. Other witnesses corroborated this. Dr Reynolds deposed that he had no doubt that death took place on the same day as the deaths of the other constables. There was a large wound in the centre of the sternum, caused, it was supposed, by a charge of shot fired at a very short range. It passed completely through the body, coming out of the back. It was believed to be a shot wound from its size and the appearance of the rent through the clothes. There was also another wound directly under the right arm, which was probably given when Kennedy held up his arms. Upon escaping, and on seeing that the murderers would show no mercy, he had fallen. The gang, then coming up, had put the muzzle of a gun close to his breast and shot him through the body, which was in an awful state. Father Scanlon has arrived to be present at the burial. About

200 attended Kennedy's funeral, which was headed by Father Scanlon, the Bishop of Melbourne and the Reverend Sandiford, Church of England clergyman. Mrs Moorhouse performed the gracious act of placing a wreath of flowers on the coffin. The service was conducted by Father Scanlon. All business places were closed. The wire has been interrupted since eleven o'clock and is supposed to have been cut by some of Kelly's confederates. Four troopers left here at daylight this morning. No news has arrived from any search party. It has been raining heavily all day.

The residents of Benalla have been interested by the constant arrival of bodies of police to join in the pursuit to strengthen the protection at the smaller townships, which it was thought might be stuck up, and to patrol the Murray. The authorities adopted the plan of securing all the mounted men who had ever been stationed in the north-eastern district, and as a consequence they have got together a body of men well acquainted with the district and at a great advantage over members of the force unaccustomed to the bush. Benalla contributed its quota. From Sandhurst, Kyneton and the Western District, as far as Balmoral, men were brought, and after a brief stay to rest themselves and horses, were told off for duty in the district by Superintendent Nicholson, who is in charge in the place of Mr Sadlier. We had a look at one body of these men at the station, dressed in common dress, and certainly they are a class of men in every way to be relied on for dangerous service. The men were all roughly dressed, but well dressed, although not so well mounted. The horses, as a rule, are not the best for active service and there seems good reason for the complaint that country troopers have to put up with inferior animals, whilst the best horses are kept in and around Melbourne for show. The men had not been practised with firearms and were ill-acquainted with the arms they had to use, which appears to us to be a serious defect in the service, but they were eager to mount and be off. Amongst them was Trooper Flood, whom Ned Kelly has sworn to 'roast' if he catches him. The reason for the outlaw's hostility to this constable appears to be that Flood, whilst stationed at Greta, kept a strict surveillance over him and his friends. Sergeant Steele, of Wangaratta, is another of the force on whom Kelly has a determined 'down'. Steele was mainly instrumental in bringing the Baumgarten or 'Greta mob' to justice and revenge has been sworn by Kelly. This criminal appears to be a man of a most vindictive and bloodthirsty character. His threats of murder have been so numerous that it would be hard to recount them. When crossed by the officers of justice, or by anyone, in fact, it was his invariable custom to threaten what in bushranging parlance is called 'colonial law'. He is said to have stated before the late Beechworth assizes that he would wait to see if his mother was convicted. If she were not he would give himself up to answer the charge of horse-stealing preferred against him, whilst if she were he would shoot every man concerned in bringing about the conviction. Mrs Kelly was convicted and Kelly appears to be taking his revenge on the force. As showing the nature of the murderer, we may mention that he has also threatened to do for Mr McCarthy O'Leary, Barrister, of Benalla, the only reason apparently being that Mr O'Leary ordered him out of his office on one occasion when the fellow was talking about giving 'colonial law' to certain members of the police force.

The Chronicle

Williamstown Chronicle, 2 November 1878

Throughout the length and breadth of the colony horror and indignation have been aroused in the minds of all classes of the community by the outrages committed by Kelly and his murderous associates during the past week in the Mansfield district. The murder of the three constables, Scanlon, Lonigan and Kennedy, in cold blood, has annihilated every trace of mercy and the four young men have by their own diabolical acts delivered themselves over to a terrible retribution. In justice to society they have been branded as outlaws, everyman's hand raised against them and a price set upon their heads. The action of the Government of the day in promptly offering a reward for each of the miscreants, dead or alive, and proclaiming them outlaws, meets with the full concurrence of every right-minded member of the community, and should these steps be insufficient to secure them, the authorities will be expected to take such further means, however extreme they may be, to vindicate the law and relieve the country of such fiends incarnate. While upon this subject, we may be excused making a few comments on what we regard as the carelessness or folly which has been shown in the equipment of the parties who have been sent out to follow up the murderers. We hear that the troopers and civilians who form these parties are armed only with revolvers. It is known that Edward Kelly has a splendid breechloading rifle and that his accomplices are also well armed. The police feel the disadvantage they are under if they should succeed in overtaking the bushrangers.

Now, what is there to prevent each member of the party being armed with a breechloading rifle and well supplied with ammunition, as well as being supplied with a revolver? There are hundreds of such arms in the possession of the volunteers and we apprehend there could be no difficulty whatsoever in obtaining from that source a sufficiently large number to arm every man in the search party. The necessity which has unfortunately arisen this week for employing the police in active duty of this kind must be our excuse for referring to the matter of their equipment generally. In Williamstown, the police are provided with muzzle-loading Enfield rifles, the only use ever made of them being periodical cleanings of lock, stock and barrel. Not a shot is ever fired from them and the constables, being absolutely unpractised in the use of their weapons, would as a consequence be conspicuous failures if they were called upon to go out on active service. We are told that the same state of things exists in other districts, and if it be the case with those unfortunate men who have been ordered to the Mansfield district to follow Kelly and his companions in crime, we can only express our deep commiseration for them. Policemen are always liable to be called upon to use firearms in the maintenance of law and order and they should certainly be thoroughly well practised, not so much in polishing the brass mountings of their weapons as in their use.

The Mansfield Bushrangers

The Bendigo Advertiser, 2 November 1878

The interest excited locally in the Mansfield outrage and the sympathy for the unfortunate men who were so cruelly murdered by the bushranging gang continues unabated. Every fresh piece of news is eagerly looked after and the probability of the early capture of the ruffianly gang eagerly discussed amongst all classes. There is a great indignation expressed as to the want of arms among the Victorian police and the Government yesterday purchased 300 suitable short rifles, which have been sent up and will be served out with ammunition to police and volunteers. Mr Graves, M.L.A., has been telegraphed to call attention in the House to the miserably deficient arms of the police.

Thursday's search party, numbering 24, had only three rifles, and the men had to exchange arms at each watch. There was not a single revolver or gun in the police camp on Thursday night. Constable Hodgson, who was formerly stationed at Echuca, but latterly in the Sandhurst and Eaglehawk district, has been ordered to join in the search after the murderers. It was his intention to leave the Sandhurst Station by the 4.15 train this morning for Echuca. Any four men could bail another man up and represent themselves to be the notorious Kelly gang, and the mere mention of the name would be sufficient to produce terror in any single individual. By this means it might be hoped to distract the attention of the pursuers from the locality in which the gang are actually hiding, awaiting a more favourable opportunity of getting across the border, or going in whatever direction they might deem safest. It does not seem probable that at the present time, while an alert watch is kept on every hand, these men would leave the vastnesses of the wild country in which the outrage was committed, every hole and corner of which is well-known to them and in which they might hide secure from discovery at least for a considerable time unless betrayed, for the more open country lying to the north, in which they could not long hope to retain life or liberty. Most are of the opinion that the gang have not moved far from the scene of the atrocities which have created so much indignation throughout the whole colony and we hope that the search of the King district will continue.

The inquest on the body of Sergeant Kennedy has just been held. Henry Sparrow deposed to finding Kennedy's body about half a mile from the camp, near a tree. The tree had bullet marks on it. The spot was an open space of about 10 yards. The tree was between Kennedy and the camp. Constable Orr said there were no signs of a struggle having taken place where the body was found. He should suppose that upon Kennedy's attempting to escape, when he saw the murderers would show no mercy he was shot and fell and that the gang then came up to him and put the muzzle of a gun close to his breast and shot him through the body. Father Scanlon arrived to be present at the burial, which takes place this afternoon. The Sketcher artist is here, but finds it difficult to get volunteers to accompany him unarmed to the scene of the outrages. All the available police in the district are now out searching for the gang, the Albury township police included. Two troopers are stationed at all the bridges, in the event of the bushrangers attempting a rush across, and all the crossing places and punts are under police surveillance. At the Wahgunyah bridge over the Murray, last night, the tallgate was kept locked, while the only available policemen, together with about half-a-dozen civilians fully armed, kept watch, and as each passenger, horseman or driver of vehicles crossed, he was challenged and examined. Strong reinforcements of police have arrived, and have been placed all along the border, so that if they have not already crossed it will be impossible for them to do so now. The warrants issued by the Victorian authorities for the arrest of the gang for murder have been backed by New South Wales. Great excitement still prevails.

The Police Murders

The Argus, 4 November 1878

Constable McIntyre is now in the police hospital at the Richmond depot, having been sent there on Saturday in consequence of the impaired state of his health. The terrible scene which he witnessed his own jeopardy and narrow escape, occasioned a great shock to his nervous system, the effects of which he is now realising, and when in his race for life he fell from horseback he sustained much injuries and bruises to his back as would be alone sufficient to throw him off duty for a time. He was and still is most anxious to be after the murderers of his comrades, but, it is doubtful if he will be allowed to return to the bush until all danger of his being assassinated is over. Being the only eyewitness of the slaughter, it is thought that the bushrangers or their friends might attempt to destroy him, and it is stated that his life has actually been threatened. He says, however, that he has no fear on that account and that the only threat he knows of was made when he was arresting 'Wild' Wright, who muttered to him, "You have escaped once, but you won't next time".

A contemporary on Saturday represented McIntyre as saying that on the Friday evening before the murders he fired several shots at kangaroos and that it was this foolish conduct which had probably attracted Kelly and his mates. McIntyre desires us to contradict this and to say that he never made any statement to that effect. The facts were that on Friday evening Sergeant Kennedy said he had seen several kangaroos in the bush and asked McIntyre to shoot them. McIntyre found that the game had disappeared and returned to the camp without firing a shot. McIntyre also gives us the following particulars which will further explain some points in the tragedy. When

Kennedy and Scanlon left the camp it was with the view of reconnoitering and determining their exact position. There had been a difference of opinion as to what creek it was they had encamped at, some of them thinking that it was Holland's Creek and others that it was one of the sources of the King River. It was their intention, having ascertained their position, to strike eastward and form their next camp on the King River. They believed that they were fully 20 miles from the Kelly's, as they had information that they were to be found in the ranges near Greta. Between their tent and the creek and a little to the left were two fallen trees, one lying over the other at right angles. In the angle facing the tent McIntyre, on Saturday afternoon, kindled a large fire to make the night cheerful. After he had prepared tea at a small fire at a stump of a tree nearer the tent, he was standing in front of the large fire whilst Lonigan stood in the opposite angle of the fallen trees.

The four men suddenly emerged from tall grass on the right of the camp and advanced in skirmishing order. Edward Kelly was the man on the extreme right of the line and consequently nearest to the policemen. Some have asked why McIntyre, on seeing Lonigan fall, did not spring forward to seize his revolver and make a fight, it may be well to point out that the fire and fallen trees intervened between him and Lonigan, and that in addition to this the desperadoes advanced upon him immediately with levelled guns and would have shot him on the spot if he had stirred. Ned Kelly appropriated all the firearms about the camp before he would allow McIntyre to lower his hands. He inquired particularly as to how the fowling-piece was loaded and on finding that it only contained round shot he picked them out and replaced them with bullets. This weapon he then exchanged with one of his accomplices for a single-barrelled rifle. Kelly had thus two rifles, one of his mates a double-barrelled fowling-piece, loaded with bullets, and the other two one gun each, besides revolvers. When they appropriated the tea which had been prepared, they asked McIntyre if it was poisoned, and it was probably for the purpose of satisfying their minds on that point that they required McIntyre to drink the beverage with them. When Kennedy and Scanlon were approaching the leader of the gang, Edward Kelly, placed one of his men in the tent, stationed his brother Daniel and the other ruffian in the tall grass already referred to and concealed himself within the angle of the fallen trees where Lonigan was shot. He ordered McIntyre to sit upon the cross-tree and told him that one of his rifles was for him and that if he did not act as directed he "would make a hole in him". These arrangements were so made that when Kennedy entered the camping ground he was covered by the rifles of Daniel Kelly and the other two unknown offenders. Scanlon was only a yard or two behind. Both men dismounted together. Kennedy walked a few paces from his horse, was challenged by the bushrangers, and fired at.

McIntyre had, in accordance with Kelly's orders, walked up to the sergeant and advised him to surrender. Although Kennedy called out "Stop it boys", the villains continued shooting and Scanlon was killed. McIntyre, seeing then that the miscreants intended to slaughter them all, looked about for a way of escape. Kennedy's horse frightened at the firing and was rearing about beside him. With a spring he was soon seated in the saddle and his feet slipped easily into the stirrups. The horse shied, and in urging it forward with his heels he lost a stirrup. Seizing the horse's mane he leaned to one side to catch the stirrup with his hand. The assasins had evidently just fired at him and concluding from this movement that he had been wounded, they set up a fiendish yell of delight. With the aid of a small branch which he snatched from a tree as he was passing, he was able to gallop out of their sight. He could not look back to see what had become of Kennedy, for if he had done so he would have been sure to dash his head against some tree. After a perilous ride he fell from the horse, how he cannot tell, but supposes he was caught by a branch.

The photograph of Kelly which has been circulated amongst the police is, he says, a good likeness, but the outlaw presents a rather altered appearance, as he now wears a square-cut moustache and a short beard, at least he did so when he stuck up the camp. There can be no doubt that this deplorable affair has found the police in the districts contiguous to the outrage very inadequately equipped. In addition to what has been already stated on this subject, it appears that the fowling-piece possessed by Kennedy's party was borrowed from the Reverend Sandiford, of Mansfield. The mounted troopers are well trained in sword exercise, which is very well in its way, but it seems to be considered unneccessary to train them to the use of rifles or carbines. For 12 or 18 months before the butts were removed from Sandridge the men of the Richmond depot were regularly exercised at them in revolver practice, and in commending this practice in September last year we suggested that the troopers should also be furnished with carbines and taught the use of them, a suggestion which has not yet been adopted. The revolver now used by the police is called Webley's, and notwithstanding reports to the contrary, is a most elective and reliable weapon. Adams and Colt revolvers were both discarded for it. When the men where practising at the butts, Sergeant Fegan, their drill instructor, tested its throwing power and found that at a distance of 200 yards the bullet struck the target with as much force as if it were fired from a carbine.

The 30 fowling-pieces purchased the other day by the Government have cartridges containing 18 or 20 round shot and are said to be deadly at a long distance. A fear has been expressed that the parties out hunting for the bushrangers might mistake each other in their disguise and shoot each other down. This fear was not without grounds as whilst police patrolling both banks of Murray. The Wahgunyah party were fired on last night by another party of police, fortunately without injury. Some understanding should be come to so that the various police and volunteer parties might recognise each other and so prevent such a dangerous mistake being repeated. It was an old trick of Power's to elude the police by appearing to cross into New South Wales and Kelly is quite capable of the same ruse. Eleven troopers disguised left here in haste about 11 o'clock this morning for Benalla. Large reinforcements of police have already been received on the border and specially selected men from other districts are expected to arrive today (Saturday). There is now a strong cordon of police right along the border and parties stationed back from the border, so that they can be met if they break through the first line. Every possible crossing is being closely watched by strong parties of police.

The Mansfield Bushrangers

The Bendigo Advertiser, 4 November 1878

On Saturday evening Constable Couch of Marong proceeded to the scene of the outrage for the purpose of joining in the search. We shall not be surprised to hear of this officer distinguishing himself in his perilous task, for to our own knowledge he has been proved to possess all the requisite qualifications for work of this description. Some years since, when he was stationed in the Murray district, he was known as a smart and courageous officer, and on several occasions, when having to deal single-handed with very rough characters, who had devoted themselves to horse-stealing and like pursuits, he acquitted himself in a particularly creditable manner. He is a good bushman and being a 'light weight', an essential qualification for the work in which he is now engaged, though one which is frequently unduly depreciated, his horse can take him over almost any country. It would, we think, be a matter for congratulation if many more men of the same stamp as Constable Couch were sent up to join in the search after the desperate villains who have perpetrated the shocking deeds which have evoked such a strong feeling of indignation throughout the colony. Nothing would afford the police greater relief than to hear positively that Kelly has taken to the open country. There is one reported fact which gives some colour to the statement namely, that four armed men, taken for police, were seen on the top of the range about 20 miles from Mansfield, on Sunday. They were on the track which Kelly would be likely to follow if he wanted to make the Murray, but all reports of this sort, even when circumstantially related, have to be received with the greatest caution. For the next few days every party of strange horsemen will be taken for the Kellys.

The *Herald* of Saturday publishes an account of an interview between a reporter and Constable McIntyre, who escaped from the bushrangers. In the course of the interview McIntyre is reported to have said:

> I really believe they intended to shoot me and only kept me alive in order to obtain information as to the movements of our party and perhaps because they did not want to fire, as it might have alarmed Kennedy and Scanlon, whose horses they expressed their determination to obtain. It was a dreadful time for me when the men hid, just as the poor sergeant was approaching the camp. I didn't know what to do. I have been blamed by some persons for not warning Kennedy, but after having begged Kelly on my knees to spare my mates' lives without producing any effect upon him, I thought it advisable, to wait till Kennedy came to camp.
>
> When the firing commenced it was pretty hot. I counted six shots as fired by the rascals. Ned Kelly had a double-barrelled gun or rifle, and discharged both barrels. When Lonigan fell I thought the best thing I could do was to endeavour to clear out, as I might, if I lived, be able to arrest the murderers. When I left the camping place, Lonigan was kneeling, his head hanging down, whilst the blood was pouring out of his side. Sergeant

Kennedy had just dismounted and cried out to the gang, "Stop it, boys! Stop it!" I thought it was all up with us, but as a last hope I sprang into Kennedy's saddle. The animal seemed scared at the firing, and not having my spurs on I had a little difficulty in getting the horse to move. I had just time to lean over and place my foot in the right stirrup, when the scoundrels, seeing I was making off, stopped firing at Sergeant Kennedy and commenced shooting at me. They evidently thought they had hit me when I leaned over for the stirrup-iron, for they set up a diabolical laugh all round. At this juncture I pulled a small branch from a tree, and striking the horse, managed to get out of shot. I hope to be well by Monday, when I intend asking the 'Chief' to permit me to follow up the trail. Sub-Inspector Pewtress is a fine fellow and considering that he has been stationed in town for so many years, does very well in the ranges. He acts promptly, discreetly and pluckily. After I returned to Mansfield I only had a slight breakfast, and volunteered again immediately. Sub-Inspector Pewtress said I could please myself, but did not press me to resume duty and I had to be carried by two men to my saddle. I wish you would mention this fact, sir, as I feel sorry that some persons have questioned my conduct.

The same journal gives an account of the proceedings of two of the search parties, which returned to Mansfield on Friday night:

Both parties met in the Glenmore Ranges, about 30 miles from here, and arrived at eight o'clock last night, drenched to the skin. The weather was awful at night. The men were miserably armed. There was one rifle in Steele's party and one in James's. Each man, however, had a revolver, but these weapons are no good at a long range. They were also short of ammunition, and James's party had only two blankets for the lot. Affairs have been very badly managed, Steele, whom the Kellys want, is a splendid shot and a fine bushman. He carried a Spencer rifle, with a range of 800 yards. He is equally as anxious to meet Kelly as Kelly is to meet him. The men prefer breechloading rifles, which are not nearly so heavy as the Spencer and are easier handled. It rained the whole time the party was in the ranges. One hill in the Glenmore Ranges, which the police had to climb, is nearly a mile up, which took an hour and a half to get up. Several horses got knocked up.

The following telegram from Detective Kennedy was received by the Chief Commissioner today:

> Benalla 1st November. Myself and party searched Murray flats since three o'clock this morning. Found marks of shod horses and traces of recent fire in hollow log. A man named Gideon Margarey says he saw four men on the flat on Wednesday morning. One of them winged. They asked him for bread, which he supplied. A small bit of cheese and two empty bottles were found in a log. Margarey cannot, or will not, describe the men. One of them had a face like a Chinaman. On the whole we incline to believe that Kelly and his mob may have been there and cleared out yesterday, as the river is rising fast. Probable direction Greta. One of the men told Margarey, so he says, that he was Kelly the bushranger and that he intended calling on a man named Whitty, at Moyhu, about some horse-stealing case. If the information be correct, Kelly and his mates are hard pushed for food. Close watch should be kept about Greta and Moyhu. Margarey says he saw some horses with the party. Colours of the horses: a very dark brown, a chesnut and a dark bay. Assuming, as I have said, there may be some truth in the information, still he says it in a way not to inspire confidence. Don't think they have crossed the Murray. Will continue search. – D.S. Kennedy, Senior-Detective, Wodonga Police Station.

The Police Murders

The Argus, 5 November 1878

A special train was run from Broadford to Chiltern yesterday morning with reinforcements for Superintendent Nicholson, consisting of mounted constables called in from outlying districts. The railway gates at Tarrawingee were not opened, and the train dashed through them, happily without any serious result. No information as to the operations of the police can be obtained from official sources. There is nothing definite to report up to the present time concerning the bushrangers. There are several parties out in the direction of Rat's Castle, where the gang are believed to be secreted. This place is situated between the Indigo Creek and Yackandandah and is a most inaccessible place. It is confidently believed that the miscreants are on this side of the border, as the River Murray is running very high at the present time and is almost impossible to be crossed.

Yesterday afternoon an application was made to his Honour the Chief Justice by Mr Gurner, the Crown Solicitor, under the *Felons Apprehension Act* recently passed, for an order requiring Edward and Daniel Kelly and their two associates to surrender themselves. The application was based upon an affidavit sworn by Captain F.C. Standish, the Chief Commissioner of police which was as follows:

> On the 1st November, 1878 information made on oath was sworn by W.A. Mainwaring before Frederick Call Esquire, a Police Magistrate in and for the Colony of Victoria, and a Justice of the Peace in and for the said colony, that Edward Kelly, of Greta, in the said colony, on the 26th October, 1878, at Stringybark Creek, near Mansfield, in the northern bailiwick of the said colony, in company with one Daniel Kelly and two other men whose names are unknown to the said William Mainwaring, did feloniously and with malice aforethought kill and murder one Michael Scanlon.
>
> 1. A warrant was, on the 1st November, thereupon duly issued by the said Frederick Call, as such Police Magistrate and Justice of the Peace as aforesaid, for the apprehension of the said Edward Kelly, charging him with the offence as aforesaid, which is a felony punishable by law with death.
>
> 2. The said Edward Kelly, so charged as aforesaid, and the beforenamed Daniel Kelly, and two men whose names are unknown, are mounted, armed, and associated together, and they did, on the said 26th October, at Stringybark Creek, resist and kill the said Michael Scanlon and Michael Kennedy and Thomas Lonigan, officers of justice.
>
> 3. The said Edward Kelly so charged as aforesaid is at present at large, and will probably resist every attempt made by ordinary legal means to apprehend him.

> 4. The Attorney-General has directed an application in chambers on his behalf to be made to one of the judges of the Supreme Court, in pursuance of the *Felons Apprehension Act* 1878, for the issue of a Bench warrant, under the hand and seal of the said judge, for the apprehension of the said Edward Kelly, and in order to his answering and taking his trial for the aforesaid offence of which he so stands accused.

There was a similar affidavit made by Captain Standish as to Daniel Kelly and the two other men whose names are unknown, and the order was asked to be issued against each of them. His Honour made the order against each of the accused, directing them to surrender at Mansfield on the 12th instant, for the purpose of taking their trial for the offences alleged against them. The summons reciting the order requiring them to surrender was directed to be published in *The Argus* and *The Australasian* and the other metropolitan daily and weekly newspapers and the newspapers at Beechworth, Chiltern, Benalla, Wangaratta, Jamieson, Mansfield and Wahgunyah and in the *Government Gazette*. By the provisions of the Act if the accused fail to appear, or if, having been arrested, they escape, an affidavit is made to that effect, a judge of the Court may then enter a declaration on the records of the Supreme Court that any of them is an outlaw, and on such declaration being approved by the Governor-in-Council, the offenders can be shot down by anyone going to arrest them without any other summons.

The following is a copy of the order directing Edward Kelly to surrender, the orders against the others being in similar terms:

> To Edward Kelly, of Greta, in the colony of Victoria. Whereas, on the fourth day of November, one thousand eight hundred and seventy-eight, a Bench warrant was issued, in pursuance of the *Felons Apprehension Act* 1878, under my hand and seal, in order to your answering and taking your trial for that on the twenty-sixth day of October, one thousand eight hundred and seventy-eight, at Stringybark Creek, near Mansfield, in the northern bailiwick of the said colony, you did, in company with one Daniel Kelly and two other men whose names are unknown, feloniously and of malice aforethought kill and murder one Michael Scanlon. And whereas, in pursuance of the *Felons Apprehension Act* 1878, I did on the fourth day of November, one

thousand eight hundred and seventy-eight, order a summons to be inserted in the *Government Gazette* requiring you, the said Edward Kelly, to surrender yourself on or before the twelfth day of November, one thousand eight hundred and seventy-eight, at Mansfield, in the said colony of Victoria, to abide your trial for the before mentioned crime of which you, the said Edward Kelly, stand accused. These are, therefore, to will and require you, the said Edward Kelly, to surrender yourself on or before the twelfth day of November, one thousand eight hundred and seventy-eight, at Mansfield, in the said colony of Victoria, to abide your trial for the before-mentioned crime of which you so stand accused, and hereof you are not to fail at your peril. Given under my hand and seal, at Melbourne, this fourth day of November, in the year of Our Lord one thousand eight hundred and seventy-eight. William F. Stawell, Chief Justice of the Supreme Court of the Colony of Victoria.

News arrived regarding the party of men seen at Barnawartha. They had five horses and one of them bore a bell brand – the brand of the packhorse which was taken out from Mansfield by Sergeant Kennedy. Another horse had the ordinary broad arrow upon it. Ready cooperation is afforded to the police by the Railway Department and the telegraph office. The message received from Superintendent Nicholson, at Chiltern on Sunday, rendered it necessary to despatch some extra men forthwith, and by 11 p.m. a special train was placed at the disposal of Superintendent Sadlier. Six or seven of the men who arrived at nine p.m. from Mansfield were sent off by this train, under the command of Sergeant Steele. They had a good rest at Mansfield after their three days of hard bushwork, and though they and their horses had just come off a 40 mile journey, yet they were prepared to start again in little more than an hour. They would get a short rest in the train before they took the road again. From the telegraph office the police authorities received invaluable aid, and the wires are available each night until a late hour. The Stationmaster (Mr Sax) appears to do all the work himself, and he deserves to be honourably mentioned for the courtesy he has afforded to the press, and the close attention he has given, long after ordinary closing time, to the transmission of special messages.

Today a short talk was had with Senior Constable Kelly (no relation to Ned Kelly), a member of the party who came across the ranges, via Mansfield, under Sergeant Steele. Though some of the information received from him maybe now a little old, the narrative should nevertheless possess some interest, particularly where it touches on the movements of some suspected friends of the Kellys'. The tracks of the party cannot be indicated very closely on the map, on account of the few known landmarks in the region drained by the King River, but the general direction can be shown. If the map be looked at it will be seen that the King River runs pretty nearly due north from the ranges to Wangaratta, where it enters the Ovens. The best plan therefore will be to find Wangaratta, and then trace the river southwards to its source. Greta, the well-known hotbed of the Kellys, Lloyd's and sundry other folks of evil reputation, will be noticed between Moyhu on the King, and Winton, on the north-eastern railway line. The Fifteen Mile Creek can be traced backwards through Greta in a direction parallel with the King River. This minor tributary of the Ovens rises near Wombat Hills and close to the sources of the Holland River which flows in a north-west direction to Benalla. Stringybark Creek, the scene of the murders, runs into Ryan's Creek, which runs into the Holland.

If the King be followed up through Whitfield, a point will be reached where the river divides into two important branches, one of which comes down from the Wombat Hills on the west and the other from the Great Dividing Range on the south-east. A good deal of land has been taken up by selectors, but they have kept quite close to the river, and above Whitfield the selections simply form a chain along the course of the stream up to the point at which the two branches unite, settlement then abruptly terminates. Nearly the whole of the upper selections are in the hands of an intelligent body of Chinese, occupied in the cultivation of tobacco, peanuts, etc. They appear to thrive and one of them keeps a small store. The junction of the two branches of the river is an important point, for 'Quinn's Paddock', a notorious place in Power's time, lies just above it. This paddock, part of an old pre-emption, stretched across the whole of the river flat from precipice to precipice, and completely blocked the entrance to the ravines in which Power lay concealed.

The police when in pursuit of Power had to steal by Quinns' place in the dead of night in order to escape notice, but they passed it boldly in daylight when they returned with their prisoner. The arms they carried prevented any display of hostility on the part of the Quinns'. A police station was subsequently established close to Quinn's settlement and two constables were stationed there. The presence of the police proved very disagreeable, and when it was found that they could not be dislodged, even by burning down their stables when they were absent, the Quinns sold out and their land fell into the hands of a respectable settler. It was not considered necessary to maintain the police station after the Quinns left, and the constables were therefore called in. The department has reason just now to regret that this important outpost was closed. On the way up the King, one of the police parties fell in with John Quinn, uncle of Edward Kelly, and a man named George Johnston. They learned that Quinn had made a number of inquiries of the selectors, with a view to find out who the police supposed the two strange men of Kelly's party to be. It should be remarked in parenthesis, that James Quinn, one of the occupants of the paddock in Power's time, is at present in Pentridge. Quinn and Johnston kept ahead of the police all the way up to Glenmore, at the junction of the two branches before alluded to, and then struck off to the left, in the direction of an apparently impassable range which the police supposed would compel them to turn back and exhibit themselves ere long, but no more was seen of Quinn and his companion in that neighbourhood. They told some of the settlers that they were looking for horses and others that they were gone up for a bull.

Usually when Quinn has a mission of importance in hand which he does not wish to make public, he brings a bull down from the ranges. He now has a retreat somewhat deeper in the mountains than the one which he occupied at Glenmore. It is between the Rose River, a tributary of the Buffalo, and one of the eastern sources of the King. Strange to say, the very day after one party of police lost sight of Quinn at Glenmore he was met by another party. Quinn had found a bull and his face was now directed downstream towards Greta. He was accompanied not only by Johnston, but by a man named Thomas, who if he was picked up in the same locality as the bull, must have travelled about 70 miles in two days, for he was seen on Monday in Beechworth. Thomas was not suitable company for an honest man, having been convicted not long ago of shooting with intent to wound. Quinn, of course, had no information to give the police about his nephew, but rode along, in the fashion of the Kellys and Lloyds, with his hat pulled down over his eyes. The quickness with which he had doubled back showed how intimate his acquaintance with the ranges must be.

The King was found very difficult to cross below Glenmore on account of the flood. The police had to swim their horses over obliquely, and steer carefully to avoid boulders. Some distance up the ranges they came upon an empty hut, which appeared to have been recently occupied. They found flour and also about a dozen gun cartridges concealed in the roof. They brought away the cartridges, but left the other things undisturbed, as they had some reason to believe that the hut was provisioned for the benefit of an out station hand, and not the Kellys. The two parties of police by this time had become consolidated into one and numbered 11. They ascended a very steep spur, and struck across to the Wombat. For two days it rained heavily and they had to put up with the discomfort of saturated clothes. They could not venture to light a fire, except on low ground, where they made tea.

On the high parts of the ranges almost perfect solitude prevailed. No birds were heard or seen, the crows and magpies had been left far behind. Wombats and wallabies were abundant in places, and the holes excavated by the former in the soft earth were noticed to be marvellously large. Very scanty supplies of grass could be obtained for the horses after they had left the neighbourhood of the friendly settlers. Many of the slopes were quite bare of herbage, and covered only with sharp, loose stones, which told severely on the horses' feet. In the gullies cattle tracks were numerous, and some wild cattle and a few wild horses were occasionally seen. The spur ascended from Glenmore was so steep that the horses could not go more than 10 or 12 yards without stopping to recover wind, but in this respect the country was not more difficult than that around Woods Point. No traces of the Kellys were met with between the King and the fatal camp. A few miles from the camp, in the direction of Mansfield, a call was made upon a selector named Perkins who was reported to have supplied the Kellys with provisions for three or four months past. Perkins was working in a garden in front of a small bark hut. He had heard nothing of the Kellys.

On the previous Sunday, when a member of the first search party called, and reported to Perkins's daughter that two constables had been shot, the news appeared to cause no astonishment. The only remark was "Yes", and no particulars were asked for. One of the constables saw Perkins give a peculiar grin as the dead bodies were carried past. Mrs Perkins, however, came out and said, "Excuse a woman's curiosity, but how many were shot?" When Steele's party of police reached Mansfield on Friday, they were able not only to get into good quarters, but to buy dry clothes. The breeches of some of them were so much injured with wet and wear that they tore into rags as they were pulled off. It is to be hoped that the Government will deal somewhat liberally with the police employed in searching for the Kellys and not cut them down to the new regulation allowance of 1s. 6d. a day. Small as his allowance is a commercial traveller would raise his eyebrows at the amount, yet it would nearly cover the authorised expenses of five constables.

Between Mansfield and Benalla on Sunday the police met the two Wrights. It had not taken the pair more than three days to go across country to Greta and back, if they went away at all. As Kennedy's body was found the day after 'Wild' Wright got his release there was no occasion for his special services. No details have yet reached Benalla to enable us to determine whether the Kellys are still near the Murray, or have turned back to Greta. The ranges haunted by the Kellys are prolonged beyond the north-eastern line. One obstacle they would meet with if they turned back immediately is the flooded state of the Ovens, which they would hardly be able to cross on horseback with safety between Bright and Wangaratta or even lower down. On Sunday Father Scanlon, at the Roman Catholic Church, called upon all right-minded people to help the police and maintain the authority of the law. He said that numerous friends had consoled with him on account of the death of Constable Scanlon whom they had heard was his cousin. There was no relationship between them, but the manner in which the deceased trooper had conducted himself in the district would have made him (Father Scanlon) proud to call him a kinsman. The reverend gentleman is bestirring himself about the erection of a monument in the Mansfield Cemetery.

No communication has been received from Superintendent Nicholson since morning. Strahan's party, who have been patrolling between the King River and Wombat Hills since the day before the murders, have today, for the second time, reported themselves at Mansfield. They have been over a great deal of ground. They state that they have seen tracks of horses which they propose to follow up, but it is probable that they have merely crossed the trail of Steele's party, of whose presence on the ranges they could not have been aware. The men are stated to be in good health in spite of the bad weather and ready to set out again on receipt of fresh instruction. The main body of the party have not come into Mansfield. The weather has improved since the afternoon.

The Police Murders

The Argus, 12 November 1878

The authorities here very properly refuse to make known what is to be done by each party sent out, for if they were to do so the gang of which they are in search would soon know all about the proceedings. The men sent out do not know in what direction they are going, that only being confided to the non-commissioned officer or man who is put in charge. The authorities here are greatly annoyed at a statement that appeared in one of the morning papers to the effect that a Government horse had been found by one of the parties recently despatched from here. This fact was known on Saturday, but as it was hoped that it would lead up to something further there was a desire that it should not be made known. The confidence having been broken, it may now be said that when a party was returning from the Murray in the Yarrawonga direction they came upon horse tracks, and after some searching a brown horse, bearing the Government brand, was found in the Warby Ranges, not more than six miles from this town. It was minus its shoes, and had evidently been travelled at such a rate that the gang were obliged to abandon it. This horse, which is said to be 20 years old, was one of those attached to Sergeant Kennedy's party as a packhorse, and had at least been abandoned, owing to the hard work in the ranges having incapacitated it for further effort. The horse will be brought in this evening, but from a further investigation that has been made of the locality, it is believed that the tracks seen in the vicinity of the place where the horse was found were at least a week old.

The only advantage derived from the discovery is, therefore, the almost certainty of the gang of desperadoes having doubled back on their tracks towards the Murray. The untoward publication of this fact about the discovery of the horse has quite upset one plan arranged by the authorities, and very naturally causes them to be much more reticent in giving information. Some little excitement was caused today by the guard of the morning up train stating at Benalla that he had seen four armed men sticking up a bushman on the old main road between Glenrowan and Benalla. To the great amusement of all who had heard the statement, however, it turned out that the armed party was that of an officer of police, with his men, who had considered it necessary to interrogate a man whom they met on the road. This is one sample of the rumours that get afloat in the district. Superintendent Sadlier arrived here by the morning train to confer with Superintendent Nicholson, and he brought with him a copy of the threatening letter which had been sent to Mr Monk at Wombat Hills, between Mansfield and the scene of the murder. "To E. Monk, You think you have done a great thing by searching for the traps, but you have made a great mistake, for your friend Kennedy is gone, although we made him confess many things, and many little things you have told him in confidence. And we heard you say you could track us, and our horses, but we will track you to hell, we will have you. We will make your place a Government camp, and give them some more bodies to pack when we come. What a fine thing it is to cut their ears off, but we will poke your eyes out. Yours until we meet, E. and D. Kelly." The handwriting is not disguised, and there was no difficulty in tracing it home to the writer, who is now in the Mansfield lockup. The letter plainly shows what an amount of sympathy is felt in the district towards the desperadoes, and to what an extent the system of terrorism is being carried on towards those who are supposed to be giving any information or assistance to the police, and also how necessary it is for the authorities to be very reticent as to their proposed movements, so as to prevent any knowledge of their intentions to leak out.

There is, however, one satisfaction, and that is the knowledge that tomorrow the provisions of the *Outlawry Act* come into operation, and then certain persons who can't at present be touched by law can be most severely dealt with. From what I can see at present, the police, who are working their hardest, do not receive the assistance from the general public that they are entitled to, especially in such a work as this. Some people are under the impression that the police are solely working for the £2000 reward which has been offered by the Government for the arrest of Kelly and his confederates, but this view should be at once put aside, when it is stated that the police can't share in the reward. The men are working with the sole desire to bring such hardened criminals to justice, and so avenge their murdered comrades. As showing the hard work which has been done recently, it may be stated that several of the police horses had to be sent out to the paddock today for a few days' rest, in consequence of the difficult country they had had to go through in the ranges having made their feet sore. There is, however, a good supply of spare police horses in the district, so that no party will be delayed from going out whenever ordered

The Police Murders

The Argus, 15 November 1878

There has been absolutely nothing doing here today. None of the search parties that are out have sent in any information as to their movements. There is no doubt that the weather that prevailed during the past week has been very favourable to the Kelly gang. There has been a bright moon at night-time, which they could utilise so as to travel rapidly among the fastnesses which they know so well, while at the same time the hot sun has made the ground so hard that their tracks can be followed with difficulty. It was different when rain prevailed, as then the tracks were more easily discernible, and it is believed that had not the hot, dry weather set in the tracks which were lost in the Warby Ranges the other day might have been followed up until the party was traced. There are many people here who believe that these tracks were not those of the Kelly party, but that some of their friends have taken out in that direction the packhorse belonging to Sergeant Kennedy's party was found, with the sole object of misleading the troopers and putting them on a false scent, so as to allow the gang to get away in the direction of the head of the Murray, and so cross into New South Wales at a point where it is probable that there is not a very strong force kept, and which might be more easily evaded than at some of the better-known crossing places. A rumour was current here this evening to the effect that a party of four armed men had been seen in the vicinity of the Darling, but it could not be traced to any authentic source, nor could it be ascertained at which particular spot on the River Darling they had been seen. It is therefore more than probable that it is only another attempt of some of Kelly's friends to mislead the authorities. This morning Superintendent Nicholson came down from Wangaratta, and has been in close consultation with Superintendent Sadlier during the day. A keen eye is kept by certain parties on the movements of the troopers, and it is rumoured that the men now in the police camp are to be despatched on a search expedition during the night.

This only shows how every movement of the authorities is watched, and notice no doubt promptly despatched to the outlaws by their friends. Some people who profess to know the Kellys are of the opinion that if ever the gang of ruffians are brought to bay Ned Kelly will make a hard fight of it, and will not be taken alive, but that Dan Kelly will show the white feather directly Ned is shot down and will at once give in. Of the other two men little is known, but on all hands it is agreed that Ned Kelly is the moving spirit of the band, and that if he were once disposed of the others would not hold out. Some men in uniform were seen to arrive by the train last night, and as several gun cases were seen with them, the rumour at once gained ground that the Government had sent up some of the Victorian Artillery to assist the police in searching for the ruffians. It turned out, however, that the men in uniform were some of the volunteers on their way to Sydney to take part in the Intercolonial Match.

The Police Murders

The Argus, 18 November 1878

There are no fresh tidings of the whereabouts of Kelly and his mates, and the people in the district are beginning to complain about the desperadoes being at large for such a length of time. Superintendent Sadlier, with two blacktrackers, went out yesterday in the direction of Winton, but it is not known with what success, as everything is kept very quiet. More troopers arrived here last night, and a host of men are now awaiting orders to proceed. Their destination is kept secret, but hopes are entertained of valuable information being obtained tomorrow. Detective Ward passed through Benalla last night. It is believed that the publication of the outlawing proclamation will have a good effect, and may frighten some of the murderers' friends or mates and induce them to give information.

Further Outrages by the Kelly Gang

The Geelong Advertiser, 12 December 1878

The Chief Commissioner of Police has given to the Press the following particulars of the robbery of the National Bank at Euroa by the Kelly gang on Monday last, and of other outrages committed by them:

Euroa is a post and telegraph station on the Seven Creeks, 102 miles north east of Melbourne (County of Delatite). It is on the main line of road between the metropolis and Beechworth, and is now reached by the north-eastern railway, and has a station and a goods shed. The land in the neighbourhood is principally of a pastoral character, but it is now being much taken up for farming uses. There is one flour-mill in the township, a sawmill, a branch of the National Bank, and a State school. The population is about 200, and rapidly increasing. The Kellys stuck up Mr Younghusband's station at Faithfull's Creek on Monday morning, and remained in possession of it during the whole day. On Tuesday the outlaws approached the township of Euroa, only a few miles distant, leaving, it is presumed, one of their number in charge of the station.

They then cut the telegraph wires between Melbourne and Euroa, and removed a considerable length of wire. They then went to the bank, the robbers being Edward Kelly, Daniel Kelly, and Steve Hart, who were armed with revolvers, and stuck up the clerk and manager, taking with them nearly £300 in sovereigns, and a quantity of notes amounting, as is estimated, to 14 or 15 hundred pounds. They compelled the manager, with his clerk and family, to get into a vehicle, in which they were taken to the Faithfull's Creek station, and retained there till near midnight, when they were liberated. Superintendent Nicholson arrived in town on Tuesday night, and left yesterday afternoon for the scene of operations with a number of policemen. Arms have been forwarded to Euroa. The gang took possession of the township and kept charge of it for some hours. The manager of the National Bank, Melbourne, received a telegram from the local manager yesterday. He says that the bank was stuck up by the two Kellys and Steve Hart. Edward Kelly and Hart presented revolvers at the clerk's head, and the other Kelly took charge of him, while Hart and Edward Kelly glided noiselessly into the room of the manager, whom they secured. Kelly had a revolver in each hand, and Hart one in his right hand, and there was nothing for it but to surrender. The bank was then ransacked, and the manager states that the outside of what was taken away was from £200 to £300 in specie, and between £1400 and £1500 in notes.

A gentleman thoroughly conversant with the district in which the Kelly outlaws are carrying on their depredations furnishes the *Herald* with the following probable account of their movements since they were in the Warby Ranges:

> In all probability they found the Warby Ranges afforded insufficient shelter, and, therefore, would cross the main road

and railway line, a few miles from Glenrowan, thence keeping in the direction of Tatong. The Broken River would be crossed between Samaria and Mansfield, after which the gang would at once cross into the thick, rangy, and sparsely inhabited country which leads into the Strathbogie district, at the back of Violet Town, Euroa, and Longwood. The Strathbogie Ranges are very difficult to travel in, and at one time afforded a refuge to Morgan, Power, and other notorious scoundrels. The distance from the Kellys' haunts is not great, and the gang could travel almost the whole way through difficult rangy country. The probable course of the outlaws will now be to lie concealed for a time in some of the steep granite gorges of the Strathbogie. It is evident they have provisions and ammunition, but the fact of their being still together ought to ensure their capture at no remote date. They have had only a very short start of the police, but lest they should try to make back to their old haunts at the head of the King River, a cordon should be drawn along the Broken River at once. After the outrage at Euroa, we may expect to hear of McKellar's station on the Broken River, and even the Mansfield or Alexandra banks, being stuck up, unless the bushrangers are overtaken. Kelly and his three mates stuck-up Faithfull's Creek station on Monday afternoon, about two o'clock.

The surprise was so sudden that no one thought of resisting. The station hands were ordered into one of the apartments and locked up, one of the gang keeping guard. The others went away, and we learned subsequently that they had cut the telegraph line between Euroa and Violet Town to prevent information being given, and had besides removed a quantity of wire, believing that it would delay the repairs. The people at the station were kept locked up all Monday night, and the gang openly declared their intention to stick up the Euroa bank. They left the station at about 3.20 on Tuesday afternoon for Euroa, leaving one man in charge of the captives, who numbered 20 persons, and who were crowded into a small log hut. At four p.m. on Tuesday Ned Kelly walked into the National Bank at Euroa and presented a cheque, purporting to be signed by Mr McCauley, the overseer of Faithfull's Creek station, and requested Mr Bradley, the teller, to cash it. Mr Bradley said it was after bank hours, and refused to honour it, whereupon Kelly presented two revolvers at him and told him to "bail up," saying at the same time that he was Ned Kelly. Kelly then asked where the manager was, and still keeping Bradley covered, entered the room of Mr Scott, the manager, and ordered him to hand over the keys of the safe. A few words passed, when the keys were duly handed over. Meanwhile two others of the gang had entered the bank and kept their revolvers pointed at the manager and assistants, while Ned Kelly helped himself to the notes, gold, and securities. The servant girl at the bank recognised one of the gang as Steve Hart. Having plundered the bank, the robbers ordered Mrs Scott (the manager's wife) and her six children to enter a buggy that was at the door, and the rest of the inmates of the bank, including the manager and clerks, to get into a covered wagonette in waiting.

This latter they had taken from a hawker two hours previously. Two of the robbers drove the vehicles to Faithfull's Creek station, the third following on horseback, revolver in hand. When they arrived at the station, the men were crowded into the log hut with the other prisoners, the women being disposed of in another building. They were detained until 10 o'clock at night, when they were released, and got back by various means to Euroa.

The people of Faithfull's Creek station this afternoon are in a state of great excitement. At four o'clock this morning a large body of troopers arrived at the station with a blacktracker from Benalla. Kelly told the station people before he left them that he had made a good haul, having robbed the bank of £3000. (The actual sum, I believe, is nearly £2000–£2500 in cash, and £1500 in notes.) He told them also that if he was hard pressed by the police, he would return to the station and fight it out with them. While at Faithfull's Creek one of the station hands drove up in a spring cart and raised the alarm that the Kellys were returning. The frightened crowd scampered off at once, and took refuge in a crop of wheat that hid them from view.

Presently the report of a rifle was heard, but it proved to be only one of the hands on the station, who was practising in view of future contingencies. The troopers have just returned to the station without finding any trace of the gang. Nine troopers, with a blacktracker, headed by Superintendent Nicholson, have just started from here in pursuit of the gang. Mr Fitzgerald, the working overseer on Faithfull's Creek station, informs me that neither Kelly nor any of his gang left the station till after three o'clock in the afternoon. The police have received information that three of the horses ridden by the Kelly gang were unshod. It is anticipated that this and the weight of coin carried will retard their flight. Superintendent Nicholson is in pursuit, and Captain Standish is going to the district tomorrow.

The Mansfield Murderers

The Argus, 17 December 1878

The Kellys and their two mates have not yet been met with by the police. The search for them in the Broadford district was continued yesterday, but without success. There is no reason to doubt the truthfulness of the charcoal-burner who reported having seen them there, but as no corroboration of his statement can be obtained, it is considered that his judgement must have been at fault, and that he had mistaken other men for the murderers. A further search, however, has been ordered. As there is still some misunderstanding as to whom will receive the rewards offered by the Government, Mr Nicolson, the Assistant Commissioner of Police, desires us to state distinctly that the police will not be entitled to any part of them, as in pursuing the gang they are only performing their duty, but that the money will belong to any person or persons who give information which will lead to the capture of the murderers, even although the informant or informants are not present thereat. Seeing, however, that there is now no police reward fund, the Government may be reasonably expected to deal liberally with members of the force who may take part in the capture.

It may be mentioned that the guard duty at the Treasury and Government House was resumed by the garrison corps yesterday so that the city police are consequently relieved from that extra call upon their presently limited numbers. Superintendent Nicholson's eyes are not suffering from blight, as was at first reported. The inflammation, his doctors say, is caused by some eyelashes growing inwards and producing irritation, this being the result of the low physical condition to which he has been reduced by his late arduous duties. Under medical treatment they are now gradually improving and he hopes to be shortly able to return to the bush. With regard to the statement that there is a feeling of dissatisfaction amongst the members of the police force at the way in which they are officered, he denies that anything but the most friendly relations exist between the officers and the men, and says that they are all anxious to meet the outlaws.

The courage of the men was never called to question and the testimony from all quarters has been that they are always eager to meet with the murderers and their comrades. They have certainly been disappointed and disheartened at the non success of their expeditions, but they have become again reinspired by the recent energetic steps which have been taken by the department and the Government. The Government continues to receive offers from private persons to start on expeditions, at a small remuneration, in search of the murderers. The latest offer has been received through the Minister of Education from nine State school teachers of Ballarat a number of them being members of the Prince of Wales Light Horse, who desire to spend their three weeks holiday in pursuit of the gang, only asking in return to be supplied with arms and provisions. Major Smith has undertaken to lay their proposal before the Chief Secretary. We would here warn private individuals who wish to take part in the pursuit that, unless they are well acquainted with the Strathbogie Ranges and adjoining country, they would, most probably, get lost in the bush, and if so, the search for them would occasion nearly as much trouble as the search for the Kellys.

It has been stated that the widow of Sergeant Kennedy is in comfortable circumstances. It is true that her husband left her some small means, but as she has not yet taken out administration to his Will, she would have been seriously inconvenienced for want of money had it not been for the assistance of friends. The widow of Constable Lonigan was in most impoverished circumstances, and but for the kindness of friends, and especially of Mr F. McDonald, the ex-president of the Shire of Benalla, would have found herself in a very awkward position. It is, therefore, satisfactory to learn that, by the prompt action taken by the Chief Secretary upon the statement made in these columns on the matter, the wants of the bereaved widows and their families have now been relieved. A gentleman who is in a position to be well informed on the subject has supplied us with the following information which he has gleaned from what he believes to be reliable sources:

> Sergeant Kennedy was not shot dead by Ned Kelly, but by his brother, Dan. The death wound was inflicted by the shotgun which was carried by Dan whilst Ned had only two rifles. It is believed that the gang is now broken up, and that whilst the two Kellys have elected to remain in their own haunts, and are now probably in the Puzzle Ranges. Police have now identified the other two gang members. They are Joe Byne and Steve Hart. The police believe Byrne and Hart are endeavouring to make their way to New South Wales. Hart is thoroughly acquainted with the neighbouring colony, as he was a long time there droving cattle. It was in consequence of his knowledge of that country that the gang first attempted to cross the Murray, but on approaching the river they learned to their surprise that Constable McIntyre had escaped alive, and that their crimes were known, and being therefore afraid to trust themselves in open country, they returned to the ranges near Mansfield. They always travelled during night, and rested in some concealed stronghold during the day, and there was always one of their number keeping guard.

There have been very few rumours respecting the whereabouts of the Kellys afloat. A large and well armed search party left Benalla last evening, but the direction they intended taking was, of course, kept secret. Today, two parties came into Benalla after being out in the ranges for several days. The weather has been frightfully hot of late, especially in the bush, where there is no circulation of air, and the close, oppressive heat has had great effect both on men and horses. Many of the latter are completely knocked up with their exertions. One of these parties searched the ranges as far as Mount Separation, which is about 20 miles to the rear of Euroa. At only one place did they come upon anything bearing the slightest resemblance to the trail of the gang. At an old deserted hut, traces were found of a party having encamped there within the last two or three weeks, and the reason it is thought that this was the Kellys was the fact that on the trunks of many of the trees surrounding the hut were the marks of bullets, as if some target practice had taken place.

An apparently trivial circumstance occurred in this township on Saturday, but as every trifle has to be carefully attended to in this affair, the matter is now being enquired into. The criminal sessions commence here on Thursday, when the principal case in the list is the trial of the man Walter Lynch who was committed for trial from Mansfield on the charge of having sent a threatening letter signed "E. and D. Kelly" to Mr Monk, of the sawmills near Mansfield. The police authorities here recently made an application to have the venue changed to Melbourne, and it has been semi-officially notified this evening that the application has been acceded to, and that the case will be tried in Melbourne. At all events, it is not intended to proceed with the case here at the coming session, but an application will be made to the judge for a postponement until the next assizes. Superintendent Hare has just returned from Avenel, where he was met by Sub-Inspector Baber, who is stationed at Kilmore. This officer reported that on Saturday afternoon a charcoal-burner came into Broadford and informed the police there that he had seen four men sitting on a log with guns in their hands. This was about four miles from Broadford, in the direction of the ranges. As soon as this man noticed the gang, he concealed himself behind a fence in order that they should not perceive him, and made the best of his way to Broadford. The police constable there, knowing that Sub-Inspector Baber was in the neighbourhood of Yea, at once sent a message for him upon his arrival in Broadford. He organised a party, and taking the man who had given the information with them, proceeded to the spot.

This was found to be a retired place in a bend of Sunday Creek, and a very likely place for the gang to take a rest in, as it is very seldom visited. The logs on which the four men were sitting were pointed out by the charcoal-burner, but although a careful search was made until late last night, no trace of any men or horses could be found. Sub-Inspector Baber has been instructed to make a further and more extended search tomorrow. From Seymour news has been received that on Friday afternoon last, the overseer of an outstation near the Black Ranges found the tracks of four shod horses coming down from the direction of the ranges. Subsequently, he and his wife heard two shots fired in the vicinity of their place, and becoming frightened of a domiciliary visit from the Kellys, they made their way as rapidly as possible to the home station, and the occurrence was not notified to the police until the next day. No great importance is attached to it, however, as there are a great number of selectors in that locality, and any of them might have fired off their guns.

The authorities have, in order to make sure, carefully examined all the punts and crossing places on the Goulburn, but have not come upon any trace of persons having crossed. A horseman who was travelling between Longwood and Seymour on Saturday last was arrested by the police on suspicion of being Ned Kelly, his appearance being identical with the description given of the leader of the gang. The man, however, conclusively proved that he was an inoffensive traveller making his way from New South Wales to Melbourne, and he was therefore at once released. The man's appearance so much resembles that of Ned Kelly that it has become a regular nuisance to him, this being the third time he has been detained by the police on suspicion of being that notorious individual. It appears that for the past three weeks, Kelly's gang was residing in a hut in the Blue Ranges, between Gobur and Longwood, reconnoitering the surrounding stations and watching the roads to and from all the adjacent townships. The police at the time were many miles distant, and so secure did the gang feel, that they went riding about through the ranges quite unconcerned, inwardly laughing at the attempts which were being made to capture them in a totally different part of the district. They were supplied with provisions by a Chinaman, whom they bound by solemn promises not to tell the police where they were, threatening to shoot him if he gave any information. All the gold was removed from the Union Bank here today and sent to Melbourne. It was rumoured here yesterday that one of the gang was seen at the end of the week not far from Seymour, near which place, it is believed, they have friends. There is a proposal to employ the garrison corps to protect the neighbouring townships while the police are sent in pursuit of the Kelly gang is most cordially endorsed throughout the district.

With the present police arrangements, the gang may never be captured, unless by the merest chance. The officers-in-charge of the various stations are hampered with red tape and departmental instructions from their superiors, who reside scores of miles away, and who know nothing of the geography or requirements of the district. Will it be believed that upon the receipt of important information, when instant action is necessary, the officer-in-charge is actually compelled to telegraph to his superior officers for instructions. He dare not act until a reply is received. Generally instructions arrive too late to allow the information received to be of any value. This has positively occurred within the past few days. Everything now depends on prompt and soldierly action, and the police should be in a position to start in pursuit at a moment's notice on receipt of reliable information. I do not know a more efficient or energetic officer than Sub-Inspector Pewtress who is stationed here. Although he has spent years in the city office, he has, since the outrage, shown an aptitude for bush work that should put to shame more experienced men, and I firmly believe that if a score of good men were placed under his sole charge, with carte blanche to act on an emergency, some great good would result, but at present it is well known that his hands are tied, in consequence of the absurd regulations to which I have referred. I think it also my duty to inform you that a party of police left Mansfield on Friday with breechloading guns, and what do you think? The cartridges were made of nothing but No. 2 shot or small slugs, which are bound to scatter before they are 20 yards from the gun. The police here are under the impression that, in the event of their taking the Kellys, they will not receive one penny of the reward. If they are mistaken, I think they should be set right as it might make a difference in their efforts.

Meetings are being held here for the purpose of organising a fund to erect a memorial, in the town of Mansfield, in memory of Sergeant Kennedy and Constables Lonigan and Scanlon.

The Mansfield Murderers

The Argus, 18 December 1878

The mysterious letter from the Kellys has arrived in Melbourne. It was addressed to Mr Donald Cameron M.L.A. Mr Cameron, it will be remembered, put a question in the Assembly to the Chief Secretary as to whether inquiries had been made as to the cause of the outbreak and very much to his surprise he has been honoured with the outlaws' confidence. The circumstance proves that the men are readers of the papers and are aware of what takes place in Parliament. The letter was delivered by post at Parliament House and was received by Mr Cameron in the afternoon. Never thinking that it was a communication from the outlaws, he allowed it to lie unattended to for some time, and eventually opening it, he tore up the envelope. On seeing what the contents were, he gathered up the fragments of the envelope, and found that it bore the Glenrowan postmark of December 14. He declines to give the document to the press until he has first consulted the Chief Secretary and police authorities. It may, however, be stated that the letter is evidently composed with the object of obtaining public sympathy and it appears to be perfectly genuine. It is written by a clever illiterate person in red ink, covers some 22 pages and is signed "Edward Kelly, a forced outlaw". The place from which it was written is not stated. Kelly relates his whole history from boyhood.

He charges members of the police force with having wronged his relatives and with being the cause of his crimes. These charges have been repeated more than once, but as they are such as are often made by criminals, they would require corroboration before they could receive the slightest consideration. The letter concludes with certain fiendish threats, which Kelly says he will carry out if justice is not done to his mother. Mr Cameron, whilst very judiciously suppressing the letter until he could consult with the Chief Secretary on the question of whether it should be published or not, will notify the nature of the threats to the authorities concerned, so that by precautions being taken their execution may be prevented. Just before closing his lengthy epistle Kelly says that he had something more to write, but that he would be unable to do so unless he "robbed" for more paper. Captain Standish, the Chief Commissioner of Police, was yesterday gazetted a justice of the peace for all the bailiwicks, in order that he might have more power for suppressing the active sympathisers of the murderers. A person who arrived by the early up train this morning made a statement to the effect that Byrne, was playing billiards in a public room in Wangaratta last evening, but that as soon as he noticed that some persons left the room for the purpose of giving information to the police, he decamped, and was seen no more. The informant was unable to explain why the persons in the room did not secure him at once, instead of going to fetch the police. Of course, the whole story is looked upon as a fabrication. I was shown a photograph of Steve Hart today, which has been taken since he came out of gaol in June last. In appearance he is a mere youth, slight of build, smooth of face, and with nothing bad looking in his countenance, and from his looks no one would anticipate that he would ever take part in such a bloodthirsty proceeding as the murder of the three troopers.

It was stated here this afternoon that a horseman stuck up some men who were engaged in harvesting operations at the Broken Creek, about 12 miles from here. It was said that he rode up to the man in charge of the reaping machine and ordered him to bail up. He then rounded up four or five men who were in the paddock, and as soon as he had got them all together he galloped away without robbing them or doing them any harm.

This is another of the idle rumours that are promulgated, or if it occurred it must have been some half-drunken bushman having a lark. There is an impression gaining ground that the gang will not be seen in this district for some time to come, but leaving the police busily engaged in searching the ranges about here, they will cross over into Gippsland and make a descent upon some of the small townships. The idea of amateur search parties going out in pursuit is not looked on at all favourably. Unless the men are thorough bushmen, and have some knowledge of the country in this district, they had far better remain at home. They have no idea of the difficulties they would have to contend with in scouring these ranges and would, in all probability, be lost in the bush before they had been out 24 hours. All the search parties that go out have attached to them, or are under the command of, a trooper or non commissioned officer, who knows the country well. From indications that have been met with by some of the search parties, it is believed that the four men of the gang do not travel all together but, fixing upon a point of rendezvous, they divide into two parties, so as to move through the bush with the less likelihood of attracting attention. Some of the troopers have been supplied with the new Martini-Henry rifle.

Outlaws in Camp

The Australasian Sketcher with Pen and Pencil, 21 December 1878

Our artist has here given an imaginary view of a camp of the gang of outlaws whom the police are now searching for in the ranges around the head of the King River. The sketch tells its own tale, one of watchfulness and strained attention, listening for sights or noises to indicate the approach of the avengers of blood and agents of justice.

No. 75.—VOL. VI. MELBOURNE, SATURDAY, DECEMBER 21, 1878. [WITH LARGE COLOURED SUPPLEMENT] PRICE 6d.

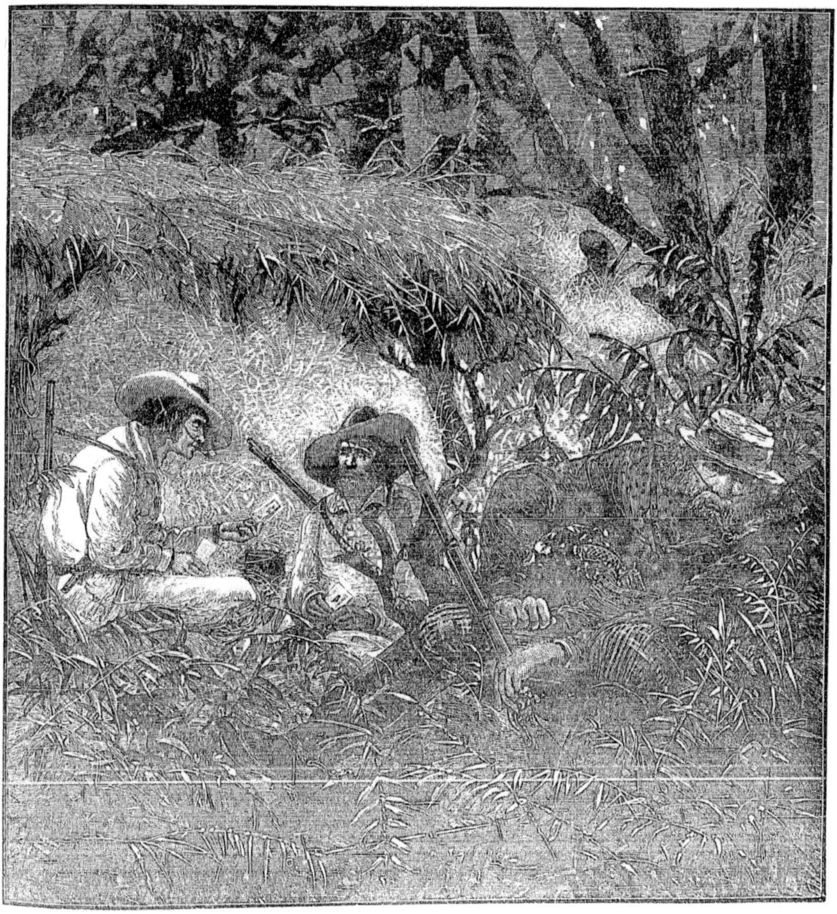

OUTLAWS IN CAMP.

The Bushranging Tragedy Scenes and Incidents

The Australasian Sketcher with Pen and Pencil, 21 December 1878

Troopers starting in pursuit of the Kellys

Head of King River

Daring Outrage by the Kelly Gang of Bushrangers

The Australasian Sketcher with Pen and Pencil, 21 December 1878

Below are two accounts of the audacious deeds of the Kelly gang in sticking up Mr Younghusband's Faithfull's Creek station on 9 December and the robbing of the National Bank at Euroa on 10 December. The first eye witness statement is that of Mr Robert Scott, manager of the National Bank of Euroa. The second is that of Mr Robert McDougall, who was one of the captives at the Faithfull's Creek station.

Mr Robert Scott's Statement:

> At about five minutes to four o'clock on Tuesday afternoon, December 9, a man came to the bank door and told the accountant that he wanted a cheque cashed. He entered and presenting a revolver at the accountant's head, ordered him to bail up. He then forced his way into my room and I found that it was Ned Kelly. Taking his stand near the end of a table at which I was sitting, he presented his revolver at my head and called upon me to bail up. He was followed by another man named 'Steve', who had a revolver in each hand. I did not bail up at first and they called again upon me to do so. I had a revolver, but it was lying on the opposite side of the table from me and I could not reach it without placing myself in the certain danger

of being immediately shot. On their again ordering me to throw up my arms I said, "It is all right", and raised my hands to the armpits of my vest. Hart then kept guard over me and Ned Kelly ransacked the bank and took possession of what money we had in use, which amounted to £300 or £400 in notes, gold and silver. Kelly next proceeded in the direction of my private apartments where my wife, family and servants were. Fearing that he would do them harm I said to him, "Kelly, if you go there I'll strike you, whatever the consequences may be". Thereupon Hart presented his revolvers at my head, and Kelly passed through. My wife and family, contrary to my expectations, took the visit very calmly and were not injured.

On returning to the bank Kelly said he knows I had more money than they had got and demanded it. I refused to give him anything and he made the accountant give him the specie and notes in the safe. He took in all about £1500 in notes, about £300 in sovereigns and about £90 in silver, besides 31 oz of gold. He also entered the strongroom, but left the bills and securities undisturbed. Frequently he remarked that there was no use resisting, as he had eight armed men outside whom he could call to his assistance in a moment. The story about the eight armed men was, however, only a pretence.

I afterwards found that they bailed up a hawker and his boy at the station and took possession of his cart. They rehabilitated themselves from his stock and called for his bill, which they promised to pay "if they were lucky". They had also taken a spring-cart from the station. In approaching the bank the two Kellys came in the spring-cart, and Hart upon one of Younghusband's horses, whilst they made the hawker's boy drive his van, which was a covered one, to my backyard. As Ned Kelly and Hart were entering the bank in front, Dan Kelly went round to the back and spoke to my domestic servant.

Before this I had heard nothing about the gang being in the neighbourhood. Steve Hart tied his horse up at De Boos's Hotel, where he afterwards had lunch. After the fellows had appropriated all the money in the bank, and my revolver and cartridges, Ned Kelly requested me to harness my horse into my buggy. I said, "No, I won't, and my groom is away. Do it for yourself". He replied, "Well, I will do it myself". He accordingly harnessed the horse and put Mrs Scott and the family into it. He then said to me, "Will you get in?" but I refused, saying, "No, I won't, it is too heavily loaded already". Kelly rejoined, "Now, none of your larks. You will, then, have to go with me", and pointing his revolver at me, he made me enter the spring-cart with himself and my servant. Before this I had asked the fellows to have a drink and they accepted the offer, but made me drink first, no doubt to make sure that I was not attempting to drug them. I also tried to bustle them about, in order to gain time, but it was no use and they drove us away to Younghusband's station.

Every person about the bank was taken. There was myself, my wife and her mother, my seven children, four boys and three girls, the eldest being a boy 13 years of age, the accountant, clerk and two servants. The hawker's van was placed in front, then followed my buggy, which Mrs Scott was driving. The spring-cart, driven by Ned Kelly, came next and Steve Hart brought up the rear on horseback. I may say here that when the bank was stuck up my wife and family were all in one room, preparing to go out for a walk and I was making ready to attend a funeral. Our arrangements were, however, rudely upset and it appeared for the time that my own funeral would be the next. The distance between Euroa and Younghusband's station is about three miles and a half.

On the way thither I had some conversation with Kelly and he chatted away very freely. I asked him, "What would that fellow Hart have done if I had struck you when you were going into my private house?" He replied, "He would have shot you dead on the spot". In reply to a question by me he admitted that it was he who shot Constable Lonigan and I saw a gold watch in his possession said to be Kennedy's. I afterwards found that he told someone at the station that the watch he wore was Kennedy's. He further said that he had heard a good deal about me and had been told that he would find me a difficult person to deal with, and that whilst the hawker he bailed up had been bad, I had been worse, and was in fact the worst and most obstinate fellow he had ever met with. The hawker, I believe, was very impertinent to him. He also said I have seen the police often and have heard them often. He did not seem a bit afraid of the police, but, on the contrary, laughed at them and at their efforts to capture him and his mates. The other ruffians appeared to have as little dread of their pursuers. I asked Hart which way he was going when he left the station and Kelly answered carelessly, "Oh, the country belongs to us. We can go anywhere we like". He said, however, that he was getting sick of bushranging life. In reply to a question as to how Constable McIntyre behaved when his comrades were murdered, he simply said that that officer made no resistance. He would not say where he and his gang had been concealing themselves nor what they as outlaws wanted with the money he had stolen.

I presume however, that they intend the money for their relatives. As we were moving along I remarked that I knew the road well and asked permission to drive. Kelly at first refused and soon afterwards got into a bad road and in going up a rough bank the cart was upset. We were nearly all thrown out. I jumped out and got hold of the horse and Kelly lifted out the servant. He then got the horse released, harnessed it again and we started afresh. After driving a little he said, "You drive very well, you had better go on". I was then proceeding to take a short cut to Younghusband's station for we had been informed that it was our destination, when Kelly, suspecting that I was misleading him, said, "If you play me any pranks I will make it hot for you". I told him that the others had taken the wrong road, or rather a longer one, and he allowed me to proceed. The notes stolen from the bank were lying beside me and I felt sorely tempted to regain them, but restrained myself. The company arrived at the station all about the same time.

I then found a number of shearers, railway labourers and farmers, who had been found by the gang when going to work, and the station hands were stuck up. They were standing beside the hut and the fourth man of the gang, who is named Byrne, was marching in front of them with two guns and his belt stuck full of revolvers. Ned Kelly had previously threatened to roast them alive and to do all sorts of things to them. There were 22 men in all bailed up here.

I now learned that the ruffians had arrived at the station about midday on Monday and that they had stayed there all night and the men they had secured were bailed up all the time. The station was a handy place for making a descent from upon the bank. Mr Younghusband was not present and in his absence Ned Kelly pounced upon McCauley, his overseer, and ordered him to write out a cheque that he might cash at the bank in Euroa. McCauley refused, saying he would lend himself to no such business. Kelly then ransacked the desk on the premises and found a cheque on the Oriental Bank, Melbourne, for £1 4s. which had been drawn out and this was the one he presented at the bank. It, of course, was not cashed and on going back to the station Kelly returned it to the overseer.

In the morning McCauley went to look at the bushrangers' horses, which had been placed in a paddock. Kelly had observed him and on Tuesday night challenged him with having been taking a note of the brands on the animals, but McCauley denied that he had been doing so. He said, "I could describe the horses, but took no notice of brands", and Kelly appeared to be satisfied, for he replied, "Then that is all right".

The horses were all fine-looking animals and as they had a day's rest they started on Tuesday night in a fresh condition. Three of them were bays and one a grey. Ned Kelly's one was a bay and its two hind feet were white. They were, however, very heavily laden, especially Ned Kelly's one, for it carried the gold and silver. The men themselves were in good condition and had evidently been feeding well and they were rigged out in the new clothes they had obtained from the hawker's van. They were also fully equipped with arms and had plenty of ammunition. Daniel Kelly is exactly like the picture of him in the papers. Ned is a good-looking man, with reddish whiskers. A man who had been sent down to repair the telegraph lines walked unsuspectingly into Younghusband's station, and was immediately placed amongst the rest of the prisoners. It had been arranged that a train should stop near the station to pick him up. The gang did not know of this arrangement and when the train stopped, Ned Kelly said, "Here comes a special with bobbies, but we are ready for them. We don't care how many there are, we will fight them". The train, after waiting a short time, moved on.

At about half-past seven o'clock in the evening the prisoners were placed inside a hut, and were ordered to remain there for three hours, one of us being made responsible for the obedience of the rest. I looked at my watch and said, "Then we will leave at 11 o'clock". Ned Kelly replied, "No, not until half-past 11. You must stop here for three hours and if any of you leave before then we will find you out and make it hot for you". Just before they left, the man Byrne returned to the door of the hut and said, "I want to see Mr Scott. Give me your watch". I said, "No, I won't. You can take it if you like", and he accordingly unhooked it from my vest and carried it away. They rode off at about nine o'clock and went up the Violet Town road. We left at about 11 o'clock. Mrs Scott drove my family home in the buggy and I walked behind them. My servants walked home along the railway line. My house is within a stone's throw of the railway station and about a quarter of a mile from the police office, but no one in the township knew what had taken place until we were released. They, however, suspected that something was wrong on some persons finding my house deserted at nine o'clock.

Constable Anderson was the only policeman in the township, but of him I have heard nothing. In the morning at about four o'clock, a blacktracker and a number of policemen arrived from Benalla and the latter told me that the bushrangers had gone a short distance in the direction of Violet Town, but had doubled-back. The hawker's boy who drove the van into my backyard did not attempt to give any alarm. The men threatened to shoot him if he did so, but he really seemed to enjoy the affair as an amusement.

Mr Robert McDougall's Statement:

While the Kellys and their companions were in possession of Younghusband's station they evidently kept a good watch on the approaches so that no information might reach Euroa that would interfere with the successful carrying out of their plan of robbing the National Bank. About two o'clock on Tuesday afternoon, December 10, a party of four men, named McDougall, Dudley, Casement, and Tennant, who were returning from the Strathbogie Ranges, were stuck up by two of the gang near the station and compelled to join the other captives there. We had just reached the railway gates, about 100 yards from Younghusband's station, three of us driving in a spring-cart and Mr Tennant on horseback.

The gates were shut and nothing being further from our thoughts than the idea of the Kelly gang being close to us, we were laughingly speculating to each other on the chances of the gates, which are private ones leading into the run, being locked. Mr Tennant getting down from his horse and finding the gates unlocked was opening them when two men suddenly made their appearance, one coming from behind us on horseback and the other advancing on foot in front. Both held revolvers presented and called upon us to "bail up". The one on horseback (who I afterwards learned was Ned Kelly, the leader of the gang) cried out, "Surrender or you'll be shot". As both the men looked like troopers in plain clothes and held up handcuffs in their left hands, and as they also accused us of stealing our own trap, we at first thought they were troopers and Mr Dudley cried out, "What right have you to arrest us?", and appeared as if he was not going to take any notice of their summons.

Edward Kelly, then riding close up to him, shouted in a threatening manner at the same time presenting the revolver at his head, "I'll shoot you dead on the spot if you give me any cheek". Fearing Kelly was going to carry out his threat I interposed, and asked Dudley to surrender quietly as it was no use resisting and told Kelly not to shoot an old man. Kelly then said he would not harm the old man if he surrendered quietly. The two bushrangers (the second being a tall, sandy, young man), then compelled us to drive up to the station. As we approached the gate leading to the station, one of the station hands opening it said in a laughing manner, pointing to Ned Kelly, "Gentlemen, allow me to introduce you to Mr Edward Kelly". This was the first positive information – though we had suspected who were our captors – that we were in the hands of the Kelly gang and the sensation created by the information did not tend to reassure us.

In fact, we were all greatly frightened and for myself I may say "My heart was in my mouth". On reaching the station we found the two others of the gang (Dan Kelly and Steve Hart) guarding the storeroom in which the manager, Mr McCauley, and about 20 others were imprisoned and where they had been, with a few intervals outside allowed to them separately by the gang, for the last 26 hours. The storeroom is a wooden building about 20 yards away from the rest of the premises and as it had only one window near the door, it was very easily guarded. Our party of four were put into the room with the others, and there being no means of ventilation we soon found the atmosphere oppressively hot and close. In the meantime the gang had thrown everything out of our cart, but there was nothing there of any value to them except some firearms and ammunition, a rifle and a double-barrelled gun, 80 bullets, two flasks of powder and three boxes of caps. Our imprisonment in the storeroom lasted for about eight hours, during which time, however, we were allowed, several of us, to go out occasionally to obtain a draught of fresh air and some water, but we were never allowed out of sight. The prisoners in the store room, I may mention, were all men, the female cook and some other women employed at the station being allowed to remain in the house.

None of the women were molested as far as I learnt in any way, though from some remarks dropped by Dan Kelly (who appeared the greatest ruffian of the lot and a thorough type of "larrikin"), he did not desire to leave them untroubled. He said something about "having a lark with the women", but apparently he was restrained by his brother. During the time we were in the storeroom four trains passed, two each way, and when any of these were heard approaching we were kept close and told not to make any noise.

Among the prisoners was a hawker who had arrived at the station with a spring-cart full of goods on Monday night intending to pass the night there. He found himself bailed up, however, on his appearance and he was put into the storeroom with the others. His arrival was regarded as a piece of specially good luck by the gang, as they were in want of new clothes and his cart contained materials for providing them all with a new outfit, even to the boots. They had all on their new clothes when we got to the station, and we saw their old ones burning.

At about half-past two o'clock the gang – who openly stated their intention of robbing the Euroa bank – proceeded to destroy the telegraph communication, leaving us guarded by one of their number. They got tomahawks and cut down one of the telegraph posts, tearing away also the wire for a considerable length, so that it could not be repaired with the usual quantity of wire carried by a line repairer. While doing this they made a further capture of four men who were working on the line and who saw them cutting the wires. The men on being told to surrender and learning that their captors were the Kelly gang made no resistance whatever and were at once marched up to the storeroom, into which they were put with the rest of us.

The severance of the telegraph communication was apparently very soon learned at Euroa, or else the line had been cut before, as the up goods train, which came in sight not long afterwards, let down a line repairer opposite the station. The gang concealed themselves and we could see the man's movements from the window. He evidently soon saw that the line had not been injured by accident and he was coming up to the station for assistance when he was suddenly pulled up by a summons to put his hands up, which he did with the most rapid obedience. He was then, having been searched, put in the storeroom with the others. We learned that his name was Watts and several questions were put to him by the bushrangers as to the number of police at Euroa and Violet Town. Ned and Dan Kelly and Steve Hart started for Euroa for the purpose, as they expressly stated, of robbing the bank. They left their horses in the paddock and drove away in the two spring-carts, ours and the hawker's. The tall, unknown bushranger was left to guard us, which he did by patrolling round the building continually. He was very heavily armed, having two revolvers in his belt, a double-barrelled gun in his hand, and two rifles placed within easy reach. While the Kellys were away, finding that there were some 15 or 16 axes stored in the building, I suggested that if parties of men commenced simultaneously assailing the four sides of the building with the axes we could soon get free, as it would be impossible for the one bushranger to look after all sides at once.

The proposition, however, was condemned by the manager and found no support indeed at all, as it was evident that at least one of us must be shot in the attempt and each one appeared to think it likely that he would be the 'one'. Besides, it was generally urged we had nothing to gain by the attempt which would compensate for the great risk, as we were pretty sure of being released when the Kellys had returned from robbing the bank. The distance from the station to Euroa is under four miles and we calculated that the rest of the gang could not be long in returning if they succeeded in their enterprise.

This proved to be correct, as it was only about half-past five o'clock when they made their reappearance with a large further addition to their list of captives. They brought with them Mr Scott, the bank manager, Mrs Scott and seven children, two servants, the accountant of the bank and the clerk. The men were put with us in the storeroom and Mrs Scott and the children and servants were sent into the station house. Besides the spring-carts, the bushrangers on their return had brought with them Mr Scott's buggy in which Mrs Scott and some of the other prisoners were driven out. Tea was made by the servants soon afterwards and was given to Mrs Scott (who was not apparently very much frightened) and the children. Having had their tea we soon saw, much to our relief, the gang making evident preparations for their departure. The spoil they had taken from the bank was packed up and distributed among the gang, with the firearms they had taken from us and Mr Scott. Two hours more elapsed, however, before we got rid of them. Having then mounted their horses (three of which were bays and that ridden by Edward Kelly an iron grey, all being good animals and in excellent condition), the men began to ride up and down in a boastful and braggadocio manner.

After a few flourishes of this kind Edward Kelly, who had assumed the leadership of the gang throughout and did most of the speaking, came over to the storeroom and announced that they were going away, warning us that we were not to stir for three hours. It was then about half-past eight o'clock. "If one of you leaves this spot," said he, "within three hours I will shoot that man dead. You can't any of you escape me in this country, I can track you anywhere and I'll keep my word." He then called to Mr McCauley to come to the front, when he told him he would hold him responsible for the escape of any of the prisoners until the period he named had expired. "Mind, if you let one of them go," said he, "I'll meet you some time or other and then you may consider yourself a dead man." After they were gone some of us talked of getting away, but as it was feared they might have left one of the gang to watch for some time, the majority were for remaining until the three hours had nearly elapsed.

The station hands took the matter very easily and cards being forthcoming they passed the time away chiefly in playing. Knowing that nothing serious was likely to happen to them, most of them looked upon the affair as a good joke, which had cost them nothing beyond their confinement. At length, at half-past 10 o'clock, we all agreed that it was time to get out which, of course, we had no difficulty in doing. Mr and Mrs Scott and family returned to Euroa, which they did not reach, I believe, till midnight. All the rest stopped at the station for the night, with the exception of myself and Mr Casement, who is a farmer. His house is situated not far from the station and was uninhabited during his absence. On our arrival at his house, where I spent the night, he expressed his belief that the gang had been there as there were glasses on the table and the door was open, whereas, he said he thought he had arranged the house and shut the door when he went away. As, however, some money that was left exposed on the mantelpiece had not been touched, it is probable that the gang did not enter his house. I may mention with regard to the conduct of the gang during our emprisonment that although domineering in giving their orders, no attempt at violence or roughness was made on any of us. Ned Kelly was the most communicative of the lot and conversed freely with several of his prisoners during the afternoon, asking questions as to the movements of the police and the "kickup" which the gang had created among the force. He avoided any reference to the police murders beyond displaying Sergeant Kennedy's gold watch, and I also saw that he carried the sergeant's short Spencer rifle slung across his shoulder.

The only thing of value Ned Kelly took from me was a silver watch, and on my telling him that it was a keepsake from my mother he shivered and said, "No, we'll never take that", and he returned it taking, however, a watch from Mr McCauley instead. I forgot to state also that before going to rob the bank Ned Kelly asked Mr McCauley whether he had any funds in the Euroa Bank, and on the latter not answering, Kelly demanded that he should write a cheque. This McCauley refused to do, but one of the gang, on searching a desk in the house, found a cheque already signed by McCauley and this Ned Kelly said would 'do'. It was evident that as they intended to rob the bank they did not want the cheque for the purpose of cashing it, but in order to gain entrance to the bank without exciting any suspicion. On leaving us the bushrangers were all splendidly armed and well supplied with ammunition. As to where they went my opinion is that they made direct for the Strathbogie Ranges, where it will be very difficult to capture them owing to the nature of the country.

The Kellys at Euroa

The Illustrated Australian News, 27 December 1878

THE KELLYS AT EUROA.

The Kelly Outrages at Euroa - Bank Robbery at Euroa

The Illustrated Australian News, 27 December 1878

Further information has come to light regarding the capture of hostages at Faithfull's Creek station and the robbery of the bank of Euroa. A cool, daring and skillfully planned robbery was perpetrated by the outlaws Edward and Daniel Kelly and their associates, Hart and Byrne, at Euroa. At about half-past 12 o'clock in the day a man went to the homestead at Mr Younghusband's Faithfull's Creek station, which is about four miles from Euroa. Accosting a station hand (Fitzpatrick), Ned Kelly learned that the Manager, Mr McCauley, was from home and he then signalled to three companions who had remained at some distance and when they came up he announced himself as Ned Kelly and demanded refreshments for the four and fodder for their horses. After inquiring about the number of hands on the station, Kelly locked Fitzpatrick and a lad who was present in a storeroom and three other men who came in soon after for their dinner were added to them. Mr McCauley next arrived and he also had to surrender and then the outlaws sat down to dinner, two at a time, but refused to eat or drink anything that some of the others did not first partake of. Their horses had also been stabled and fed and when Kelly and his gang had all had enough, the imprisoned men were allowed some food.

Towards evening a hawker drove to the outskirts of the station and prepared to encamp for the night and he and his boy were also secured in like manner too and placed with the other prisoners. The contents of the hawker's cart were next taken out and strewn about the ground and the outlaws treated themselves to an entirely new outfit from head to foot, with soaps and perfumery. They kept one of their number constantly on guard. Shortly afterwards they went to sleep, two at a time, the other two keeping watch. Those who were awake conversed freely with their prisoners, even respecting their murder of the three constables near Mansfield, and thus the night passed away. In the morning the first thing done was to break down all the lines of telegraph which skirted both sides of the north-eastern railway which was near to and in full sight of the homestead. This prevented communication with Benalla, where there was a large force of police. Breakfast was then had and then a spring-cart drove up to the station containing two neighbouring selectors and two visitors from Melbourne who had been kangarooing. These four men were also bailed up and placed with the other captives in the store room. A cheque bearing Mr McCauleys' signature was next taken from his desk and between three and four o'clock p.m. the two Kellys and Hart started for Euroa, leaving Byrne to guard the numerous prisoners. They took the two carts with them, the hawker's boy driving that vehicle and Hart riding a horse. When they drove to the door of the bank and Ned Kelly obtained entrance from the bank clerk on the pretence of wanting cash for the cheque he had with him. When inside he and Hart made the clerks surrender by presenting revolvers at them and they then all went into the room of Mr Scott, the Manager, and placed him under duress also. They next obtained the keys by intimidation and bundled all the notes and specie, into a sack, the amount being about £2000. They also took an ingot of 31 oz of smelted gold and a number of securities. They drank some whisky with Mr Scott, after he had first taken some, and then they made Mrs Scott, with her children and two maid servants, get ready to ride out.

The horse was put into Mr Scott's buggy, which his wife had to drive, the occupants being herself, her mother and some of the children. The clerks, the servants and Mr Scott and his other children were placed in the carts and then the cavalcade started for the Faithfull's Creek station, the hawker's cart being first with Ned Kelly in charge, then the buggy, followed by the selector's spring-cart, driven by Daniel Kelly, the rear being brought up by Steve Hart on horse back. In passing out of the town they had to go close to the one policeman who kept order in the town, the railway officials and a number of men employed in building a new station, but they were unheeded and they went on and reached Mr Younghusband's station in time to take tea. They found that Byrne had increased the number of his prisoners, he having captured a line repairer who had been sent to put the wires into order and who on arrival had found them in such a state that he had to seek for aid and went to the homestead for that purpose. The outlaws did not hurry themselves, but waited until about nine o'clock p.m. before they took their departure. Previously to doing so, however, they liberated Mr McCauley, and directed him to keep the other men shut up until they had been gone three hours, but he let them out about a quarter of an hour after they left. Information was then conveyed to the police and efforts made to follow the gang, who are believed to be in the Strathbogie ranges.

The Kellys' Visit to the Police Station Jerilderie N.S.W.

The Illustrated Australian News, 21 February 1879

THE KELLYS' VISIT TO THE POLICE STATION, JERILDERIE, N.S.W.

A Search Party in the Wombat Ranges

The Illustrated Australian News, 21 February 1879

A SEARCH PARTY IN THE WOMBAT RANGES.

A Search Party in the Wombat Ranges

The Illustrated Australian News, 21 February 1879

The outlawed Kelly gang are still at large, notwithstanding the strenuous efforts that have been made to capture them. Many times during the past few months the police have received information that appeared to be so accurate in all its details that no doubt of encountering the gang was entertained, but in each case a thorough investigation proved that some harmless individuals had been mistaken for the outlaws. On the evening of the 28th of January, intelligence was received that a man who for many years had been in the water police, and was well-known to be of a reliable character, had seen the Kellys on a spur in the Wombat Ranges, about 17 miles from Euroa (the scene of the sticking-up of the National Bank by the gang). A special train was instantly despatched from Benalla with a strong force of troopers and their horses, and a few hours afterwards the detachment arrived at Euroa. Superintendents Hare and Sadlier arranged the preliminaries, and at two o'clock in the morning the party, which consisted of Senior Constable Johnson, Constable Dwyer and a number of picked men, under the command of Superintendent Sadlier, started for the spot. The moon shone out clearly, and the ride through the wild and dangerous country which characterises the ranges in the district became intensely exciting as the party drew near to the locality, at which a desperate struggle was expected. Very much to the regret of the men, nothing was seen of the gang, and inquiries at the place, an old bush shanty, revealed the fact that the supposed Kellys were four peaceful farmers who had simply called there for refreshments. Our artist has been successful in faithfully depicting the scene from which a slight idea may be gathered of the wild and dangerous nature of the country in which the police are searching for the gang.

The Kelly Bushrangers at Jerilderie

The Illustrated Australian News, 21 February 1879

In the annals of crime in the Australian colonies there is hardly a more remarkable instance of audacity than that displayed by Ned Kelly and his associates in taking armed possession of Jerilderie and robbing the local branch of the Bank of New South Wales in open daylight. The raid on the Euroa Bank was considered the very acme of daring and coolness, but that exploit has been completely eclipsed by the foray across the border. Jerilderie is a small township about 35 miles north of the Murray containing a population of about 200 persons. The country as it is approached from the south is a dead-level plain only here and there relieved by patches of timber. It is the resort at certain seasons of shearers and station hands and at times business is brisk enough. The Kellys would appear to have fully matured their plans before starting on Saturday the 8th instance. They evidently regarded the presence of nearly 200 hundred men engaged in their pursuit and scattered throughout the district where their haunts were known, to be of no importance whatever. They left the Strathbogie ranges on the night previous, crossed the Murray before daylight and took their time across the open country in the direction of Jerilderie, which they entered after nightfall. They first proceeded to the police station where there were two police constables and their families quartered. Pretending that the assistance of the police was required to quell a row at one of the hotels, the constable in charge was soon roused and immediately answered the summons by opening the front door in his night dress, where he was immediately bailed up. Having secured both constables and placed them under lock and key in the room usually allotted to offenders, their families were secured in another portion of the station.

The design of the desperadoes was to plunder the bank on Sunday, but for some unexplained reason they did not do so. On Sunday, however, Ned Kelly was not idle. He compelled Constable Richards to go abroad with him through the township and by a show of familiarity completely allayed suspicion. Doubtless the confederates of the outlaws were about and it is not improbable that the chance of Mr Tarleton, the manager of the bank, returning with a large amount of ready cash induced Kelly to postpone the robbery until the following day. However, the constables and their families were kept under strict surveillance from Saturday night till Monday at noon, without anyone in the township supposing for a moment that such dangerous individuals were in the locality.

The sticking up of the bank proved after all a simple matter. Mr Tarleton, the manager, had just returned from a long ride and was enjoying a cold bath. His assistants, two young men, were standing behind the counter of the bank in readiness to attend to customers. Mr Living heard the noise of approaching footsteps from the rear, but thinking it was the manager paid no attention to the circumstances until roused by the entrance of Byrne, one of the gang, who immediately ordered him to bail up, stating at the same time that he was Ned Kelly and presenting a revolver. Mr Living and his fellow assistant saw that resistance was useless and surrendered. They were then marched off to the Royal Hotel where they found the Kellys had placed a number of persons in a room, whom they threatened to shoot if they offered the least resistance. Kelly inquired for Mr Tarleton and brought back Mr Living to the bank to find him. The manager was then surprised in his bath and bailed up after the usual fashion. He was utterly incapable of course of doing anything other than he was directed. The bushrangers then proceeded to rob the safe and after some little trouble they succeeded in securing over £2000, principally in gold. The money was placed in a sack and conveyed away, the bank officials being brought back to the hotel. It should, however, be mentioned that while in the bank two men entered, one named Rankin and the other Gill. Upon making their appearance Kelly ordered them to bail up, whereupon they turned and fled precipitately, Ned Kelly following in close pursuit. Gill contrived to escape and remained hidden in a creek adjacent until the danger had passed, but Rankin was not so fortunate. He was overtaken by the outlaws and very roughly handled. Indeed, his chances of life were not worth much, as Kelly seemed in a terrible rage and desirous of shooting him. His life was only saved by the intercession of those in the hotel. Constable Richards seemed to be a special object of revenge to the desperadoes.

Ned Kelly resolutely declared that Richards should die, as he had been engaged in pursuing him. However, Mr Tarleton's good offices appear to have saved the man's life, as the outlaw gradually relented and did not carry his threat into execution. The telegraph operator and his assistant were next waited on and the wires having been cut and the insulators destroyed, those officials were also conveyed to the hotel, where there were now about 25 persons inside, expecting every moment that something might occur that would cause bloodshed. The men were so disposed that in the event of resistance and one being overcome another stood ready with a loaded rifle at a short distance ready to fire. Ned Kelly shouted for several persons and became quite conversational. He expressed a desire to have a document printed giving a sketch of his life and sought Mr Gill, who is publisher of a local paper, for that purpose. But Mr Gill remained non est, and his wife was consulted. She expressed her unwillingness to comply with the request and the document was then given to Mr Living, who undertook to have it published. In the meantime Byrne had mounted his horse and with the money taken from the bank in his possession he took his departure in the direction of the Murray. To facilitate his escape with the plunder, the Kellys and Hart remained about the hotel for several hours. Before leaving they directed the telegraph stationmaster not to connect the wires before morning or he might expect condign punishment. Finally, towards dusk the remainder of the gang followed Byrne, stating that they were going to stick up the Bank of Urana. They had no sooner left the township than immediate steps were taken to restore telegraphic communication, and in the course of a few hours Sydney and Melbourne were in possession of the startling intelligence. Such are briefly the circumstances connected with the robbery of the Jerilderie Bank by the Kellys.

Destruction of the Kelly Gang

The Argus, 29 June 1880

At last the Kelly gang and the police have come within shooting distance and the adventure has been the most tragic of any in the bushranging annals of the colony. Most people will say that it is high time too, for the murders of the police near Mansfield occurred as long ago as the 26th of October, 1878, the Euroa outrage on 9th and 10th December of the same year, and the Jerilderie affair on the 8th and 9th of February, 1879. The lapse of time induced many to believe that the gang was no longer in the colony, but these sceptics must now be silent. The outlaws demonstrated their presence in a brutally effective manner by the murder of the unfortunate Aaron Sherritt on the 25th June 1880 at Sebastopol. Immediately on the news being spread the police were in activity. A special train was despatched from Melbourne at 10.15 on Sunday night. At Essendon, Sub-Inspector O'Connor and his five blacktrackers were picked up.

They had come recently from Benalla, and were en route for Queensland again. Sub-Inspector O'Connor, however, was fortunately staying with Mrs O'Connor's friends at Essendon for a few days before his departure. Mrs O'Connor and her sister came along thinking that they would be able to pay a visit to Beechworth. After leaving Essendon the train travelled at a great speed, and before the passengers were aware of any accident having occurred, we had smashed through a gate about a mile beyond Craigieburn. All we noticed was a crack like a bullet striking the carriage. The brake of the engine had, however, been torn away, the footbridge of the carriage shattered and the lamp on the guard's van destroyed. Guard Bell was looking out of the van at the time and had a very narrow escape. The train had to be pulled up, but after a few minutes we started again, relying on the brake of the guard's van. Benalla was reached at half- past one o'clock, and there Superintendent Hare with eight troopers and their horses were taken on board. We were now about to enter the Kelly country and caution was necessary. As the moon was shining brightly, a man was tied upon the front of the engine to keep a lookout for any obstruction of the line. Just before starting, however, it occurred to the authorities that it would be advisable to send a pilot engine in advance, and the man on the front of our engine was relieved. A start was made from Benalla at two o'clock, and at 23 minutes to three when we were travelling at a rapid pace, we were stopped by the pilot engine. This stoppage occurred at Playford and Desoyre's paddocks, about a mile and a quarter from Glenrowan.

A man had met the pilot and informed the driver that the rails were torn up about a mile and a half beyond Glenrowan and that the Kellys were waiting for us near at hand. Superintendent Hare at once ordered the carriage doors on each side to be unlocked, and his men to be in readiness. His orders were punctually obeyed and the lights were extinguished. Mr Hare then mounted the pilot-engine, along with a constable, and advanced. After some time he returned and directions were given for the train to push on. Accordingly we followed the pilot up to Glenrowan station and disembarked. No sooner were we out of the train than Constable Bracken, the local policeman, rushed into our midst, and stated with an amount of excitement, which was excusable under the circumstances, that he had just escaped from the Kellys, and that they were at that moment in possession of Jones's public house, about a hundred yards from the station. He called upon the police to surround the house, and his advice was followed without delay. Superintendent Hare with his men and Sub-Inspector O'Connor with his blacktrackers, at once advanced on the building. They were accompanied by Mr Rawlins, a volunteer from Benalla, who did good service. Superintendent Hare took the lead, and charged right up to the hotel. At the station were the reporters of the Melbourne press, Mr Carrington, of *The Sketcher*, and the two ladies who had accompanied us.

The latter behaved with admirable courage, never betraying a symptom of fear, although bullets were whizzing about the station and striking the building and train. The first brush was exceedingly hot. The police and the gang blazed away at each other in the darkness furiously. It lasted for about a quarter of an hour, and during that time there was nothing but a succession of flashes and reports, the pinging of bullets in the air and the shrieks of women who had been made prisoners in the hotel. Then there was a lull, but nothing could be seen for a minute or two in consequence of the smoke. In a few minutes Superintendent Hare returned to the railway station with a shattered wrist. The first shot fired by the gang had passed through his left wrist. He bled profusely from the wound, but Mr Carrington, artist of *The Sketcher*, tied up the wound with his handkerchief and checked the haemorrhage. Mr Hare then set out again for the fray and cheered his men on as well as he could, but he gradually became so weak from loss of blood that he had reluctantly to retire and was soon afterwards conveyed to Benalla by a special engine. The bullet passed right through his wrist, and it is doubtful if he will ever recover the use of his left hand. On his departure Sub-Inspector O'Connor and Senior Constable Kelly took charge, and kept pelting away at the outlaws all the morning. Sub-Inspector O'Connor took up a position in a small creek in front of the hotel and disposed his blackfellows one on each side and stuck to this post gallantly throughout the whole encounter. The trackers also stood the baptism of fire with fortitude, never flinching for one instant.

At about five o'clock in the morning a heart-rending wail of grief ascended from the hotel. The voice was easily distinguished as that of Mrs Jones, the landlady. Mrs Jones was lamenting the fate of her son, who had been shot in the back, as she supposed, fatally. She came out from the hotel crying bitterly and wandered into the bush on several occasions, and nature seemed to echo her grief. She always returned, however, to the hotel, until she succeeded, with the assistance of one of the prisoners, in removing her wounded boy from the building, and in sending him on to Wangaratta for medical treatment. The firing continued intermittently as occasion served and bullets were continually heard coursing through the air. Several lodged in the station buildings and a few struck the train. By this time the hotel was completely surrounded by the police and the blacktrackers and a vigilant watch of the hotel was kept up during the dark hours.

At daybreak police reinforcements arrived from Benalla, Beechworth and Wangaratta. Superintendent Sadlier came from Benalla with nine more men and Sergeant Steele, of Wangaratta, with six, thus augmenting the besieging force to about 30 men. Before daylight Senior Constable Kelly found a revolving rifle and a cap lying in the bush, about 100 yards from the hotel. The rifle was covered with blood and a pool of blood lay near it. This was evidently the property of one of the bushrangers, and a suspicion therefore arose that they had escaped. That these articles not only belonged to one of the outlaws but to Ned Kelly himself was soon proved. When day was dawning the women and children who had been made prisoners in the hotel were allowed to depart. They were, however, challenged individually as they approached the police line, for it was thought that the outlaws might attempt to escape under some disguise. At daylight the gang were expected to make a sally out, so as to escape, if possible, to their native ranges, and the police were consequently on the alert. Close attention was paid to the hotel, as it was taken for granted that the whole gang were there. To the surprise of the police, however, they soon found themselves attacked from the rear by a man dressed in a long grey overcoat and wearing an iron mask. The appearance of the man presented an anomaly, but a little scrutiny of his appearance and behaviour soon showed that it was the veritable leader of the gang, Ned Kelly himself.

On further observation it was seen that he was only armed with a revolver. He, however, walked coolly from tree to tree and received the fire of the police with the utmost indifference, returning a shot from his revolver when a good opportunity presented itself. Three men went for him, Sergeant Steele of Wangaratta, Senior Constable Kelly and a railway guard named Dowsett. The latter, however, was only armed with a revolver. They fired at him persistently, but to their surprise with no effect. He seemed bullet-proof. It then occurred to Sergeant Steele that the fellow was encased in mail and he then aimed at the outlaw's legs. His first shot of that kind made Ned stagger, and the second brought him to the ground with the cry, "I am done – I am done". Steele rushed up along with Senior Constable Kelly and others. The outlaw howled like a wild beast brought to bay and swore at the police. He was first seized by Steele and as that officer grappled with him he fired off another charge from his revolver. This shot was evidently intended for Steele, but from the smart way in which he secured the murderer the sergeant escaped. Kelly became gradually quiet and it was soon found that he had been utterly disabled. He had been shot in the left foot, left leg, right hand, left arm, and twice in the region of the groin. But no bullet had penetrated his armour. Having been divested of his armour he was carried down to the railway station and placed in a guard's van. Subsequently he was removed to the stationmaster's office and his wounds were dressed there by Dr Nicholson of Benalla.

What statements he made are given below. In the meantime the siege was continued without intermission. That the three other outlaws were still in the house was confirmed by remarks made by Ned, who said they would fight to the last and would never give in. The interest and excitement were consequently heightened. The Kelly gang were at last in the grasp of the police and their leader actually captured. The female prisoners who escaped during the morning gave corroboration of the fact that Dan Kelly, Byrne and Hart were still in the house. A rumour got abroad that Byrne was shot when drinking a glass of whisky at the bar of the hotel about half-past five o'clock in the morning and the report afterwards turned out to be true. The remaining two kept up a steady defence from the rear of the building during the forenoon and exposed themselves recklessly to the bullets of the police. They, however, were also clad in mail and the shots took no effect. At 10 o'clock a white flag or handkerchief was held out at the front door and immediately afterwards about 30 men, all prisoners, sallied forth holding up their hands. They escaped whilst Dan Kelly and Hart were defending the back door.

The police rallied up towards them with their arms ready and called upon them to stand. The crowd did so and in obedience to a subsequent order fell prone on the ground. They were passed, one by one and two of them, brothers named McAuliffe were arrested as Kelly sympathisers. The precaution thus taken was highly necessary, as the remaining outlaws might have been amongst them. The scene presented when they were all lying on the ground and demonstrating the respectability of their characters was unique and, in some degree, amusing. The siege was kept up all the forenoon and till nearly three o'clock in the afternoon. Some time before this the shooting from the hotel had ceased and opinions were divided as to whether Dan Kelly and Hart were reserving their ammunition or were dead.

The best part of the day having elapsed, the police, who were now acting under the direction of Superintendent Sadlier, determined that a decisive step should be taken. At 10 minutes to three o'clock another and the last volley was fired into the hotel, and under cover of the fire Senior Constable Johnson, of Violet Town, ran up to the house with a bundle of straw which (having set fire to) he placed on the ground at the west side of the building. This was a moment of intense excitement and all hearts were relieved when Johnson was seen to regain uninjured the shelter he had left. All eyes were now fixed on the silent building and the circle of besiegers began to close in rapidly on it, some dodging from tree to tree and many, fully persuaded that everyone in the hotel must be hors de combat, coming out boldly into the open. Just at this juncture Mrs Skillion, sister of the Kellys, attempted to approach the house from the front. She had on a black riding habit with a red underskirt and white Gainsborough hat and was a prominent object in the scene. Her arrival on the ground was almost simultaneous with the attempt to fire the building. Her object in trying to reach the house was apparently to induce the survivors, if any, to come out and surrender. The police, however, ordered her to stop. She obeyed the order, but very reluctantly and, standing still, called out that some of the police were ordering her to go on and others to stop. She, however, went to where a knot of the besiegers were standing on the west side of the house.

In the meantime the straw, which burnt fiercely, had all been consumed and at first doubts were entertained as to whether Senior Constable Johnson's exploit had been successful. Not very many minutes elapsed, however, before smoke was seen coming out of the roof, and flames were discerned through the front window on the western side. A light westerly wind was blowing at the time, and this carried the flames from the straw underneath the wall and into the house, and as the building was lined with calico, the fire spread rapidly. Still no sign of life appeared in the building. When the house was seen to be fairly on fire, Father Gibney, who had previously started for it but had been stopped by the police, walked up to the front door and entered it. By this time the patience of the besiegers was exhausted, and they all, regardless of shelter, rushed to the building. Father Gibney, at much personal risk from the flames, hurried into a room to the left, and there saw two bodies lying side by side on their backs. He touched them, and found life was extinct in each. These were the bodies of Dan Kelly and Hart, and the reverend gentleman expressed the opinion, based on their position, that they must have killed one another. Whether they killed one another or whether both or one committed suicide, or whether both being mortally wounded by the besiegers they determined to die side by side, will never be known.

The priest had barely time to feel their bodies before the fire forced him to make a speedy exit from the room, and the flames had then made such rapid progress on the western side of the house that the few people who followed close on the reverend gentleman's heels dared not attempt to rescue the two bodies. It may be here stated that, after the house had been burnt down, the two bodies were removed from the embers. They presented a horrible spectacle, nothing but the trunk and skull being left, and these almost burnt to a cinder. Their armour was found near them. About the remains there was apparently nothing to lead to positive identification, but the discovery of the armour near them and other circumstances render it impossible to be doubted that they were those of Dan Kelly and Steve Hart. The latter was a much smaller man than the younger Kelly and this difference in size was noticeable in their remains. Constable Dwyer, by-the-by, who followed Father Gibney into the hotel, states that he was near enough to the bodies to recognise Dan Kelly.

As to Byrne's body it was found in the entrance to the bar-room, which was on the east side of the house, and there was time to remove it from the building, but not before the right side was slightly scorched. This body likewise presented a dreadful appearance. It looked as if it had been ill nourished. The face was black with smoke and the arms were bent at right angles at the elbows, the stiffened joints below the elbows standing erect. The body was quite stiff, and its appearance and the position in which it was found corroborated the statement that Byrne died early yesterday morning. He is said to have received the fatal wound, which was in the groin, while drinking a glass of whisky at the bar. He had a ring on his right hand which had belonged to Constable Scanlon, who was murdered by the gang on the Wombat Ranges. The body was dressed in a blue sac coat, tweed striped trousers, Crimean shirt and very ill-fitting boots. Like Ned Kelly, Byrne wore a bushy beard. In the outhouse or kitchen immediately behind the main building the old man Martin Cherry, who was one of the prisoners of the gang and who was so severely wounded that he could not leave the house when the other prisoners left, was found still living, but in articulo mortis from a wound in the groin. He was promptly removed to a short distance from the burning hotel and laid on the ground, when Father Gibney administered to him the last sacrament.

Cherry was insensible, and barely alive. He had evidently suffered much during the day, and death released him from his sufferings within half an hour from the time when he was removed from the hotel. It was fortunate that he was not burnt alive. Cherry, who was unmarried, was an old resident of the district and was employed as a plate-layer, and resided about a mile from Glenrowan. He was born at Limerick, Ireland and was 60 years old. He is said by all who knew him to have been a quiet, harmless old man and much regret was expressed at his death. He seems to have been shot by the attacking force, of course unintentionally.

While the house was burning some explosions were heard inside. These were alarming at first, but it was soon ascertained that they were cartridges burning. Several gun barrels were found in the debris, and also the burnt carcase of a dog which had been shot during the melee. All that was left standing of the hotel was the lamp-post and the signboard bearing the following device, which, in view of the carnage that had just been perpetrated within the walls of the hostelry, read strangely: THE GLENROWAN INN, ANN JONES, BEST ACCOMMODATION. In a small yard at the rear of the buildings four of the outlaws' horses, which had been purposely fired at early in the day, were found and were killed at once, to put them out of their agony. They were poor scrubbers. Two of them were shod. The police captured Byrne's horse, a fine animal. About the same time that Mrs Skillion appeared on the scene, Kate Kelly and another of her sisters were also noticed, as were likewise 'Wild' Wright and his brother Tom, and Dick Hart, brother of one of the dead outlaws. Mrs Skillion seemed to appreciate the position most keenly, her younger sisters appearing at times rather unconcerned. Dick Hart, who was Steve Hart's senior, walked about very coolly.

Interview with Ned Kelly:

After the house had been burnt Ned Kelly's three sisters and Tom Wright were allowed an interview with him. Tom Wright as well as the sisters kissed the wounded man and a brief conversation ensued, Ned Kelly having to a certain extent recovered from the exhaustion consequent on his wounds. At times his eyes were quite bright, and although he was of course excessively weak, his remarkably powerful physique enabled him to talk rather freely. During the interview he stated:

> I was at last surrounded by the police and only had a revolver, with which I fired four shots. But it was no good. I had half a mind to shoot myself. I loaded my rifle, but could not hold it after I was wounded. I had plenty of ammunition, but it was no good to me. I got shot in the arm and told Byrne and Dan so. I could have got off, but when I saw them all pounding away, I

> told Dan I would see it over, and wait until morning." "What on earth induced you to go to the hotel?" inquired a spectator. "We could not do it anywhere else," replied Kelly, eyeing the spectators, who were strangers to him, suspiciously. "I would," he continued, "have fought them in the train, or else upset it if I had the chance. I didn't care a – who was in it, but I knew on Sunday morning there would be no usual passengers. I first tackled the line, and could not pull it up, and then came to Glenrowan station." "Since the Jerilderie affair," remarked a spectator, "we thought you had gone to Queensland." "It would not do for everyone to think the same way," was Kelly's reply. "If I were once right again," he continued, "I would go to the barracks, and shoot every one of the – traps, and not give one a chance." Mrs Skillion (to her brother) "It's a wonder you did not keep behind a tree.

Ned Kelly:

> I had a chance at several policemen during the night, but declined to fire. My arm was broke the first fire. I got away into the bush and found my mare, and could have rushed away, but wanted to see the thing out, and remained in the bush.

A sad scene ensued when 'Wild' Wright led Mrs Skillion to the horrible object which was all that remained of her brother Dan. She bent over it, raised a dirge-like cry and wept bitterly. Dick Hart applied for the body of his brother, but was told he could not have it until after the post-mortem examination. The inquest on the bodies will be held at Benalla. Michael Reardon, aged 18 years, was shot through the shoulder, but it is apparently only a flesh wound. The boy Jones was dangerously shot in the thigh. Both have been sent to the Wangaratta Hospital. A cannon was brought up as far as Seymour, but as the burning of Jones's Hotel had proved successful, it was countermanded. According to Ned Kelly, the gang, after shooting Sherritt at Sebastopol, rode openly through the streets of Beechworth and then came on to Glenrowan for the purpose of wrecking any special police train which might be sent after them, in the hope of destroying the blacktrackers. They descended on Glenrowan at about three o'clock on Sunday morning and rousing up all the inhabitants of the township bailed them up. Feeling unable to lift the rails themselves, they compelled the line-repairers of the district and others to do so. The spot selected was on the first turning after reaching Glenrowan, at a culvert and on an incline. One rail was raised on each side and the sleepers were removed. The diabolical object in view was the destruction of the special train. Having performed this fiendish piece of work Kelly returned to the township and, bailing all the people up, kept them prisoners in the stationmaster's house and Jones's hotel.

By three o'clock on Monday morning, they gathered all their captives into the hotel, and the number of those unfortunate people amounted at one time to 47, as already stated. The police then arrived, and the prisoners escaped at intervals during the night. The first attack of the police was a brilliant affair. They approached the house quickly but stealthily. Their arrival, however, was expected, and they were met with a volley from the verandah of the hotel. Special trains were run during the morning between Glenrowan and Benalla and Mrs O'Connor and her sister, who may justly be called the heroines of the day, for they behaved bravely, were taken on by one of them to Benalla in the forenoon. Ned Kelly, after being secured, quieted down and became absolutely tame. He is very reserved as to anything connected with his comrades, but answered questions freely when his individual case was alone concerned. He appeared to be suffering from a severe shock and exhaustion, and trembled in every limb. Now and again he fainted, but restoratives brought him round and in his stronger moments he made the following statements:

Ned Kelly's Statements:

> I was going down to meet the special train with some of my mates and intended to rake it with shot, but it arrived before I expected and I then returned to the hotel. I expected the train would go on and I had the rails pulled up so that these – blacktrackers might be settled. I do not say what brought me to Glenrowan, but it seems much. Anyhow, I could have got away last night, for I got into the bush with my grey mare and lay there all night. But I wanted to see the thing end. In the first volley the police fired I was wounded on the left foot, soon afterwards I was shot through the left arm. I got these wounds in front of the house. I do not care what people say about Sergeant Kennedy's death. But I am satisfied it is not true that Scanlon was shot kneeling. He never got off his horse.

> I fired three or four shots from the front of Jones's hotel, but who I was firing at I do not know. I simply fired where I saw police. I escaped to the bush, and remained there overnight. I could have shot several constables if I liked. Two passed close to me. I could have shot them before they could shoot. I was a good distance away at one time, but came back. Why don't the police use bullets instead of duck-shot? I have got one charge of duck-shot in my leg. One policeman who was firing at me was a splendid shot, but I do not know his name. I daresay I would have done well to have ridden away on my grey mare. The bullets that struck my armour felt like blows from a man's fist. I wanted to fire into the carriages, but the police started on us too quickly. I expected the police to come.

Superintendent Sadlier, "You wanted, then, to kill the people in the train?" Kelly, "Yes, of course I did, God help them, but they would have got shot all the same. Would they not have tried to kill me?" When the first attack subsided, the outlaws were heard calling, "Come on, you –, the – police can't do us any harm". The armour in which each member of the gang was clad was of a most substantial character. It was made of iron a quarter of an inch thick and consisted of a long breast-plate, shoulder-plates, backplate and helmet. The helmet resembled a nail-can without a crown and with a long slit at the elevation of the eyes to look through. All these articles are believed to have been made by two men, one living near Greta and the other near Oxley. The iron was procured by the larceny of ploughshares, and larcenies of this kind having been rather frequent of late in the Kelly district the police had begun to suspect that the gang were preparing for action. Ned Kelly's armour alone weighed 97 pounds, a considerable weight to carry on horseback. There are five bullet marks on the helmet, three on the breast-plate, nine on the backplate and one on the shoulder-plate. His wounds so far as at present known, are: Two on the right arm, several on the right leg, one on left foot, one on right hand and two near the groin.

The Stationmaster's narrative:

The stationmaster at Glenrowan, states:

> About three o'clock on Sunday morning a knock came to my door. I live at the gatehouse within 100 yards of the station

on the Melbourne side. I jumped out of bed and, thinking it was someone wishing to get through the gates in a hurry, I proceeded to dress, and after getting half my clothes on I went to the door. Just as I arrived at the door it was burst in. Previous to that there was some impertinent talk outside to get me to open quickly. When the door was burst in I asked, "Who are you, what is this for?" The answer was, "I am Ned Kelly". I saw a man clad in an overcoat, who walked in with me to my bedroom. Mrs Stanistreet and the children were there in bed. There were two little girls and one infant. Ned Kelly said to me, "You have to come with me and take up the rails". I replied, "Wait until I dress", and I completed my dress and followed him out of the house on the railway line. I found seven or eight men standing at the gate looking over the line near Mrs Jones's Glenrowan Inn. Ned Kelly, speaking to me, said, "Now you direct those men how to raise some of the rails, as we expect a special train very soon". I objected, saying, "I know nothing about lifting rails off the line. The only persons that understand it are the repairers and they live outside and on the line".

Ned went on alone to Reardon the platelayer's house, which stands about a quarter of a mile along the line southward. I and the other men were left with Steve Hart. Ned Kelly went on to Reardon's house. Steve Hart gave me a prod with his gun in the side and said, "You get the tools out that are necessary to raise those rails". I replied, "I have not the key of the chest". He said, "We'll break the lock", and he got one of the men to do so. They took all the tools out of the chest, which lay in a back shed or tool house between the station and the crossing. Soon afterwards Ned and two of the repairers, Reardon and Sullivan, arrived. Ned, accompanied by these two men, proceeded down the line towards Wangaratta. We stood with Hart in the cold at the hut for about two hours. At last Ned Kelly and the repairers returned.

Ned inquired about the signalling on the line, how I stopped trains with the signal lamps. I told him white is right and red wrong and green generally "come along". He then said, "There is a special train coming, and you will give no signal". Then, speaking to Hart, he said, "Watch his countenance and if he gives any signal shoot him". He marched us into my house, and left us under the charge of Steve Hart. Subsequently other persons were made prisoners and lodged in my house to the number of about 17. They were the Reardon family, the Ryan family, Tom Cameron, son of a gatekeeper on the line, and others whom I don't remember. We were locked up all day on Sunday, but we were allowed out under surveillance.

The women were allowed to go to Jones's hotel about dark. All the men but myself and family went to the hotel soon afterwards. Steve Hart remained with us all night. During the night Dan Kelly relieved Hart and he was afterwards relieved by Byrne. Just before the special train arrived this morning I was ordered by Hart, who was on and off duty throughout the night, to follow him over to Jones's, and not to signal the train. I went into the back kitchen and found there Mrs Jones, with her daughter, about 11, and two younger children. There was also a man there named McKean. By this time the train had arrived and firing was going on furiously and we all took shelter about the chimney.

The house is a mere shell of a structure. The gang disappeared from me when the firing commenced. A bullet passed right through the kitchen and grazed the temple of Jane Jones, aged 11, daughter of the landlord. She exclaimed, "I am shot", and as she turned to me I saw her head bleeding, and told her it was nothing serious. Poor Mrs Jones commenced to cry bitterly. I left the kitchen and went into the backyard and passed the gang there. They were standing together at the kitchen chimney. I cannot say whether there were three or four of them. One of them said, "If you go out you will be shot". I walked straight to my house. Firing was going on, but I was uninjured. Of course I was challenged as I passed through. I omitted to state that on Sunday night Steve Hart demanded my revolver from me, and I had to give it up.

Robert Gibbons' Narrative:

farmer, living at present with Mr Reynolds, states:

I came to the railway station with Mr Reynolds's brother at about eight o'clock on Sunday night to bring Mr Reynolds' little boy home. He had gone to Sunday school and we could not understand what was detaining him. We called at the stationmaster's house and Mrs Stanistreet informed us that Mr Hart was inside and that they had been stuck up since three o'clock that morning. We went in and saw Steve Hart, who presented his firearms and told us we had to remain there. We had been there about two hours when Ned Kelly came. Hart then ordered us all to come outside. Ned told us we would all have to go with him to the police station. We went and he kept us there about two hours. He left us for a time and returned after about an hour and a half with the constable. Byrne was in charge of us during Ned's absence. Ned told Mr Reynolds' brother and myself to return with him to Jones's hotel. We went with him and he put us all in the sittingroom.

We remained there from 10 o'clock on Sunday night until three o'clock this (Monday) morning. During that time we went from one room to another, but were not allowed to go outside. Byrne was in charge of the back door and the front one was locked. Ned and Dan Kelly were walking about the house quite jolly. Hart was at the stationmaster's house until about three o'clock. The bushrangers were drinking and making themselves quite jolly. At about three on Monday morning Ned Kelly came into the sittingroom and told us we were not to whisper a word of anything that was said there, or seen about him. "If I hear of any one doing so," he said, "I will shoot him." He went to the door of the room and said, "Here she comes", evidently thinking that the train was about to be wrecked. With that they seemed to me to be making preparations.

The gang went out to the back for a few minutes, and on coming back they proclaimed that the first man who left the house would be shot. Two of the gang mounted their horses and rode away. I saw them through the window. They returned in about

10 minutes. I saw two, one of them being Dan Kelly, go into a small room. They came out soon afterwards fully armed and prepared for a fight. Then the other two did the same. Not long after that the police arrived, when the firing commenced. There must have been about 10 men, women and children prisoners in the house at this time. There was a great shrieking of the women and children. Mrs Jones's eldest daughter (about 14) got shot in the side of the head and her eldest boy was shot in the thigh. We all lay down on the floor for safety, as the bullets were rattling on the house. We were packed so close that we had to lie on our sides, and lay in that position until we came out at about 10 o'clock. Those next to the door led the way and we were prompted to leave by hearing the police, as we thought, giving the gang their last warning. We feared, in fact, that the firing would be commenced again heavier than ever. We did not see any of the gang when we left, as they were in the back room. We were not maltreated in any way.

STATEMENT OF MRS REARDON:

I am the wife of James Reardon, plate-layer. We live in a house near the Glenrowan railway station, on the opposite side of the line to Mrs Jones's hotel. On Saturday night our family, consisting of my husband, myself and our children, a boy 18, a girl seven, and a boy three years old, went to bed. At three o'clock on Sunday morning we were awakened by the dog barking. My husband asked how it was the dog had got out of the stable. I replied I had heard a horseman jump the fence. My husband got up and opened the door, where he was met by Ned Kelly and another plate-layer named Sullivan, whom Kelly had taken. We were bailed up, and taken to the stationmaster's house, and kept there until Sunday evening.

We were allowed to walk about and foolishly walked to Jones's hotel. There we found a large number of prisoners, amongst whom were John Delaney of Greta with his brothers William and Patrick, W. S. Cook, Martin Cherry, plate-layer, John Larkin, a farmer, William Mortimer, a farmer, Edward Reynolds, Robert Gibbons, a brother of the postmaster, two of the McAuliffes, and many others I don't remember. I made several attempts to escape from the hotel. At daybreak this (Monday) morning I came out with my infant child, and got refuge in one of the railway carriages.

Sergeant Steele's Statement:

Sergeant Arthur Loftus Maule Steele, of Wangaratta, states:

I arrived at Glenrowan with five men about five a.m. Others came down by train. I was challenged in the vicinity of the hotel by the police, and I informed them who we were. I scattered my men around the hotel. I went up to the nearest tree behind the back door. Heard no firing up to that time. A woman and child came to the back door screaming. I told her to run on quick and she would not be molested. A man then came to the back door, and I called upon him to throw up his hands or I would fire on him. I was only about 25 yards from the house. The man did not hold up his hands, but stooped and ran towards the stable. I fired at him and he turned and ran back into the house. I am certain that the man must have been injured, as he screamed and fell towards the door. I was firing with slugs. There was then some hot firing and bullets were whistling all round. From the ring of the slugs I at once recognised that the man wore mail. I then heard some men roaring out. It was then just breaking day.

When I looked round I saw Ned Kelly stalking round behind me in the bush. He was marching down on the house quite deliberately and from his rig-out I supposed him at first to be a blackfellow, but seeing him present a revolver and fire at the police, I knew he must be one of the gang. I could see the bullets flying about his head and chest, and concluded that he also had armour on. I then made a run for him and got within about 10 or 15 yards of him, when he turned round and aimed at me with a revolver. I immediately shot at his legs and he staggered. He still aimed at me, so I gave him the second barrel, also in the legs about the knees. I was at this time in the open. He fell on my second charge, and said, "I'm done, I'm done". I ran up to him then, and just as I got up he tried to get the revolver pointed on me again. I ran behind and he could not twist round fast enough. I got up to him, seized hold of the revolver, turned it off from me and he fired it off in my hand. Senior Constable Kelly came up at this juncture and caught hold of him and in a few seconds there was quite a group of people around us.

We disarmed and secured him. We only found one revolver on him. Having divested him of his armour, we carried him to the railway station. Just after I had seized him the rush of the other people knocked Kelly and me over and I received a rather awkward twist and his armour injured my side.

Statement by Charles S. Rawlins:

I accompanied the detachment of police which went from Benalla. On arriving at Glenrowan I went with Superintendent Hare towards the hotel where the Kellys were lodged. Hare went straight towards the house, and I went to the railway gates. Two of the blacktrackers were with us. They got into a ditch, and I got behind one of the railway gate posts. I fired at once, three times, and then I heard Hare say, "I am shot, anyway". After a few minutes I took him to the stationmaster's house, which is close to the railway gates. Then I took him to the railway station and subsequently, at Mr Hare's request, I got some ammunition and went round the line distributing it.

Statement of Constable Hugh Bracken:

I am stationed at Greta, five miles from Glenrowan. At 11 o'clock on Sunday night I was called by Edward Reynolds, I was then at the police station, which is one mile from the railway station. I had been suffering from a bilious attack and was very weak. At first I didn't reply, but another voice called me and then I opened the door. Just as I did so, Ned Kelly presented a revolver at my head. He was masked with an iron helmet and I didn't at first know it was Ned Kelly. The mask was like a nail-can. He told me to bail up and throw my hands up. I said, "You are not Ned Kelly, you are only one of the police trying my mettle'. He continued, "Throw up your arms, or you are a dead man". I put one hand up and he said, "Put the other up, we want no nonsense". I complied. He then took my gun and revolver and asked me for cartridges. I told him I had only those the gun and revolver were loaded with. Then he said, "I believe you have a very fast horse". He referred to a horse called 'Sir Solomon', which I possess. "Sir Solomon is crippled", but I had a good horse in the stable. He ordered me to lead him to the stable and I did so.

We saddled the horse, bridled it and then he told me to mount. Ned Kelly was accompanied by Byrne. Both were mounted, and a man named Reynolds was with them on foot. Byrne took hold of my horse's bridle and Ned Kelly followed up behind with Reynolds on foot. We proceeded to Jones's hotel. Robert Gibbons, another prisoner, also accompanied us. When we arrived at the hotel, we found a lot of people stuck up there. We were in one of the rooms of the hotel. The gang were all armed with revolvers and rifles. There were only three of them there. Hart being, I believe, at the postmaster's house at the time. Byrne locked the front door and I watched where he put the key. He laid it carelessly near the chimney. Believing a special train would be coming up with police, I secured the key when Byrne's back was turned and put it in my pocket. I heard the special train arrive. Thereupon the gang went into a backroom. This was my opportunity and I quietly went to the front door, unlocked it and rushed out. I ran to the railway station, found the train had arrived and the police on the platform, I told them where the Kellys were and asked them to surround the place immediately. After a few minutes, Superintendent Hare returned with his arm wounded. I then secured a horse and rode off to Wangaratta, about 12 miles distant. Told the police there what had happened and sent telegrams all over the district and the police of Wangaratta immediately started for the scene, I returning with them."

Statement of the very Reverend M. Gibney:

I am a Catholic priest, of Perth, West Australia. I was travelling on the north-eastern line, having left Melbourne by the first down train in the morning. On arriving at Glenrowan station, having heard, while going there, that the Kelly gang were at Jones' hotel, I got out of the train, abandoning my intention to proceed further on. Consequently my presence at the scene was, so to speak, accidental. I got out at Glenrowan, because I thought I might be of use in my clerical capacity. The train arrived at Glenrowan between 12 noon and one o'clock and I went at once into the room where Ned Kelly was lying at the station. I don't think he is dying. He is penitent and shows a very good disposition. When I asked him to say "Lord Jesus have mercy on me", he said it and added, "It's not today I began to say that". I heard his confession, which I shall not be expected to repeat. As I at first thought he was dying I annointed him.

Statement by Senior Constable Kelly:

When we started from the platform we ran down towards the railway gates, hearing that the gang were in Jones' public house. We had not time to scatter, but made at once for the front of the house, a few of the men going round to the back. As we neared the place the gang slipped out on the verandah and began to fire at us. Superintendent Hare was near me, as was also Mr Rawlins, a volunteer from Benalla. Two or three constables fired and Superintendent Hare was wounded, a bullet striking his wrist. He said to me, "Kelly, for God's sake surround the house and don't let them escape". With his right hand he forthwith fired two shots. Handing his gun to Mr Rawlins he then retired, saying, 'Kelly, place the men under cover'. I immediately placed the men around the house. Sub-Inspector O'Connor, with his trackers, took up a position in front and I went round to the further part of the premises, taking Constable Arthur with me. We crept on our faces and hands for about 400 yards, and reached a tree 50 yards from the house. We got at the back of this tree, which was in the scrub. There we found a six-barrelled revolving rifle, covered with blood and a skullcap. We kept a lookout and every time we fancied we saw anyone in the hotel we fired. We shot four horses which were saddled, and tied up at the back door, with a view to prevent escape on them.

When he left the train Constable Bracken, who had just escaped from the hotel, told us the gang were all inside. He jumped on one of our horses, which was saddled and rode off to Wangaratta

> for additional assistance. At half-past six o'clock he returned in company with Sergeant Steele and eight men, who at once assisted in mounting guard round the house. We continued firing on the house until about eight o'clock, when Ned Kelly made his appearance under the brow of the hill, about 150 yards from the hotel, and deliberately fired a revolver at me. He was heavily armoured and our men kept up a continuous fire at him, Sergeant Steele being at one side of him and myself and Dowsett (a railway guard) on the other side. Gradually we closed on him, all the while keeping up a steady fire from the rifles.
>
> Finding our shots had no effect on his body we aimed at his head, arms and legs. He walked boldly forward, as if to defy us. Some of our men retired behind trees and logs and in about 10 minutes afterwards he fell beside a fallen tree at which we were posted. We at once rushed forward and caught him. I caught him by the head and Steele grasped his hand in which he held a revolver. He fired it off, but it did no damage. We took his armour off and carried him to the railway station. Found, on searching him only a 3d. piece, a silver Geneva watch and a quantity of ammunition. I asked him to tell me where Sergeant Kennedy's watch was so that I might get it for Mrs Kennedy. He replied, "I can't tell you, I would not like to tell you about it". He said "I had to shoot Sergeant Kennedy and Scanlon for my own safety and I can't tell you anymore". We then gave him over to Mr Sadlier and the medical gentlemen.

With regard to the murder of Aaron Sherritt, near Beechworth, one of the constables present gives the following narrative:

> There were four of us sent out to watch Byrne's mother's house. We were planted for a few weeks in Sherritt's hut, which is about seven miles from Beechworth. About five minutes past six o'clock on Saturday evening a man knocked at the door. Sherritt opened it and said, "Who is here?" The man replied, "I have lost my way. Can you put me on the right track for Sebastopol?" Mrs Aaron Sherritt told her husband to go out and direct the man. He accordingly went out and found that the man was Antonio Wicks, a digger, and that he was handcuffed.

Joe Byrne stood behind Wicks and the moment Sherritt stepped forward Byrne shot him through the eye. Sherritt staggered backwards and then received another bullet in the chest and died. Sherritt's wife and mother-in-law were in the house and we were in the bedroom. Byrne entered the house and asked who was in the bedroom. Mrs Sherritt said it was a man. Byrne then ordered her to bring the man out. She came in and we kept her there. Byrne then said to Mrs Sherritt. "I will shoot your mother if you don't come out". Mrs Sherritt's mother then came into the room to bring her out and we kept them back. Byrne said, "I will soon make you come out", and he, with Dan Kelly, put seven bullets through the walls of the hut.

We never got a chance of shooting at them. Dan Kelly said, "We will set fire to the – place", and he broke up a barrel for firewood. Byrne asked Mrs Sherritt if she used kerosene or candles, and when she said candles, he said he wanted kerosene to set the place alight. We heard them talking on the outside until four or five o'clock in the morning, when they must have left. Byrne asked us to surrender and we replied that we would sooner die. When they threatened to burn the house down, Mrs Barry (Mrs Sherritt's mother) said, "Do not burn down the house. I know, Byrne, you have got a soft heart". Byrne replied, "I have a heart as hard as stone. I will shoot the whole lot of them like dogs". We remained in the hut until last night, when we were relieved by another party of police.

An inquest was commenced today on the body of Aaron Sherritt, who was shot by Byrne at Sebastopol on Saturday evening. His father, mother-in-law and brother and the doctor gave evidence. There were two bullet wounds, but no bullet was found in the body. The inquest was adjourned until Wednesday for the attendance of the policemen who were in the hut when the murder was committed. Sherritt was buried this evening.

Destruction of the Kelly Gang

The Argus, 30 June 1880

The excitement that was created in Melbourne by the intelligence of the latest outrage of the Kelly gang, and of their capture at Glenrowan, was intensified yesterday when it became known that Edward Kelly, the one survivor of the band of desperadoes, was on his way to Melbourne. Crowds of persons collected at the newspaper offices and at street corners, eager for further information. Rumours of a conflicting nature were in circulation, some affirming that Edward Kelly had succumbed to the injuries received in the last affray at Glenrowan. It soon became known, however, that the authorities had made arrangements for bringing him to town yesterday, and the utmost curiosity was manifested as to the probable time of his arrival in town. It was understood that he would be brought down by a special train, to arrive shortly after the ordinary midday train.

In the anticipation of obtaining a view of the notorious bushranger, a large number of persons assembled at the Spencer Street station, and it was found necessary to bring the barricades used on occasions of unusually heavy traffic into use in order to keep the people clear of the trains. A goodly number of people also went to the Essendon station, believing that the prisoner would be removed from the train there, and taken as quietly as possible to the Melbourne Gaol. At the North Melbourne station, which had been selected as on the whole the most convenient place for taking him out of the train, several hundreds of people had assembled to await the arrival of the train from Wodonga. Shortly before two o'clock the ordinary train arrived at North Melbourne station, and the passengers soon informed the excited crowd that Kelly was in the van of the train.

Despite all the efforts of the police and the railway officials, who had been extremely reticent, and had adopted every precaution to prevent a crush at the station, the crowd interfered to some extent with the officers. The platform was rushed, and the crowd tried every means of obtaining a glimpse of the prisoner. Dr Charles Ryan travelled in the van in order to give Kelly the medical attention he required. Dr Ryan was unremitting in his attention to his patient during the long journey. On the arrival at North Melbourne station, Inspector Montford took charge of Kelly, who was placed on a stretcher, and lifted into a wagonette waiting for him. His removal was to some extent impeded by the crowd, which pressed round the van and was with difficulty kept back. The patient lay perfectly helpless. His face wore a wan appearance indicative of prostration, and his hands and foot were bound up. Although he looked at the crowd with some interest, all the look of bravado had gone. There was no demonstration of any sort made by the crowd, although the female section expressed commiseration for the worn-out, broken-down and dejected appearance of one who had become known to them as a man of reckless bravery and of great endurance. The wagonette was rapidly driven by a direct course to the Melbourne Gaol. Along the route, numbers of men, women and children rushed out from factories, shops and private residences and followed the wagonette, eager to obtain a glance at the prisoner.

At the gaol 600 or 700 persons had assembled. The wagonette drove up at a brisk pace, and was taken into the gaol yard before the people had time to obtain even as much as a glimpse at it. As it entered the gaol yard three cheers were called for, and mildly responded to by the crowd, but the manner in which they were called for and given left it a matter of doubt whether they were intended as a recognition of the success of the police officers, who drove up behind their captive, or as a manifestation partly of sympathy with and partly of recognition of the prisoner's reckless daring. When safely lodged within the gaol walls, the prisoner was given over into the hands of the governor, Mr Castieau, who had him immediately removed to the gaol hospital. Dr Shields, of Hotham, the health officer for the gaol, was sent for, and was soon in attendance. He found the patient to be in a feverish state. A wound on the left foot showed that a bullet had passed through it. In the right arm there were two serious wounds, which had been caused by a bullet going right through the fleshy part of the lower arm. The right hand was seriously injured, and in the right leg there were found no less than eight or nine slug-shots. Dr Ryan also in attendance, and the opinion of both medical gentlemen was that Kelly would in all probability recover from his injuries, serious as they were, and notwithstanding the despondency and loss of spirit shown by the prisoner, who has never concealed the fact that he would rather die in any way than allow the law to take its course.

During the afternoon the prisoner's condition improved, and he became more communicative than at the time of his departure from Glenrowan. Almost immediately after his admission to the gaol, Kelly was visited by the Reverend J.P. Aylward, who had a short interview with him. Upon that reverend gentleman devolved the duty of conveying to Kelly's mother, who is undergoing her sentence in the same gaol, the first intimation of the destruction of the gang, of the death of Dan Kelly and Hart, and of the capture and removal to Melbourne of Edward Kelly. On the journey to Melbourne and after his arrival Kelly conversed tolerably freely at times with those round him, but divulged little that was new with regard to the proceedings or intentions of his gang. He was specially reserved in his references to his late mates, and as a rule declined to say anything about them. In reply to a question as to whether he had on any previous occasion been in Melbourne, he said that he must decline to answer it. He stated that the police had taken the gang unawares, and that finding that the police had discovered their whereabouts through the murder of Sherritt, the attempt to upset the special train was recourse to a desperate last resort. Kelly spoke frequently of his determination to bring the blacktrackers to grief, and alluded to that as one strong motive for the act in question. At a late hour last evening Kelly was progressing favourably, and his medical attendants considered him out of danger.

Superintendent Hare returned to town by the train in which Kelly was brought, which was, as previously stated, an ordinary passenger train, and brought down a very large number of passengers. The superintendent proceeded direct to Spencer Street. The large crowd, which had gathered there in anticipation of seeing Kelly himself, soon recognised Superintendent Hare, and cheers were given for him with enthusiasm as he alighted the train. He was in a weak state, having suffered from great loss of blood through the wound in his wrist, which proved to be much more serious than was at first thought. Fears were entertained that amputation of the left arm would be necessary, but Dr Ryan, who was attending him, held out strong hopes of the hand being healed without serious permanent injury. Superintendent Hare, immediately on his arrival in town, proceeded to his residence at Richmond, and was in an improved state of health last night, though still weak. Edward Kelly now awaits his trial for the series of outrages by which he and his late companions attained their notoriety. He has been brought to Melbourne on a remand warrant requiring him to appear before the Central Criminal Court at its sittings commencing on the fifth. It is very doubtful, however, whether, even if his recovery be assured, his condition will permit of his removal from the gaol hospital for some time to come, and it is probable that his trial will have to be postponed.

Dr Charles Ryan's Statement:

I came down in the same van as Ned Kelly. He spoke very little, and seemed like a man in a trance, and glared at any strangers he saw. He had had no sleep all the previous night. Most men wounded as he was would have been far more prostrated than he was, but he has a splendid constitution. Moreover, his body looked as if it had been well nourished. When I asked him if he had been pretty well fed, he said he had, but he did not add where he had got the food. I expected to find him, after the life he had been leading, very dirty, but his skin was as clean as if he had just come out of a Turkish bath. I attended to his wounds and now and then gave him some brandy and water. He seemed grateful, but gave me the idea that he wished to die.

Of course in attending to his wounds I gave him temporary pain, but he never complained in the least. His wounds would not be likely to prove mortal in an ordinary case where the patient had as strong a constitution, but the prisoner is likewise suffering from a severe mental shock, and moreover wants to die. That must be borne in mind when considering his chances of recovery. Under ordinary circumstances a strong man with such wounds might be expected to be able to walk about, not to run about, and not to have the free use of his limbs in some two months' time.

With regard to his wounds, his left arm is pierced by two bullet-holes, one above and one below the elbow. I feel confident that both wounds were caused by one bullet, which, entering below the elbow while the arm was bent, passed also through the arm above the elbow. When I asked him if his arm was bent at the time he received that wound, he said it was. There are also two slug wounds in the right hand, and seven slug wounds in the right leg. One of the slugs I got out. I don't think the wound in the right groin is very dangerous. There is a nasty wound in the ball of the big toe of the right foot. I saw him last at five o'clock (p.m.) in the gaol. He seemed better then than during

> the journey down, and much less feverish. In the tram his pulse was 125, but at the gaol it was only 114. He told me he didn't think that his brother and Hart shot themselves, because they were "two cowards', and hadn't enough pluck to kill themselves. He said that Byrne was plucky enough. The prisoner's breath smelt as if he had been drinking very bad liquor. Superintendent Hare is getting on very well. His wound is a very nasty one and seems to have been caused by a conical bullet revolving at a very rapid rate. The bones of the left wrist are very much shattered, and some portion of them has been ground to powder by the bullet. Still, I don't think amputation will be necessary. He will probably be able to use his left hand in time, but there will be a stiffness in it, particularly in the thumb.

THE OFFICIAL MEDICAL REPORT:

The following is the medical report on the condition of Ned Kelly by Dr. A. Shields, medical officer, Melbourne Gaol:

> The prisoner Kelly was rather feverish on admission to the gaol hospital, the temperature being 102 degrees and the pulse quick. Kelly is a tall, muscular, well formed man, in good condition, and has evidently not suffered in health from his late mode of life. The principal injuries are, first, a severe bullet wound near the left elbow. There are two openings, one above, the other below, the joint, the two apertures having probably been caused by the bullet traversing the arm when bent. The right hand has been injured near the root of the thumb, and from this I removed one large slug shot. In the right thigh and leg there are also several wounds, caused by the same kind of shot. These, however, seem not to be of a dangerous nature. The right foot has received a severe injury. The track of the ball here is marked by two openings, one on the top of the ball of the great toe, and the other on the sole of the foot. The bone is damaged. The last wound and the one near the elbow joint are those of the greatest import. There is, however, no immediate danger. At the same time it is very necessary that Kelly should be kept perfectly quiet, and free from all avoidable causes of excitement.

Mrs Kelly, who was no doubt very much grieved at the fate of her sons, was anxious to see Edward, but in consequence of the recommendations of Dr Shields, Mr Castieau declined to allow her to see him, but promised she should visit him as soon as the prisoner was better. About half-past 10 last evening Kelly was quiet, and appeared to be resting peacefully.

Following the Siege of Glenrowan:

> Shortly after eight o'clock this morning a spring-cart emerged from the local police barracks, and was driven down the street at a slow pace. It was accompanied by eight armed policemen on foot, and the curiosity of the townspeople was naturally excited as to what the vehicle contained. A peep over the side showed that inside, on a stretcher, lay the wounded outlaw Ned Kelly, formerly the terror of the district, but now reduced to the weakness of a child. The police were conveying him to the railway station, and were all fully armed lest any attempt might be made by sympathisers of the late gang to rescue the arch villain. On the arrival of the train he was carried into the guard's van and laid on the floor.
>
> A Miss Lloyd, cousin of the outlaw, was the only relative present, and as the train left she cried without restraint. It is understood here that Kelly has been conveyed to the hospital of the Melbourne Gaol. Just before Kelly was taken away from Benalla, Senior Constable Kelly had a short interview with him in his cell. The senior constable said, "Look here, Ned, now that it is all over, I want to ask you one question before you go, and that is, did you shoot Constable Fitzpatrick at Greta when he went to arrest your brother?" The prisoner replied "Yes, I did. I shot him in the wrist, and the statements which have been made that Fitzpatrick inflicted the wound himself are quite false". This, it will be seen, bears out the statement made by Fitzpatrick, and subsequently by Kelly's sisters.
>
> Of course it will be remembered that the shooting of Fitzpatrick was the original cause of Ned and Dan Kelly taking to the bush. The senior constable also talked with the outlaw about the police murders. He told Kelly that Mrs Kennedy had telegraphed to know whether he had got a letter for her from

her murdered husband. Ned replied that he had got no letter from Sergeant Kennedy, and that Kennedy never uttered a word after he was brought down, except "God forgive you". "I shot him," continued the outlaw. "He kept firing all the time, running from tree to tree, and tried to kill Byrne until his ammunition went done".

During the forenoon the body of Byrne was brought out of the lock-up where it lay, and was slung up in an erect position on the outside of the door, the object being to have it photographed by Mr Burman, of Melbourne. The features were composed in a natural way and were easily recognised. The face was small with retreating forehead, blue eyes, the upper lip covered with a downy moustache, and a bushy beard covering the chin, whilst his hair had been recently cut. The figure was that of a tall, lithe young fellow. The spectacle, however, was very repulsive. The hands were clenched and covered with blood, whilst blood also covered his clothes. The police therefore had the body soon removed from the public gaze. The officers, policemen, trackers and gentlemen then at the barracks, who were present at the encounter, were also photographed in a group.

During the day Detective Ward proceeded to Glenrowan and on making some inquiries discovered five of the horses of the gang stabled at McDonnell's Railway Hotel, which stands on the east side of the line, opposite to the scene of the fight. They had evidently been fasting ever since they had been stabled there, which, of course, was on the arrival of the gang two days ago. Why McDonnell did not give voluntary information to the police concerning these horses has not been explained. They were all brought to Benalla, and two of them were identified as horses which were stolen within the last fortnight from Mr Ryan's farm, on the Major Plains. One of the two was ridden by Joe Byrne when he committed the murder of Sherritt on Saturday last, a third was recognised as a packhorse belonging to Mr Fitzsimmons, of Benalla, that was stolen from his farm near Greta about 12 days ago. The other two have not yet been identified. Ned Kelly's grey mare has also been caught and will be brought on to Benalla tomorrow. On one of the horses was found one of the Government saddles taken from the police horses on the occasion of the Mansfield murders. Another of the saddles, the one on Byrne's horse, was found to have been made by Mr Bullivant of Wangaratta. It may be here mentioned that the Kellys brought packhorses with them for the purpose of carrying their armour. There is some mystery as to what has become of Sergeant Kennedy's watch. It is known that Ned Kelly wore it for a time, but the only one found on him was a small silver lady's watch and it is supposed that he has been exchanging with somebody. Two chains were attached to the latter, one gold and the other silver. All the members of the gang were comfortably clad, and they wore boots which were evidently made to order. Ned Kelly had riding boots, which showed well how he prided himself on having neat feet. When the doctor was dressing his wounds the boots had to be cut off. It was found that he wore no stockings. The gang all have the appearance of being well-fed and Byrne stated to one of their prisoners that they had always lived well, but that the want of sleep which they had often to endure was very trying.

With the view of gathering any fresh particulars obtainable concerning Monday's encounter I revisited Glenrowan today. I found the debris of Jones's hotel still smouldering, and a crowd of people fossicking among the ruins for mementoes of the gang. Two brick chimneys were all that remained standing and the black ashes of the building were covered in part by the sheets of corrugated iron which had formed the roof. The iron was pierced with innumerable bullet and slug holes, and on the chimneys were also a number of bullet marks. The wrecks of two iron bedsteads and of a sewing machine and a few tin cans, some of which contained shot marks, were the only recognisable objects in the debris. It may not be too late to explain here that the hotel was a wooden building of one storey, and contained a front parlour and bar, and two bedrooms at the back. At the rear and separated from the front tenement, stood the kitchen, a rough wooden structure. It stood about 130 yards from the railway station at about the same distance from the railway line on the west side and on the rising ground which leads up to Morgan's Lookout, which is the nearest peak of the Warby Ranges. The stationmaster's house stands on the line below the hotel. The only other houses in the immediate vicinity are McDonnell's hotel and another small private house, both of which are situated on a track running about parallel with the line, at a distance of say 150 yards on the east side. The police station, post office and State school of Glenrowan are about a mile south of the railway station, and the same side as Jones's hotel. On the east rise the Greta Ranges and the township of Greta, only four miles away. The place where the rails were pulled up is exactly half a mile beyond the station, and not a mile and a half as first reported. It was chosen with diabolical fitness for bringing about the total destruction of the special train. The line takes a sudden turn down an incline and is then carried over a gully on an embankment. There is a little creek in this gully, and to carry it under the line a substantial culvert had been built. This culvert is situated just at the end of the sharpest part of the curve and at the foot of the incline, and it was just at this point that the rails were torn up. Had the special train continued its journey without any warning having been given it would have been impossible for the engine-driver to see the breach in the line until too late, and the inevitable result would have been that the train, with its living freight, would have rushed over the embankment into the gully beneath. If it had gone on the left side it would have had a fall of about 20 feet and if on the right, a fall of about 30 feet.

Reardon, the line repairer, who was ordered by Kelly to take the rails up, gives the following narrative:

I was in bed with my wife and family, as my wife has already informed you, when Kelly called at my house. I was awakened at about 20 minutes past two o'clock on the Sunday morning by my dog barking and subsequently hearing a horse galloping. I thought it was one belonging to a friend that had got loose, and I therefore got up and dressed and went out to catch it. I was met in the yard by a mate, who said he had been arrested. I asked him what trouble he had fallen into, thinking he had been arrested by the police. Ned Kelly then stepped forward and presenting a revolver at my head ordered me to bail up and tell him who was inside. I did as he desired and all in the house were then bailed up. My children had to come out half-dressed. He then told me that I had to tear up some rails, and that if I refused he would shoot me. The tools necessary were in a box which was locked up, and I pretended not to have the key.

The lock was broken by someone, and I was directed to take out the necessary tools and to accompany a party down the line. I took along some tools, but not all that would be required, and six or seven other men were brought along with me to assist. Kelly pointed out the spot where he wanted the rails lifted and ordered me to proceed with the work. I remonstrated with him and begged to be excused owing to my position on the railway and on account of my wife and family, whom I would not be able to support if I lost my billet. He repeated his order in a peremptory manner and told me I was a dead man if I refused. I then asked that the other men should do the work and said I would direct them. To this he agreed. I accordingly showed them how to unscrew the bolts and so cut off one rail on each side. I then directed them to remove the pair of rails with the nine sleepers to which they were attached. I thought that by removing sleepers and all there would be less danger for the train. Kelly objected to this plan, and talked to me again fiercely. I represented to him that the danger would be increased if the sleepers were also removed, and that if the set of sleepers and rails were pitched over the culvert, 30 men would be unable to raise them again. I also protested that I had not the tools by which the rails could be detached. He fired up on me again, and asked if I could not draw out the bolts with my teeth. I appeased him by replying that he could not do that himself, although a stronger man than me. He persisted, however, in having the rails removed singly. I then commenced hammering at them, making a great clanking noise. He at once interfered, and said he could not stand that.

The rails and sleepers were then removed together and thrown over the embankment and we returned to the hotel. My boy was shot by the police in the shoulder when out trying to escape with his mother. I have heard from Wangaratta that he is improving, for he was able to take a good breakfast this morning.

So much for the lifting of the rails. How we received such timely notice of the plot when approaching in the special train is still surrounded with a degree of mystery. The man who stopped the train turns out to be Mr Thomas Curnow, the local schoolmaster. Mr and Mrs Curnow were stuck up at about 11 o'clock on Sunday morning by Ned Kelly and Byrne at the railway gates as they were driving towards Greta. Their horse and buggy were put up at Jones's hotel, and they themselves were lodged in the stationmaster's house. When bailing them up Kelly said, "I am sorry, but I must detain you". They were detained until about 10 o'clock at night, when Kelly and Byrne took them to the hotel, requested them to get into their buggy, and then accompanied them to the police station, where Kelly told them to go home and get to bed, and to remain quiet, otherwise he would shoot Mr Curnow. How Mr Curnow heard of the rails having been pulled up has not yet been explained and it seemed strange, seeing that he had been set at liberty before the deed was done. He, however, did receive the information, and took the risk of earning the hatred of the Kelly gang by utilising it in the interests of humanity. His house stands quite close to the railway line, and he was, therefore, able to hear the pilot engine approaching. On doing so he immediately ran out with a red handkerchief, which he held up with a lighted match behind it. By this action the special train was warned and the locale of the gang discovered.

Next-door to the police station is the post office of Glenrowan and on the Sunday night Mr Reynolds, the post-master, was interviewed by Kelly as to where Constable Bracken was to be found. Kelly, by his remarks, showed that he had a full knowledge of the constable's habits. He pointed, for instance, to a sofa, and said he expected to find him sitting there. Finding after bullying Mr Reynolds that Bracken was really not there, he left without making Reynolds a prisoner. When he stuck up Bracken at the police station, he went into Bracken's bedroom, and found Mrs Bracken in bed with her little son. He shook hands with the little boy and said, "I may be worth £2000 to you yet, my child". He then demanded handcuffs and cartridges from Bracken, who, however, defended his office where these things were by cunning evasive replies. Had Kelly got the handcuffs he would, in all probability, have put a pair on the constable, who would then have been unable to escape from the hotel as he so opportunely did. There are several tents between the railway station and the hotel inhabited by a number of stonebreakers. These men were of course also bailed up, but in a rather startling manner. Kelly, without warning, fired into one of the tents in which two men were sleeping. Fortunately neither of them were hurt, but the bullet passed through a portion of the blankets.

THE FOLLOWING ARE FURTHER PARTICULARS FROM CONSTABLE BRACKEN, WHICH DURING THE EXCITEMENT OF MONDAY HE HAD NOT TIME TO SUPPLY:

> When we were held prisoners in the hotel Ned Kelly began talking about politics. "There was one in Parliament," he said, "whom he would like to kill, Mr Graves". I asked why he had such a desire and he replied, "Because he suggested in Parliament that the water in the Kelly country should be poisoned, and that the grass should be burnt. I will have him before long". He knew nothing about Mr Service, but he held that Mr Berry was no good, as he gave the police a lot of money to secure the capture of the gang, too much by far. He then asked me "What was the policeman's oath?" I replied, "That policemen were sworn to do their duty without malice or favour, and to deal even handed justice all round". He rejoined, "Constable – of Greta, once told me that the oath was that a policeman had to lag any person, no matter whether it was father, mother, brother or daughter, if they were but arrested". He also asked if there were not 19 or 20 men in the force who were as great rogues as himself. I of course concurred with him. He then said, "We are just after shooting one – traitor", alluding to Aaron Sherritt, "and we now want that – Detective Ward, but he is not game to show up. The next I want are those six little demons", alluding to the blacktrackers, "then O'Connor and Hare. If I had them killed, I would feel easy and contented". He questioned the ability of the blacks to track in the Victorian bush, and said he himself could track an emu in Queensland. The prisoners were then all called together, and Ned said, "If any of you ever hear or see any of us crossing the railway, or at any other place, and

if the police should come and ask if you had seen any such party, you must say, 'No, we saw nobody', and if I ever hear of any of you giving the police any information about us I will shoot you down like dogs. I do not mind a policeman doing his duty so long as he does not overdo it". I remarked that the police were only earning an honest living, and asked how he, if he was an honest man, could get on without them? He turned upon me, and demanded, "And am not I an honest man". I replied, "I'm damned if you are", and nearly all laughed. Kelly next called a man named Sullivan before him, and said, "I have seen you somewhere else. Have you not been in Wangaratta lately". Sullivan replied in the affirmative. Kelly then asked if he had ever been in New Zealand and received a similar answer."How long ago?" he next asked, and Sullivan replied, "Ten or 12 years ago". In answer to other questions Sullivan said that he was in New Zealand when the notorious murders were committed there by strangling, but denied with truth that he was the Sullivan who turned Queen's evidence on his mates, and who is understood to be living in this district at present. Kelly then said to me, "£8000 has been offered for our capture. I promise to give you a similar amount if you tell me where that Sullivan is to be found, and the same amount for information as to where I can find Quinlan, the man who shot Morgan".

Between 12 and one o'clock on Sunday morning one of Mrs Jones's sons sang the Kelly song for the amusement of the gang, and his mother occasionally asked him to sing out louder. Most of the prisoners were then cleared from the front parlour and the gang had a dance. They danced an act of quadrilles, and Mr David Mortimer, brother-in-law of the schoolmaster, furnished the music with a concertina. Ned Kelly had the girl Jones for a partner, Dan had Mrs Jones and Byrne and Hart danced with male prisoners. Thinking they heard a noise, the gang broke away from the dance abruptly and Dan went outside. It was at that time that I secured the key of the door. Doubling up my trousers at the feet, I placed the key in the fold, and when I heard the special arrive I raised my leg, picked out the key stealthily, unlocked the door and bounded away. When the train

> was heard, stopping Kelly said, "You will see some play now, boys. We will shoot them all". When the constable's escape was discovered Byrne, who noticed it first, exclaimed, "Let me but catch him, and I will make a Bracken of him".

The prisoners heard Byrne fall at the bar when he was shot. He dropped down dead without uttering a word, and the bullet must have entered at the bar window. A difference of opinion exists, however, as to the hour of his death. Some say that he fell at daylight, others that it was about nine o'clock in the morning. At 10 o'clock, when the prisoners made their escape, they saw Dan Kelly and Hart standing in the passage fairly cowed. They looked gloomy and despairing and said nothing to the prisoners as they left. The gang had all been drinking and Ned has stated that he took too much liquor. His idea was that he and Byrne should clear away from the hotel after the first attack unobserved, that Dan and Hart should remain, that in the morning he and Byrne should return and charge the police, and that Dan and Hart should then sally forth and take the police in the rear. He accordingly called on Byrne to follow him into the bush, but Byrne's courage failed and he declined. The trees behind which Kelly stood when fighting in the morning are all pierced with bullets and slugs, and the place where he fell is saturated with blood. He had evidently passed the night under a fallen tree a little further up the rise, for there were found the marks of his feet and much blood.

The boy Jones has died at Wangaratta. He was shot when lying on the ground in one of the bedrooms. The bullet is said to have come through the wall, entered at his thigh and passed into his body. Cherry was shot early in the morning, and his wound was dressed by some of his fellow prisoners. None of Ned Kelly's wounds are of a deadly character. What were supposed to be shot marks in the groin are, Dr Nicholson states, only grazings.

The charred remains of Dan Kelly and Hart were handed over to their friends and taken to Mrs Skillion's place at Greta, and are there now. John Grant, undertaker, of Wangaratta, was employed by their friends to provide coffins of a first-class description, the cost being a matter of no consequence. He arrived with them in a buggy at Glenrowan yesterday afternoon, and they were seen to be high-priced articles. The lid of the one was lettered "Daniel Kelly, died 28 June, 1880, aged 19 years", and the other "Stephen Hart, died

28 June 1880, aged 21 years". How the remains are to be distinguished from each other is a problem that will not be easily solved.

During the afternoon Superintendent Sadlier telegraphed to the local police that the remains were on no account to be interfered with until the magisterial inquiries were held and steps were at once taken to carry out these instructions. The inquest on the body of the unfortunate Sherritt will be held tomorrow (Wednesday) at Benalla.

THE MAGISTERIAL INQUIRY ON BYRNE:

In the morning Captain Standish intimated his intention of holding a magisterial inquiry upon the bodies of Byrne and Cherry sometime during the day, but afterwards it was decided to hold the inquiry upon the body of Byrne alone and hold an inquest upon Cherry's body. Mr Robert McBean, J.P., was called upon to officiate, and the inquiry took place in the courthouse. The proceedings were somewhat of a formal nature, but little evidence being required. So quietly was the whole affair disposed of that no one was made aware of it, and the courthouse was almost empty, two or three of the police and some others who were at the courthouse at the time constituting the audience. Captain Standish sat upon the bench with Mr McBean, and assisted in conducting the inquiry.

Thomas McIntyre, police constable, stationed at Melbourne, stated that he was one of the party who went out in search of the outlaws from Mansfield in October, 1878. On the 26th of the same month they encountered the Kellys, Hart and Byrne. He identified the body as being that of the outlaw Joseph Byrne, who was one of the gang that shot Sergeant Kennedy and Constables Scanlon and Lonigan on that date. Louis Pyatzer, a contractor, who was one of those present at the capture of the gang on Monday last, stated that he was compelled by them to enter and remain in Mrs Jones's hotel at Glenrowan.

He identified the body as being that of Joseph Byrne, the outlaw, who was one of the gang. Byrne assisted the Kellys in resisting the police. Edward Cenny, a police constable, stationed at Benalla, said that he had known Joseph Byrne at the Woolshed and other places for over eight years. The body now in the possession of the police was that of Byrne, the outlaw, who was one of the Kelly gang of bushrangers. Inspector Sadlier produced the proclamation issued in the Government Gazette in October and December last, offering £4000 for the capture of the gang of outlaws, consisting of Edward Kelly, Daniel Kelly, Joseph Byrne and Steve Hart. The two latter were at first stated to be men by the names of King and Brown, but were afterwards known to be Hart and Byrne. He also produced the proclamation issued in the *New South Wales Government Gazette* offering a similar reward for the capture of the gang. He stated that the rewards were to be withdrawn at the end of the present month, but as the gang had been captured before that time the reward was still in force. This concluded the evidence taken in the matter and a verdict of justifiable homicide was returned by Mr McBean in the following terms:

> The outlaw Joseph Byrne, whose body was before the Court and in the possession of the police, was shot by them whilst in the execution of their duty. The body was subsequently handed over to the friends of the outlaw, who were waiting in Benalla to receive it, and they conveyed it to Greta. They intend to bury it with the bodies of Hart and Dan Kelly in the Wangaratta cemetery, after the magisterial inquiry upon the latter has been held.
>
> The boy John Jones died from his wounds in the Wangaratta Hospital this morning. The burial of the remains of Dan Kelly and Steve Hart had been fixed for noon today, but it being found necessary to hold a magisterial inquiry the burial was stopped. Mr Foster, P.M., and Mr Wyatt, P.M., being both engaged with inquests, Mr Bickerton, J.P., has consented to hold the inquiry on the bodies of the outlaws at Glenrowan tomorrow and Mr A. Tone, J. P., will be asked to hold the inquiry at the hospital. The girl Jones is progressing favourably. The boy Reardon is lying in a critical state, and is not expected to recover.

With regard to the part taken by Sub-Inspector O'Connor and the Queensland blacktrackers in the encounter at Glenrowan, Sub-Inspector O'Connor makes the following statement:

> I went down by the special train on Sunday night at the request of Captain Standish. I collected my troopers and started three hours after I received notice. I agreed to go on condition that the Government of Victoria would see me held blameless, as we were under orders to leave for Queensland. On our arrival

at Glenrowan we heard that the rails had been taken up some distance further on. We thought the best course would be to get the horses and proceed to the spot. Bracken then appeared, and informed us that the Kellys were at Jones's public house. Superintendent Hare, myself and four or five men rushed up to the house. When we got within 25 yards we were received with a single shot, and then a volley. We returned the fire. Hare said, "O'Connor, I'm wounded – I'm shot in the arm. I must go back". He left immediately. We remained, and our incessant fire drove the outlaws into the house, which we heard them barricade. Superintendent Hare returned to the station, stayed a short time there and then went to Benalla. I stood at my post until half-past 10 o'clock in the forenoon, when I was sent for by Superintendent Sadlier. I was within 25 yards of the house the whole time. At daybreak I got behind shelter. One of my troopers was shot alongside me, cut across the eyebrows. He jumped on the bank, fired five shots into the house, and said, "Take that, Ned Kelly". It seemed to afford him great relief, but rather amused us. I was in charge of the men from the time Superintendent Hare left until Superintendent Sadlier arrived on the ground.

Destruction of the Kelly Gang

The Argus, 2 July 1880

Further particulars of an interesting character relating to the tragedy at Glenrowan have transpired. The most startling item is that Cherry, the plate-layer, was not accidentally killed, but was deliberately shot by Ned Kelly at the beginning of the fray, because he refused to hold back a window curtain in the hotel while Kelly fired at the police. As to the survivor of the gang, he was visited yesterday by Dr Shields, who reports favourably of his condition, and his speedy recovery is confidently expected. No one else was allowed to see him, Mr Castieau having received instructions from the Chief Secretary to admit no one without a special order. Superintendent Hare's wound has not proved quite so serious as was anticipated and there is every prospect of his shortly recovering the use of his arm. He is staying at Sunbury now as a guest of the Honourable W. J. Clarke.

A report was circulated in town yesterday that a fresh outbreak of bushrangers had taken place at Stanley, near Beechworth. On inquiries being made it was ascertained that the police authorities had received no communication on the subject and that the report was without foundation. Since the tragedy, Glenrowan has been visited by crowds of people who have inspected the ground in the vicinity of the house in which the outlaws took refuge with eager curiosity, but there is a sufficient force of police on the spot to keep order. Superintendent Sadlier is still at Benalla and reports that everything is quiet there. Among those who contributed a share towards the destruction of the Kelly gang, Mr H.E. Cheshire, acting postmaster at Beechworth, deserves to be mentioned. There is no telegraph office at Glenrowan and Mr Cheshire therefore, on hearing that the Kelly gang had broken out there, proceeded with the Beechworth detachment of police by train on Monday morning and on arrival had the wires cut and connected with a small pocket telegraph instrument, thereby placing Glenrowan in telegraphic communication with the city. He did all the telegraphing himself, on his own account, and it must be admitted that he rendered a very important service in the interests of justice and humanity.

The engine-driver and fireman of the special train which was dispatched on Sunday night also deserve some recognition for the readiness they displayed in placing themselves in a position of danger. It appears that in running through the Craigieburn gates damage was done to the gear of the brake, rendering it entirely useless. The pilot engine being provided with a brake, the driver of the special train, H. Alder, suggested that this engine should take the train, at the same time volunteering his services as driver of the pilot engine. The fireman of the special train, H. Burch, also volunteered his services for the pilot engine. After running at a fair speed for some time in front of the train containing the police party, speed was slackened on account of the curves, and in order to keep the train that was following in sight. When a strange signal was observed the pilot engine approached cautiously and on the nature of the signal being ascertained, a stop was made and the driver then went cautiously back and related to Superintendent Hare what he had been told by Mr Curnow.

Ever since the Jerilderie affair many people imagined that the gang had finally left the colony and were accustomed to shake their heads and look as sagacious as possible when told that the police authorities had positive information that the outlaws were still hiding in the north-eastern district. Of course the authorities in question could at any time have proved their words if such a course had been judicious. Assistant Commissioner Nicolson, who had charge of the police in that district from May 1879, up to the beginning of June 1880, has stated that never a month passed without his receiving authentic information of movements of the outlaws. Such was the terrorism, however, that the latter caused and such their cunning, that in most instances the information received by the police came too late to be of any use. It will be remembered that very soon after Assistant Commissioner Nicolson took charge of affairs the permanent garrison men were withdrawn from the district and the police force there was considerably reduced, the number of constables left being 60.

With this reduced force Assistant Commissioner Nicolson improvised a new system of operations, which new system was continued in force after his removal to another district and until the destruction of the gang. Previously to the introduction of the new plan the course adopted was to send large bodies of police numbering perhaps, a dozen, with 15 horses out into the district to look for the Kellys. These troops would have no idea when they started where or in what direction the Kellys were and would have no such idea when they returned to the point of departure. They attracted much attention, cost a lot of money, were sufficiently numerous to feel tolerably secure and in fine weather enjoyed themselves immensely.

The leading feature of the new system was the dispersal of the force in small parties of four men, or fewer, stationed in places likely to be attacked or haunted by the gang. These men were not in uniform and it is, by the by, a singular fact that policemen in uniform were often able to pick up more information than those in plain clothes. In what is known as the Kelly country, a stranger is, because he is a stranger, and no matter how he is dressed, an object of suspicion to such persons as the Kellys and their friends, and they have been so much on the alert that no one would have been thought to have dreamt of sending a constable in uniform to obtain particulars regarding them. Knowing this, men in uniform, when ostensibly engaged in performing ordinary routine duties, have often been able, simply because they were not suspected of having any other designs, to obtain genuine information as to the proceedings of the gang. The small parties of police scattered through the country received instructions to act on their own responsibility and sometimes had to conceal themselves for weeks when watching a place.

Prior to the withdrawal of the blacktrackers, Assistant Commissioner Nicolson found them so useful that he reported, about three weeks ago, that if they were taken away the gang would be most likely to commit another outbreak. The blacktrackers not only frightened the Kellys, but caused them much inconvenience and hard work. For instance, it is well known that bushmen of the Kelly type object to walking much and always ride on horseback if they get a chance. The presence of the Queensland Aborigines in the district often compelled the gang to walk, in order to avoid giving the Aborigines a chance of following horses' tracks, when they would otherwise have ridden. Some time ago people used to wonder how the bushrangers when mounted could cross the railway line or bridges without being seen.

It was ultimately ascertained that the plan they adopted was to ride up to the railway fence, say, and then dismount, hand over their horses to sympathisers, and cross the line on foot. The sympathisers would ride the horses boldly through the nearest level crossing and no one would suspect that the animals were those of the gang, the members of which would receive back their horses at some spot agreed upon. During the past few months traces of the gang were often discovered by the blacktrackers. Sometimes the trace would be the marks where bridles had been hung round a tree and sometimes a gunyah. If a track was new and had not been crossed and recrossed, the blacks could follow it with unerring certainty, and their astuteness in that direction astounded and terrified Ned Kelly, than whom there are few better white bushmen. Although the bushrangers were in the district, they were seen by comparatively few of their friends.

There were various signals by which the gang communicated with their friends. Sometimes a couple of stones placed in a peculiar position would be the signal and sometimes an eccentric horse's track. Thus, one of the gang would ride in a circle near a sympathiser's hut and then jump a fence and again ride circuitously and finally strike off in the direction where the outlaws were hid. The sympathiser, on seeing this track, would carry provisions in the direction indicated. When carrying provisions for the gang, the sympathisers would adopt all sorts of devices to avoid discovery. Occasionally they would pretend to be drunk and make the night hideous with their cries. Hearing the wild fellows about, honest residents of the district would retire into their homes, but the gang would also hear them and answer with a peculiar signal.

All of a sudden, when time and place suited, a member of the gang would appear, take the provisions and hurry off out of sight in a moment. The precautions devised by Ned Kelly were so elaborate that some very experienced police officers doubt whether one of the gang could have betrayed the others into the hands of the police. When they extinguished their fires they would remove the ashes and scatter them far and wide and cover over the black spot with earth. But their fires were always small, like those made by wild Aborigines. As an indication of the caution with which the gang worked it may be mentioned that they used to draw up and reduce into writing elaborate details of their proposed plan of operations prior to making a raid. It is known that the arrangements to be followed, both in the Jerilderie and Euroa affairs, were fully made beforehand and committed to paper, the object in doing so being to assist the memory. The deceased Joe Byrne, who was the best scholar in the gang and who, when a boy, distinguished himself at school for his ability, was the secretary.

For some months past the police have been gradually closing up sources through which food was conveyed to the bushrangers and the latter were suffering from an insufficiency of food. Dan Kelly and Byrne, in particular, presented of late a very emaciated appearance. The bodies of Dan Kelly and Hart were interred by their friends on Wednesday in the Greta cemetery. About a hundred friends and sympathisers were present, but there was no disturbance. Etty Hart, sister of Steve, was, however, very excited and fell into hysterics. It has transpired that the unfortunate line repairer Martin Cherry was not shot by the police but by Ned Kelly, and that intentionally. The fact was at first suppressed by those who knew it out of a fear that they might be marked men if they made the disclosure. Three of the prisoners have, however, ventured to tell the police, on the condition that their names should not be published. They were interviewed separately and their statements all correspond.

This is the fifth deliberate murder committed by the gang and it was perpetrated under the following circumstances:

When the gang fired their first volley from the verandah of the hotel they retired inside. Ned Kelly, as is already known, was wounded on the foot and arm. He went to the window of the front parlour to fire again on the police, but the blind was down and having one arm wounded he could not hold it aside and fire at the same time. He therefore ordered the old man Cherry to hold the blind up whilst he fired. Cherry refused, and Kelly at once shot him with his rifle in the groin and he fell. Kelly may have intended to fire at the poor man's legs, or being disabled, he may simply have been unable to raise his rifle higher. The fact, however, remains that it was he who did the deed and that he thus added one more fiendish murder to the black list against his name. It seems that immediately after this he made his escape by the back door and got into the bush before the police got the house surrounded. The coat which Ned Kelly wore was a long, grey mackintosh. It covered his armour and is full of bullet and slug holes. Senior Constable Kelly and his men returned from Glenrowan this morning and reported that during the night perfect quietness prevailed there.

Constable James McArthur is the man Ned Kelly referred to as being an excellent shot. He gives the following interesting narrative of his experiences:

> I was one of the first party of police who attacked the gang. As has been already stated, we were fired on from the verandah and we returned the fire. Senior Constable Kelly stationed our men at different places round the building. He took me round in the bush to a point opposite to the north-western corner of the building. We approached by passing from tree to tree and taking shelter at times under fallen timber. When 100 yards away from the building we got behind one tree and I stooped down to look round it, placing my hand on the ground. I was rather startled for I touched a rifle, which was covered with blood. A pool of blood lay near it and also a round skull cap. "Look here," I whispered to Senior Constable Kelly and we both held our arms ready, for we thought that one of the gang must be near. I indeed felt sure that Ned was behind the very tree we were standing at, but we soon found that he was not there. That he was quite close to us, however, there is now no doubt. I crept forward from tree to tree and got within 80 yards of the house, finding shelter behind a fallen tree. I fired at figures of men I saw in the hotel for some time.

There were several lulls in the firing and feeling cold I filled my pipe to have a smoke. As I was stooping down doing so a bullet, fired from the hotel, ploughed the ground under my breast. I then changed my position, going behind another tree. After I had stayed there for some time and still feeling cold, I stooped down to light my pipe. In the act of doing so I caught sight of a strange figure coming down the hill. My pipe fell out of my mouth and I gazed at the mysterious being for a minute, not knowing what to make of it. The figure approached steadily and I saw it was a man, with what I thought to be a nail-can on his head. Thinking he was someone who intended storming the hotel under the protection of the headgear he wore, I sang out to him, "Keep back, you damned fool", but he still advanced and only replied by firing at me with his revolver.

I could see that he was unable to hold out the weapon and take a proper aim and the bullet tore up the ground a yard or two away from me. I then fired at his head with my Martini-Henry rifle. The bullet hit his head and jerked off. I fired a second time with the same result and he still advanced. Seeing a slit in the helmet for his eyes I aimed at it, and the bullet hit the mark, but as I afterwards found it only bruised and discoloured his eye. It was my other bullet that blackened his other eye. This he told me afterwards.

By this time Senior Constable Kelly, Sergeant Steele and Constable Phillips and Guard Dowsett were also pelting away at him, but with no better effect. Our feelings may be easier imagined than described, for it seemed we were fighting with a supernatural being. Dowsett exclaimed, "By God, it is the devil". Senior Constable Kelly, after having another shot at him replied, "No, it must be the bunyip". Thinking that he might have no armour on his back, I made a track round to get to his rear, and in the meantime Sergeant Steele, Senior Constable Kelly and Guard Dowsett closed upon him, brought him down and secured him. Then, of course, we found that it was the veritable Ned Kelly. I came down in the train with him from Glenrowan and we entered into conversation. He said that my bullets staggered him and injured his eyes. He also stated that

> when, during the night, he stood within a couple of yards of the senior constable and me, that he could have picked us off easily. I asked him why he did not then do so. He replied, "It was not my game", and explained that his intention was to get near the hotel and so attract the attention of the police away from the building. It would then, he said, have been the part of his mates to sally out and attack the police in the rear. He indeed did call out, "Come on, I am here".

From what has transpired, it appears that the Kelly gang fully intended to make a raid on one of the banks in Benalla had their plan succeeded in upsetting the railway train. When Ned Kelly was asked whether he intended to rob the Colonial Bank at Benalla, he said, "Oh no, Brock, the manager, is a decent sort of cove, we wouldn't harm him. We should have stuck-up the other bank though". The other bank that narrowly escaped a visit from the Kelly gang is the Bank of New South Wales.

Dr John Nicholson, of Benalla, gives the following narrative:

> I was called early on Monday morning by Superintendent Hare, who said that he had been shot by the Kellys and wanted me to go to Glenrowan, where the police had them surrounded in a house. He told me to follow him to the post-office and dress his wound, and he would go back to Glenrowan if I would permit him. I shortly afterwards went to the post-office and ascertained that he had been wounded in the left wrist by a bullet, which had passed obliquely in and out at the upper side of the joint, shattering the extremities of the bones, more especially of the radius. There were no injuries to the arteries, but a good deal of venous heamorrhage, in consequence of a ligature which had imprudently been tied around the wrist above the wound. I temporarily dressed the wound, during which he fainted. Seeing the wound, although serious, was not dangerous to life, I made all haste to the railway station and accompanied Superintendent Sadlier and a party of police in a special train to Glenrowan. We arrived before daylight, but the moon was shining. The men, under Superintendent Sadlier's instructions, then immediately spread out, having first ascertained where the guard was weakest. A party headed by Superintendent Sadlier went up the line in

front of the house and were immediately fired at. Three shots were fired in one volley at first, and immediately afterwards a volley of four. The fire was sharply replied to by Superintendent Sadlier's party and also from other quarters where the police were stationed. I did not see anyone come outside and thought the return fire was at random.

The firing on the part of the police was renewed at intervals and replied to from the house, but never more than a volley of two after this. Mr Marsden of Wangaratta, Mr Rawlins, several gentlemen, reporters for the press, some railway officials and myself were on the platform watching the proceedings, sometimes exposed to the fire from the house in our eagerness to get a clear view of everything, and then, suddenly remembering that we were in easy range, quickly seeking the nearest shelter. Things remained in this state about an hour, when a woman with a child in her arms left the house and came towards the station, crying out and bewailing all the time. She was met by some of the police and taken to one of the railway carriages. From her we learnt that the outlaws were still there and at the back part of the house.

They had taken compassion on her and had permitted her to leave to save her darling child, but she was too much excited to give any definite information. About 8 o'clock we (the spectators on the platform) became aware that the police on the Wangaratta side of the house were altering the direction of their fire and we then saw a very tall form in a yellowish-white long overcoat, somewhat like a tall native in a blanket. He was further from the house than any of the police, and was stalking towards it with a revolver in his outstretched arm, which he fired two or three times and then disappeared from our view amongst some fallen timber. His movements seemed so deliberate and reckless that we thought he was mad. Sergeant Steele was at this time in front of him. Senior Constable Kelly and Guard Dowsett on his left, and Constables Dwyer, Phillips and another whose name I did not know, near the railway fence in his rear. There was also someone on the upper side, but I do not know who it was. Shortly after this a horse with saddle and bridle came towards the place where the man (whom we had by this time ascertained to be Ned Kelly) was lying, and we fully expected to see him make a rush and mount it, but he allowed it to pass, and went towards the house.

Messrs Dowsett and Kelly kept all this time stealthily creeping towards him from one point of cover to another, firing at him whenever they got a chance. The constables at his rear were also firing, and gradually closing in upon him, and we were all excited. Exclamations of "Look out, he's going to fire", "There he is behind that tree", "I can see him from here", "He's down", "Look at little Dowsett, what a plucky fellow he is", were heard on all sides and then we saw Sergeant Steele rush towards him, quickly followed by Dowsett and Kelly, and a general rush was made towards them. We were perfectly astounded when we discovered that he was clad in a coat of armour of a most massive description.

When I reached the place he was in a sitting posture on the ground, his helmet lying near him, and a most extraordinary and pitiable object he looked. A wild beast brought to bay, and evidently expecting to be roughly used. His face and hands were smeared with blood. He was shivering with cold, ghastly white, and smelt strongly of brandy.

He complained of pain in his left arm, whenever he was jolted in the effort to remove his armour. Messrs. Steele and Kelly tried to unscrew the fastenings of his armour, but could only undo it on one side. I then took hold of the two plates, forced them a little apart, and drew them off his body. Our operations were materially hastened at this time by being fired at from the house, one bullet striking close to us. He was then carried over the railway fence to the station. Senior Constable Kelly and myself brought up the rear with the armour. When we reached the station we laid him in the van, but he was shortly afterwards taken into the station-house, and placed on a stretcher. I then made an examination of his injuries, which I found to be as follows:

There were two holes in the fleshy part of the under and outer side of the left forearm, apparently produced by a revolver bullet which had passed in and out through the openings. There was a larger bullet wound about 4 inches above the elbow at the back of the same arm. It had apparently entered from behind, and had not passed out, but is lying somewhere in front of the joint.

There were several slug wounds on the outer side of the right thigh and leg, which had entered from the direction of his right side, one of them, after passing superficially through the skin at the upper part of the thigh, had grazed the skin on the lower part of the abdomen, but had not entered. Another bullet wound passed in a slanting direction backwards from the upper part of the great toe of the right foot, and terminated in a long slit-like wound at the sole, near the heel. A slug had also entered the ball of the right thumb, causing a wound, which he said was as painful as any of them, and prevented him holding his revolver.

I dressed the wounds as well as circumstances would permit. He complained of the coldness of his feet, and said they would never get warm again. He was being questioned all this time, sometimes by the police, sometimes by the reporters and sometimes by the general public, who were inconveniently crowding the room. He was besieged with questions, and very seldom had less than three to reply to at the same time. He was very weak, and replied in a listless way to most of the inquiries. His replies, as far as I heard, were in the main correctly given in the various reports. He said he had been lying in the same position nearly all night, and was cold and cramped, afraid to move, and unable to lift his revolver up for fear of making a noise with his armour, otherwise he could have shot some of the police during the night. None of the wounds were of a mortal character. He must have lost much blood during the night, as he said that the wound in his foot and the one in his arm were received at the first volley fired by Hare's party. As they were bullet wounds, they must have been caused by either Constable Phillips, Gascoigne, or McArthur, who were with Hare when

> he was shot. Hare had a shot gun, which was taken from him by Mr Rawlins. I attended to Edward Kelly during the rest of the day. He remained in the same listless, apathetic state up to the time he was taken out of my charge. The excitement caused by the capture of the Kelly gang is gradually subsiding, although the matter still remains the all-absorbing topic of conversation.

Mrs Barry and her daughters still remain here, and have not yet returned to their residences. Aaron Sherritt's house remains untenanted. It will be remembered that at the inquest Mrs Barry said that Joe Byrne was talking to her about his mother, but she did not detail the conversation. It appears that Byrne asked Mrs Barry how long it was since she had seen his mother, and Mrs Barry replied not since Mrs – 's funeral, mentioning the name of a neighbour who died some weeks previously. Byrne affected ignorance of the death, and denied having seen his mother for some time. What his object in misleading Mrs Barry was cannot, of course, be ascertained, but it is known that he was at the house several times recently. Some curiosity has been expressed as to the causes which led Aaron Sherritt to turn against the gang, with all of whom he was once on terms of intimate friendship, and go over to the police. From inquiries from the deceased man's friends and relatives, it transpires that Sherritt was on several occasions served very shabbily by them, especially by Byrne. A mob of stolen horses or cattle would be put on Aaron Sherritt's selection, and left there until they could conveniently be sold, and when these were realised upon none of the money was given to Sherritt. This led to bickerings, and gradually engendered the ill feeling, which ultimately developed into hate.

In consequence of the controversy which is still carried on with much warmth, regarding the conduct of the police in Aaron Sherritt's house on the night of his murder, the place itself has become an object of interest. The house is situated in the ranges at Sebastopol, about eight miles from Beechworth, at a spot exactly in a line with the 'Devil's Elbow'. It is a one-storey weatherboard structure with a shingle roof, and comprises two rooms. One of these rooms, which was used as a kitchen, is 15 feet by about 9 feet, and the other, the bedroom, about 11 feet by 9 feet. There are two doors, one at the back and the other at the front, nearly opposite to each other. There is no passage formed through the house, both doors opening into the kitchen, which is partitioned off from the bedroom by a wooden screen having a doorway cut in the centre of it.

The partition does not reach to the ceiling, but there is a space of about 2½ feet. There is no door in the partition, the opening being covered by a piece of grey calico which hangs down like a curtain. There are two windows, both of which are in the front of the house. The bed on which the three constables were lying when the first shot was fired is a double iron one, and is placed directly beneath one window. In front of the other window is the table on which the candle was burning, an impromptu affair constructed of a zinc-lined packing case with boards laid upon it. Directly opposite the table is the fire, which is an open one, for burning logs of large dimensions. The chimney, as in most bush houses, is built out from the house, and is close to the back door. It is built of strong weatherboards, the upper portion of the flue being constructed of pieces of kerosene tins.

It was in the angle made by the lower portion of the chimney and the side of the house that Byrne stood when he made Weekes knock at the door. From the position of the rooms, both doors of the house being open, it would be impossible to pass from the bedroom to the kitchen without being under two fires if a man were posted at each door. Whether the doors could not have been shut from the bedroom without any one leaving, by someone leaning over the top of the partition, is, however, a matter of question. The house is surrounded by large trees, affording excellent cover, and it would be almost impossible from the house to hit anyone concealed behind them. Ned Kelly's armour has been on view at the police camp all day, and has been inspected by many of the residents and visitors from Melbourne and elsewhere.

Another Cold-Blooded Murder – The Killing of Aaron Sherritt

The Australasian Sketcher with Pen and Pencil, 3 July 1880

The following particulars have been released in regards to the murder of Aaron Sherritt. At the time of the killing, in the hut were a party of police, but they did not fire a shot at the bushrangers and acted entirely on the defence. The reason given for this inactivity is that the night was dark, while there was a bright fire burning in the hut, so that, while the bushrangers were out of sight, the police would have been instantly seen and shot if they had appeared at the door or window. The Kellys fired a volley through the house and also attempted to burn it down. The gang remained outside the hut until half-past six o'clock the next morning, when it is presumed they rode away. It appears that at one time Sherritt was a friend of the Kellys, but was most intimate with Joe Byrne.

He had been several times in gaol and on one occasion was convicted with Byrne of stealing a quantity of meat. His father, John Sherritt, an ex-policeman, is a selector, now an elderly man and resides at Sebastopol, which is about eight miles from Beechworth. The deceased man had a selection of 107 acres about a mile from his father's place and it is noteworthy that he was assisted in fencing it in by Joe Byrne and Ned Kelly. He was about 24 years of age, of robust health and was noted as a runner and jumper.

His holding was on the Woolshed Creek in the county of Burgoyne and about two months ago he sold it to Mr Crawford, of the Eastern Arcade, who is also a large coach proprietor and has property to a considerable extent in the district. After selling the land he built a hut at Sebastopol about two miles away and it is there that he was shot. A few months ago he was married to Miss Burke, the daughter of a well-known farmer at the Woolshed. Prior to the Kelly outbreak, as already stated he was on very friendly terms with the members of the gang and their companions, but recently it appears that he placed himself in communication with the police and for some months has been employed by them. The information he afforded as to the movements of the outlaws proved highly valuable and it is stated on good authority that not only did the gang ascertain who was keeping the police posted, but that they also caused it to be made known in Beechworth some weeks ago that they intended to take his life. The house occupied by Joseph Byrne's mother, there is every reason to believe, was recently visited by the gang and the information that the deceased was watching the place is supposed to have been communicated to the murderers.

In fact, it is stated that the reason that Sherritt went to the house in which he met his death was that he might be the better able to watch Byrne's place. As soon as the information of the outrage was received by the police authorities efforts were immediately made to pursue the murderers. Parties of police were at once sent out from the various country depots and by special train on Sunday night blacktrackers and a further contingent of police were despatched from Melbourne.

Ned Kelly at Bay

The Australasian Sketcher with Pen and Pencil, 3 July 1880

NED KELLY AT BAY.
FROM A SKETCH DRAWN ON THE SPOT BY MR. T. CARRINGTON.

Destruction of the Kelly Gang

The Australasian Sketcher with Pen and Pencil, 3 July 1880

NED KELLY'S ARMOUR. FROM A SKETCH MADE BY MR. T. CARRINGTON.

1—THE HELMET, FRONT VIEW. 2—SIDE VIEW OF HELMET. 3—BREASTPLATE. 4—BACK PLATE. 5—BACK LAPPET. 6—FRONT VIEW OF ARMOUR.

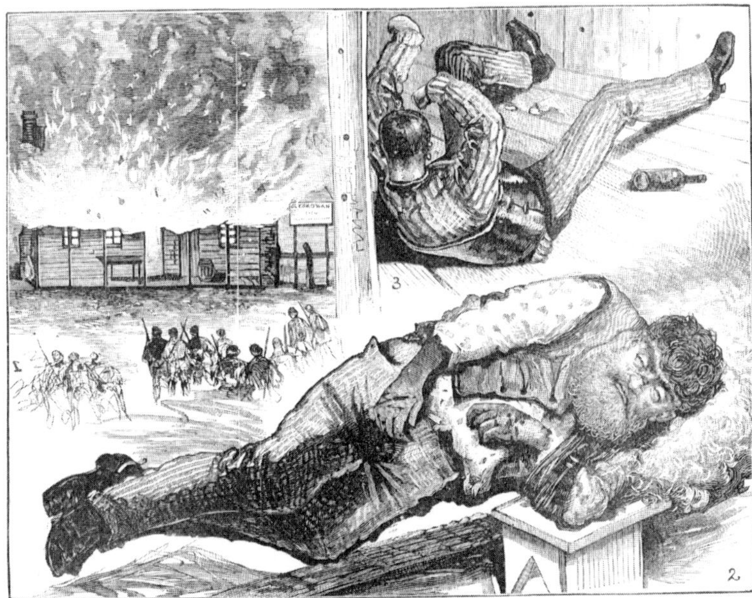

DESTRUCTION OF THE KELLY GANG. DRAWN BY MR. T. CARRINGTON DURING THE ENCOUNTER.

1—SETTING FIRE TO GLENROWAN HOTEL 2—NED KELLY LYING ON BUNK IN STATION-MASTER'S HOUSE. 3—SCENE THROUGH THE DOOR OF THE INN, BYRNE LYING DEAD ON THE FLOOR WHERE HE FELL JUST IN FRONT OF THE BAR.

Night Attack on the Glenrowan Hotel

The Australasian Sketcher with Pen and Pencil, 3 July 1880

The above sketches drawn by Mr T. Carrington during the encounter at Glenrowan:

- General view of the night attack on the Glenrowan Hotel
- Scene where Ned Kelly was shot
- The surrender of the 25 prisoners at 10 o'clock in the morning
- The bodies of Hart and Dan Kelly in the flames

The Murder of Sherritt

The Illustrated Australian News, 3 July 1880

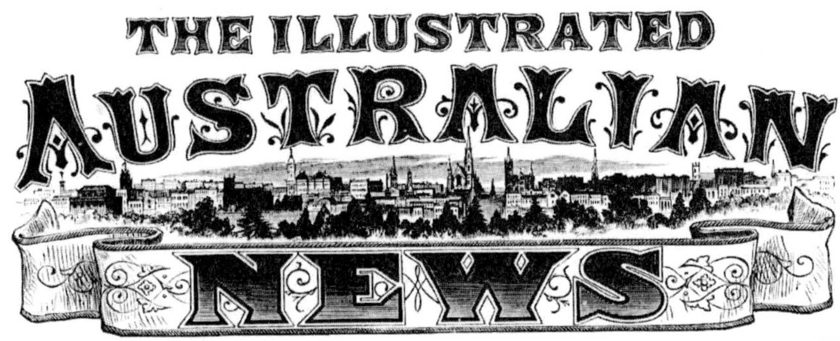
THE ILLUSTRATED AUSTRALIAN NEWS

No. 291. MELBOURNE, SATURDAY, JULY 3, 1880. PRICE {WITH TWO SUPPLEMENTS} 1s.

THE MURDER OF SHERRITT.
(FROM A SKETCH TAKEN IMMEDIATELY AFTER THE DEPARTURE OF THE KELLY GANG.)

Incidents Sketched at Glenrowan & Ned Kelly's Arrival in Melbourne

The Illustrated Australian News, 3 July 1880

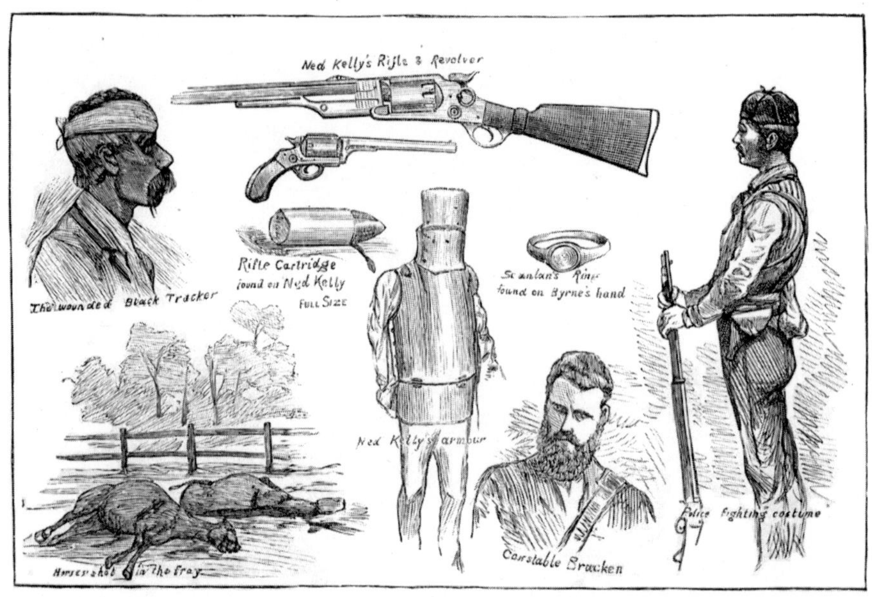

INCIDENTS SKETCHED AT GLENROWAN.

NED KELLY'S ARRIVAL IN MELBOURNE.

Portraits

The Illustrated Australian News, 3 July 1880

AARON SHERITT

NED KELLY
(SKETCHED AS HE WAS LEAVING BENALLA).

KATE KELLY.

SUPERINTENDENT HARE

The Outlaws at Bay – Scene of the Attack on Jones's Hotel at Glenrowan

The Illustrated Australian News, 3 July 1880

THE OUTLAWS AT BAY.–SCENE OF THE ATTACK ON JONES'S HOTEL AT GLENROWAN.

Finding Byrne's Body and the Capture of Ned Kelly

The Illustrated Australian News, 3 July 1880

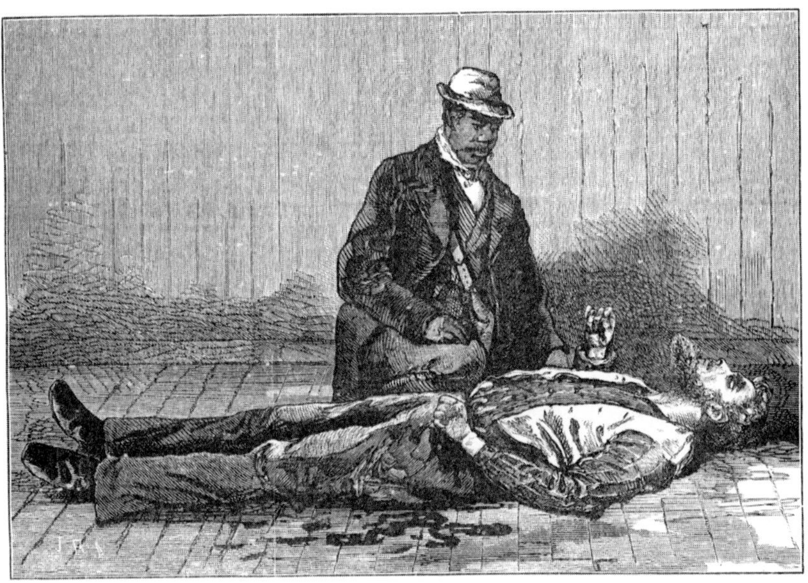

FINDING BYRNE'S BODY.—A STUDY.

THE CAPTURE OF NED KELLY.

Destruction of the Kellys

The Illustrated Australian News, 3 July 1880

Further details from Glenrowan

The leader of the desperadoes, Ned Kelly, may be considered as the most daring and bloodthirsty ruffian that the authorities of this or any other colony have had to contend with. When the body of Byrne was dragged from the ruins it was laid upon the ground in the vicinity and was an object of considerable curiosity. Not the least dramatic situation of the tragedy may be considered the blacktracker contemplating Byrne's corpse. The subject in one that might well bare elaboration and become in a manner historic. These trackers were the terror of the Kellys, as their semi-bloodhound instincts were for them, on the part of the outlaws, a sort of superstitious dread. Preparatory to leaving, Mrs Skillion and his sister, Kate Kelly, appeared on the platform for the purpose of bidding Ned Kelly farewell.

Kate Kelly is a somewhat remarkable woman and has bourne a conspicuous part in connection with the Kelly gang. Though suspected and closely watched by the police, they have never been able to sheet home to her a charge of assisting her brothers, and there cannot be a doubt that she possessed considerable pluck, powers of endurance and loyalty to her misguided brothers. The career of the Kelly gang terminated, as it commenced, with a tragedy so shocking that the whole country and the neighbouring colonies were thrown into a state of intense excitement. It opened with the cold-blooded murder of Sergeant Kennedy and Constables Lonigan and Scanlon. It closed with a tragedy, in which three of the outlaws were shot dead, and unfortunately the lives of several innocent persons sacrificed, while the leader of the gang, Ned Kelly, has been preserved for, if possible, a more ignominious fate.

It is now nearly two years since the Kellys rendered themselves notorious and during all that time they succeeded in not only evading the law, but defying the Government and the authorities. Whether in a drunken frolic, or wearied with the hunted life they led, they emerged finally from their hiding place on Saturday, 26th June and proceeded to the house of one Aaron Sherritt, who was induced by a ruse to open the door of his hut. On doing so, he was at once shot dead by Byrne, one of the desperadoes. There were four constables in the house at the time, but they declined to come out and show fight, although pressingly invited by the gang to do so. The hut was situated about 20 miles from Beechworth, and as soon as intelligence was received of the outrage the police authorities in Melbourne were communicated with. The news reached the city on Sunday evening, and immediate steps were taken to follow up the gang, who, it was anticipated, would return to their old haunts. Immediately on the receipt of the news by Captain Standish on Sunday night that the Kellys had at last broken cover and committed another diabolical outrage near Beechworth, he ordered a special train to at once start from Spencer Street. He was induced to do so because of the fact that Sub-Inspector O'Connor had, with his blacktrackers, been withdrawn from the Kelly country.

They were on the eve of their departure for Queensland and were staying at Essendon. Captain Standish ordered this special train to convey the blacks to the scene of the outrage, so that they might there pick up the tracks of the dreaded gang, but no one at that time imagined that the expedition would have such a speedy and sensational termination. That in fact, it would end in the annihilation of the band in a manner that must strike terror into the hearts of all sympathisers and men inclined to imitate the doings of the gang. When the news arrived at the station that a special train was required, all the engines were cold and it was not till a quarter-past 10 o'clock that a start was made, and the small party of press gentlemen, who in good spirits took their seats in the carriage, little thought that the journey they were undertaking was of such a perilous nature. Only one gentleman was armed. At Essendon Sub-Inspector O'Connor and his five blacktrackers were picked up, together with Mrs O'Connor and her sister, Miss Smith.

The men were evidently in excellent spirits at the prospect of an encounter. The train proceeded rapidly on its way. At Craigieburn it ran through a gate, which carried away the brake of the engine and necessitated a stoppage of about 20 minutes. After that fair progress was made to Benalla, where Superintendent Hare, with eight men and 17 horses, was in waiting and joined the party. The township of Glenrowan consists of about half-a-dozen houses, inclusive of two bush hotels, Jones's Glenrowan Hotel being about 200 yards from the station on the west side of the line, whilst McDonnell's Hotel is about the same distance on the other side of the line. In an instant the men on the platform were convinced, by the report of a shot fired from

Jones's hotel, that they were in the presence of the desperate outlaws. The next few minutes were productive of painful excitement. The police abandoned the horses and rushed to their arms. The blacktrackers sprang forward with their leader and soon took up a good position in front of the house. Superintendent Hare could be plainly seen by the light of the moon. He walked boldly towards the hotel and when within about 25 yards of the verandah, the tall figure of a man came round the corner and fired. The shot took effect Superintendent Hare's wrist, but Kelly found in him a foeman who would not shrink from him. Senior Constable Kelly and Rawlings were close too and the former promptly returned the fire, which was taken up by Hare, although wounded, and Mr Rawlings followed his example. Just before Superintendent Hare was wounded, Constable Bracken, the local policeman, who had been made prisoner in the hotel, courageously made his escape and running towards the railway station he quickly spread the information that the Kellys, with about 40 prisoners, were inmates of the hotel, which was a weatherboard building containing about six rooms, inclusive of the bar. Behind the building there was a kitchen, the walls of which were constructed of slabs. Into this the police fired.

When about 60 shots had been sent into the walls of the building, the clear voice of Hare was distinguished above the screams of the terrified women and children who were in the hotel, giving the order to stop firing. This was now repeated by Senior Constable Kelly to the men who, undercover, were surrounding the house at the back, but the Kellys fired three or four more shots, after which one of them gave vent to coarse and brutal language, calling to the police, "Come on, you b– wretches, and you can fire away, but you can never harm us." A few straggling shots were then fired, the sharp sounds of the rifle being echoed from the mount called Morgan's Lookout, at the foot of which the fight took place. Then all was silent again and after the lapse of about a quarter of an hour Superintendent Hare approached the station and stated that he had been wounded in the wrist. Superintendent Hare then became faint from loss of blood and was compelled to leave the field. He went back to Benalla on an engine in order to have his injury attended to and to send more men to the front. The shots of the police had struck the daughter of Mrs Jones, a girl 14 years of age, on the head, whilst the son, John Jones, a boy of nine years, was wounded in the hip. Very soon after this painful, hysterical screams of terror were heard from

Mrs Jones and a Mrs Reardon, both of whom were walking about the place, disregarding the danger to be feared from the volleys which the police, at short intervals, poured into the hotel. Mrs Jones's grief occasionally took the form of vindictiveness towards the police, whom she called murderers. The police frequently called upon the women to come away, but they hesitated, and Mrs Reardon and her son were frightened to accompany Mr Reardon to the station. The poor woman was carrying a baby only a few months old in her arms and she eventually ran to the station, where she received every kindness from the persons there assembled.

At various times during the morning more police arrived, but the bushrangers could not be dislodged and what was more perplexing still, the prisoners inside could not be persuaded to leave, although the police repeatedly called upon them to come out. At 12 o'clock, however, the people inside, consisting of about 30 men and youths, suddenly rushed out of the front door carrying their hands aloft. The police told them to advance towards where they were located, but many of the unfortunate people were so terror-stricken that they ran hither and thither screaming for mercy. They then approached the police and threw themselves upon their faces.

One by one they were called on, and having been minutely searched were despatched to the station. When the turn of two youths named McAuliffe came, Superintendent Sadlier directed Constable Bracken to arrest them as Kelly sympathisers. They were accordingly handcuffed and taken with the others to the railway station. Young Reardon, who with his father had been confined in the hotel, was severely wounded in the shoulder by a bullet fired from a rifle in the hands of one of the police. The unfortunate youth was at once attended to by the doctors already named. Although the wound is a serious one, it is not considered such as will prove fatal.

The police after this kept up a constant fire on the place, Dwyer and Armstrong in front of the house, Andrew Clarkesen and Senior Constable Kelly getting very close in at various quarters of attack. It was noticed that the fire from the besieged bushrangers was not returned after one o'clock, but it was believed that Dan Kelly and Hart intended to lie quiet until night and under cover of the darkness make their escape. The police for a time also ceased firing. A consultation was held amongst the officers as to what was best next to be done. During the cessation of hostilities I visited the locality where the line had been torn up. It is about three-quarters of a mile on the Wangaratta side of Glenrowan. Several lengths of rails had been wrenched from their places at a curve terminating at a rapid decline, and had not the timely warning been given by Mr Curnow, the pilot engine, followed closely by the special, would have inevitably toppled over an embankment into a defile over 30 feet in depth. I arrived back at the station in time to witness the most tragic and exciting scene of the day.

The police had telegraphed for a cannon from Melbourne, but fearing it would not arrive in time to be of any use, it was determined to adopt another mode of dislodging the remaining outlaws. Just as they were about to put this newly conceived plan into operation, Mrs Skillion, sister of the Kellys, dressed in a dark riding habit trimmed with scarlet, and wearing a jaunty hat adorned with a conspicuous white feather, appeared on the scene. Father Gibney earnestly requested her to go the hotel and ask her brother and Hart to surrender. She said she would like to see her brother before he died, but she would sooner see him burnt in the house than ask him to surrender. This, in fact, was the procedure which the police had decided upon in order to bring the outlaws from their cover.

Some 200 people by this time had arrived on the platform. The police opened up a heavy fire on the hotel from the front and rear. This was done in order to cover the operations of Senior Constable Johnson, who rapidly approached the house on the north side with a bundle of straw, which he placed against the weatherboards and set fire to. It was known that Martin Cherry, an old man, was still in the house, and when the last prisoners had escaped he was alive, though badly wounded. The thought that the unfortunate man should be sacrificed and perish in the flames with the determined bushrangers who had made so long a stand caused a feeling of horror to pervade the crowd. Kate Kelly at this juncture came upon the scene, but the only expression which escaped her lips was the one uttered in heart-broken accents, "My poor, poor brother", Mrs Skillion exclaimed, "I will see my brother before he dies", and then sped towards the hotel, from the roof of which by this time tongues of flame were beginning to ascend. The police ordered her to go back and she hesitated.

Father Gibney, who happened to be on a visit to the district, emerged from the crowd, saying he would save Cherry. The brave clergyman was encouraged on his mission by a cheer from the spectators. He walked boldly to the front door, was lost to view amongst the smoke, and a moment afterwards a mass of flames burst from the walls and roof of the dwelling at the same instant. A shout of terror from the crowd announced the fear that was felt for the safety of the courageous priest. Constable Armstrong, with some other policemen, rushed into the building from the rear, and a few seconds afterwards their forms, with that of Father Gibney, were seen to emerge, carrying with them Cherry, who was in a dying state, and the dead body of the outlaw Byrne. On reaching a place of safety they stated that Dan Kelly and Hart were lying upon the floor apparently dead. Nothing, however, could be done to rescue their remains from the fire.

Soon afterwards the building was completely demolished and on a search being made amongst the ruins two charred skeletons were raked out from the smouldering debris. 'Wild' Wright, Hart (the brother of Steve) and other well-known friends were witnesses of this terrible scene. All the bushrangers were clad in the same armour as that worn by Ned Kelly, which weighed as much as 97 pounds, and had evidently been constructed by some country blacksmith out of ploughshares. The marks on Kelly's armour showed that he had been hit 17 times with bullets. During the forenoon Colonel Anderson received information from Captain Standish that in order to dislodge the two remaining members of the gang without endangering any further life the hotel would have to be blown down and as the best for accomplishing that object a small cannon would probably be required.

Colonel Anderson arranged for the supply of a 12-pound Armstrong gun, which was quickly placed upon a truck at the Spencer Street station. A special train was soon in readiness and at 20 minutes past two it departed, carrying the formidable-looking weapon, a detachment of the Garrison Artillery under Lieutenant Nicholson and the Commandant himself. The train, in order to land the gun at the scene of action while it was yet daylight, started at a prearranged rate of 40 miles per hour. Seymour was reached in due average time, but before the soldiers had time to step upon the platform came the not altogether unexpected though disappointing news that the gun was no longer required, as the whole of the outlaws had been taken. The train proceeded no further, and the gun, officers and men returned by the first passenger goods train to Melbourne.

The scene of the encounter on the following morning was visited by a number of persons from Benalla. Photographic operators from Melbourne were also present and took some excellent views of the locality. The charred remains of Dan Kelly and Steve Hart, after being recovered from the fire, were handed over to the sisters and friends of the outlaws. They were conveyed before night to Greta, where a wake on the bodies was held.

This morning the coffins were brought here. Ned Kelly left the hotel in which his mates were secured before the special train arrived and was never seen by them afterwards. He was not in the place at all during the fight. Byrne, Hart and Dan Kelly became very anxious about his absence and seemed undecided how to act. They missed the loss of their leader greatly and were continually calling out for him.

Up to the time that Byrne was shot they indulged in a great deal of firing. Byrne used the most powder, firing whenever he got an opportunity. After he fell Hart and Dan Kelly lost all heart, and fired very seldom. Just before the civilians left the place they were unhurt, but appeared quite despondent. Dan said to Hart, "What shall we do now, Steve?" and from the answer that the latter made the people confined in the place were impressed with the belief that they intended to shoot each other. Reardon, a plate-layer, is certain that this is what they meant to do. As the last of the prisoners left the place the two outlaws went into an adjoining bedroom and it is thought then fired at one another. Their remains were found lying in close proximity and as they were divested of the armour there could be little doubt but that in their last spirit of desperation they took off the iron so as to allow their shots to take effect. John Jones, aged 11 years, who received a bullet wound in the loin and was taken to the Wangaratta Hospital, died in that institution on June 28th. An inquest will be held upon his body.

The little girl, who received a scalp wound and was supposed to be in danger, has quite recovered and was walking about the place this morning. Mr Curnow, the schoolmaster, and his wife were stuck up by the gang on Sunday night and locked up in the hotel. They were, however, afterwards permitted to leave. Curnow ascertained that the line had been torn up in order to destroy the special train and he therefore at once ran along the route for some two or three miles, and gave the timely warning which came so fortunately to hand. A general feeling of relief is experienced by the respectable inhabitants of the district and it is pretty certain that now the gang are no longer to be feared that some of their movements during the past 12 months will be made known. Already stories concerning their movements are freely circulated and from these it is apparent that the police have during the past month or six months made it very unpleasant for the outlaws.

It will be remembered that a little more than three weeks ago it was reported that Joe Byrne had been seen near his mother's residence at the Woolshed. That story was quite true and it has been suspected that they have since been lurking in the vicinity. A week before Sherritt was murdered, Superintendent Hare and Detective Ward were in his house and the dead man then expressed his conviction that the outlaws were not far distant. After perpetrating the foul murder of Sherritt, it is probable that the gang rode at once for Glenrowan, crossing the Goulburn over the Pioneer Bridge, the King River at Oxley, and thence through Greta, where Mrs Skillion and Kate Kelly reside.

The sole object of their visit to Glenrowan appears to have been to murder the police and the blacktrackers. The hatred which the leader of the gang had for the blacktrackers appears to have been very great and it is certain that the fear of them has kept the gang quiet so long. Kelly knew that the trackers had gone to Melbourne, and he correctly formed the opinion that as soon as the intelligence of the murder was made known the trackers and police would be sent on by special train. It was with the object of destroying that train that he tore up the line. The way in which this cold-blooded attempt to commit wholesale murder was frustrated appears very surprising, and although it is now known that it was Mr Curnow, the local schoolmaster, who gave the warning to the train, the reason which induced Ned Kelly to give him his liberty when he detained nearly every other person in the neighbourhood is a mystery. Mr and Mrs Curnow, with Mr Mortimer, a relative, were driving in a buggy through the railway gates when Ned Kelly bailed them up.

Mr Mortimer's Statement:

> After we were bailed up we were taken over to Mrs Jones's hotel and were kept there until it was determined by Kelly to stick-up Constable Bracken. He permitted Curnow, Mrs Curnow and myself to go with him in our buggy to the police station, which

is about three-quarters of a mile from the railway station and is not far from Mr Curnow's residence. Kelly permitted Mrs Curnow to get out of the buggy in case there might be some firing when Bracken was bailed up. I was ordered by Kelly to knock at the front door and call Bracken, and I did so, but he did not answer, and then Kelly, with a young Reynolds, whom he had just bailed up, went to the back door and succeeded in arousing Bracken, who came to the door without dressing. Byrne was with Kelly and Curnow asked Ned if he would not let him go home with his wife. Kelly replied, "Oh, yes, you may go home and have a sleep but mind you don't dream too loud". Having given this warning to him, he was permitted to go home. I do not know how he heard that the line had been torn up, but I suppose he heard it at the hotel and after he obtained his liberty he determined to warn the train of the danger. Reynolds, Bracken and myself were taken back to the hotel. We all then heard that the line had been torn up.

The whole of the members of the gang were very jolly, and Ned told us that they had come there to settle the blacktrackers and that he would be on the spot when the train ran over the culvert and would shoot all who were not killed. We knew we could do nothing and therefore did not take any steps to warn those in the train of the danger. Every member of the gang was then sober. They showed us their armour and seemed to think that the police could do them no harm. At half-post two on Monday morning Ned Kelly said something to the effect that he did not think the special train was coming, and I then asked him if we could go home. He said "Yes", and I thanked him. We could all then have gone, with perhaps the exception of Bracken, but we foolishly stopped and listen to the remarks of Kelly.

Just then, Dan Kelly, who had been standing outside, rushed in and said, "Ned, here comes the – train". Our opportunity of escape was gone. Ned Kelly rushed out, and commenced to examine his firearms. He spoke to one of the gang and then left on horseback. Byrne locked the doors and I believe that Bracken then succeeded in stealing the key. Ned Kelly returned in a few minutes, but remained outside. He asked some of the others to come out with him, but none of them did so. Just then we heard the train stopped at the station and it then became apparent that the gang expected they would have to fight. Almost immediately the firing commenced and we dropped on the floor. The bullets whizzed through the weatherboards in all directions. Our feelings at that time were indescribable. The poor women and children were screaming with terror, and every man in the house was saying his prayers. Poor little Johnny Jones was shot almost at once, and I put my hands in my ears so as not to hear his screams of agony and the lamentations of his mother and Mrs Reardon, who had a baby in her arms. We could do nothing, and the bullets continued to whistle through the building.

I do not think that the police were right in acting as they did. We were frightened of them, and not of the bushrangers. It was Joe Byrne who cursed and swore at the police. He seemed perfectly reckless of his life. But the three of them got into an inside room into which the bullets seldom penetrated. We frequently called on the police to stop firing, but we dared not go to the door, and I suppose they did not hear us. Miss Jones was slightly wounded by a bullet, and when Mrs Reardon and Mrs Jones with the children ran out, Reardon and his son attempted to follow, but as soon as the police saw the figures of the men they fired. Young Reardon was hit by a bullet in the shoulder and he and his father ran back into the house.

One of the men carried young Jones away and succeeded in passing the police without being fired on. Dan Kelly told us we had better remain in the house, because the police would shoot us if we attempted to leave. Someone said to him, "You had better go out and surrender", and he replied, "We will never surrender, but most likely we will leave directly". I think they intended to do so, but shortly after five o'clock in the morning Byrne was shot. He had just walked into the bar and was drinking a glass of whisky when a ball struck him in the groin. I heard him fall, and saw the blood spurting from him. I think he died very soon. This seemed to dishearten Dan Kelly and Hart. They had been calling for Ned all night, and they

> renewed their calls for him. We had not seen the leader of the gang since the firing commenced, and did not know where he had gone. Dan and Hart went into the inside room, and I heard one say to the other, "What will we do?" I did not hear the reply, but Reardon said he thought they intended to commit suicide. We prayed for daylight, thinking that we might then escape, but even when the morning broke we dared not venture out. It must have been about this time that poor Martin Cherry was shot. He was sitting on the floor of the kitchen at the time. There were two other men there with him, but they were protected from the bullets of the police by bags of oats, behind which they were sitting. During the morning Dan Kelly told them that Ned Kelly had been shot. After that one of our company held a white pocket handkerchief out of the door, and we all ran out. Poor Cherry could not move, and he was left behind. He was a decent honest man.

Mr Curnow was in Benalla on Tuesday and had an interview with Captain Standish. I was, unfortunately, unable to see him, but from what I could glean from Mrs Curnow, I learnt that after he returned to his house he kept a lookout for the special train and when he heard it approaching he ran along the line to give the warning. Both Mr and Mrs Curnow fear that in consequence of the action which he took the friends of the gang will do them injury. The fearful end of the gang, however, will, I imagine, deter anyone from openly exhibiting their sympathy for them. The police are in possession of information which causes them to suspect that a certain country blacksmith made the armour for the gang, and it is possible that proceedings will be taken against him. The plough-shares and mould-boards out of which the armour was manufactured were stolen from five farmers at Greta, at Easter. One of the farmers has identified some of the plates by marks on them. The police at the time were informed that it was intended by the gang to turn the mould-boards into armour, but they laughed at the idea.

After an affecting parting with his sisters at Benalla, Kelly left by the ordinary train at nine a.m. on June 29. On the journey to Melbourne he maintained a very reticent and sullen demeanour, answering any questions which were put to him very gruffly. At each station there was a great rush of people to obtain a glimpse of him, and on being asked by Senior Constable Walsh if he had any objection to their crowding round the van and looking in, he replied that he had none. He seemed much refreshed by his sleep on the previous night. Dr Ryan was most attentive and many times during the journey attended to his wounds and administered stimulants to him. As soon as it became known that Ned Kelly would arrive in Melbourne by the ordinary train from Benalla a crowd gathered, but the platform and yards were cleared.

Large numbers of people congregated in the street and from the windows opposite and drays sought to obtain a good view of what was expected to occur. They were all disappointed, however, for it was decided previously that he would not be taken from the train at that place. Inspectors Montford and Secretan, in plain-clothes, Detective Wilson and one or two policemen also without uniform, had proceeded to the North Melbourne station, and waited there in an unostentatious manner. About 50 other persons had gathered there, and at two o'clock an ordinary train from the north-east arrived at the siding. There were two brake vans attached to it.

The outlaw was in the last one, lying on a pile of mattresses, and surrounded by about a dozen armed policemen. He looked terribly emaciated. His spare countenance was rendered more wan by the terrible bruises with which it was covered, the effects of the bullets having struck the helmet which he wore when he had the fight with the police. His utter helplessness was apparent at a glance, and as he lay on the floor of the van there was something horribly pitiful in his appearance. The crowd quickly surrounded the van, but the police soon cleared a passage. A stretcher was handed in and the outlaw was laid upon it. Mattresses were then placed on a four-wheeled vehicle which stood outside the reserve, and he was carried on the shoulders of the policemen thither.

Very little time was lost in placing him comfortably in the trap, but there was ample opportunity afforded for the people to see his face and thus gratify a morbid desire. Such expressions as "Poor fellow", "I am so sorry", and other pitying exclamations were given vent to by the lower portion of the assemblage, but all further remark was cut short by instructions being given to drive on. The vehicle, which was followed by several others, proceeded up to Victoria Street, and thence to the Melbourne Gaol. All the way the sudden appearance of the escort caused people to rush from the shops with a view, if possible, of seeing Kelly, but they were not afforded that opportunity.

Near the gaol was an immense concourse of men, women and children, and although an attempt was made to give a cheer, it was remarkably feeble.

The conveyance did not stop, but drove right into the gaol, the large gates being opened for the purpose, and immediately closed. There was a strong guard of police present to prevent any rushing. Within the institution he was received by Mr Castieau, the Governor, under a warrant of remand from Benalla until the 5th July. Some warders and other prisoners removed him from the cab to the hospital, where he was at once placed on a waterbed which had been prepared for his reception. Dr Shields, the medical officer, was immediately communicated with, and on his arrival he took charge of the prisoner's case.

The Reverend P. J. Aylward was also permitted to see Kelly, and that reverend gentleman kindly undertook to acquaint Mrs Kelly, the mother of the bushranger, of the fate of himself and his brother. She was also a prisoner in the gaol, serving a sentence for having resisted and assaulted Constable Fitzpatrick in April, 1878, when he endeavoured to arrest Daniel Kelly for horse-stealing. That episode, it will be remembered, was the first of a series of outrages which was perpetrated by some of the members of the gang which was soon afterwards formed. When the mother of the prisoner was informed of the fate which had befallen her sons she expressed herself as not being surprised and explained her preparedness by stating that on Saturday night she had dreamt that the gang was being encountered and that the police were victorious.

Doctors Ryan and Shields examined him in the gaol at five o'clock. It was remarked that he was in a healthy condition and that he was exceptionally clean. The most serious wound from which he is suffering is one in the left arm. When he was struck there he says the limb was bent, and the bullet entered midway between the wrist and the elbow, passed through the arm and pierced it again about three inches above the joint. There are not any bullets in his body now, but there are marks of four slug wounds in his right thigh and leg. Dr Shields extracted the slugs from a wound in his right hand, near the thumb. This was the injury which prevented his using his rifle. He was shot in the left foot near the large toe and the bullet passed out again near the instep. With such very serious injuries it is surprising how he managed to escape being killed. The doctors, however, do not consider that he is mortally wounded, and are of opinion that, unless the severe mental depression which has supervened has a deterring influence, he should soon recover.

The Destruction of the Kelly Gang

The Argus, 5 July 1880

At a late hour last night Ned Kelly was reported to be still progressing favourably, but an increase in temperature has manifested itself and gives rise to some doubt as to his ultimate recovery. During the past few days he has grumbled considerably at the diet supplied to him, which has been chiefly of a farinaceous nature, while he requested animal food. His wishes have been complied with as far as the opinion of the resident medical officer, Dr Shields, would allow. He is under remand to appear at the City Police Court this morning to answer a charge of wilful murder. He will not, however, be sufficiently recovered to be placed in the dock and Superintendent Winch, on the authority of a medical certificate to that effect, will apply for his remand for seven days.

The application will doubtless be granted without argument. Rumour has been busy with the name of Constable Fitzpatrick in connection with the Kelly outbreak. A prisoner now confined in Pentridge, who was present when Fitzpatrick was shot by Ned Kelly, has made a statutory declaration which, if true, goes far to exonerate the constable from the charges made against him. At present the authorities deem it advisable to withhold the particulars set out in the affidavit. Superintendent Hare still remains the guest of Mr W.J. Clarke at Sunbury. He is attended daily by Dr Charles Ryan and is progressing favourably. Yesterday he was doing nicely, but there now appears to be but little doubt that he will lose the use of his left hand.

Extermination of the Kelly Gang

The Illustrated Australian News, 17 July 1880

THE ILLUSTRATED AUSTRALIAN NEWS

No. 292. MELBOURNE, SATURDAY, JULY 17, 1880. PRICE SIXPENCE.

EXTERMINATION OF THE KELLY GANG—THE EMBANKMENT WHERE THE POLICE TRAIN WAS TO HAVE BEEN WRECKED.

Bird's Eye View of Glenrowan

The Illustrated Australian News, 17 July 1880

BIRD'S EYE VIEW OF GLENROWAN.

1.—Jones's Hotel. 2.—Out House. 3.—Railway Station. 4.—Stationmaster's House. 5.—M'Donald's Hotel. 6.—Platelayers' Tents. 7.—Positions Taken by the Police. 8.—Trench : Lieutenant O'Connor and Black Trackers' Post. 9.—Spot Where Mr. Hare was Shot. 10.—Paddock where Horses were Shot. 11.—Tree where Ned Kelly was Captured. 12.—Road to Bracken's Station. 13.—Half a Mile from Here the Rails were Taken up.

Edward Kelly in the Hospital of the Melbourne Gaol

The Illustrated Australian News, 17 July 1880

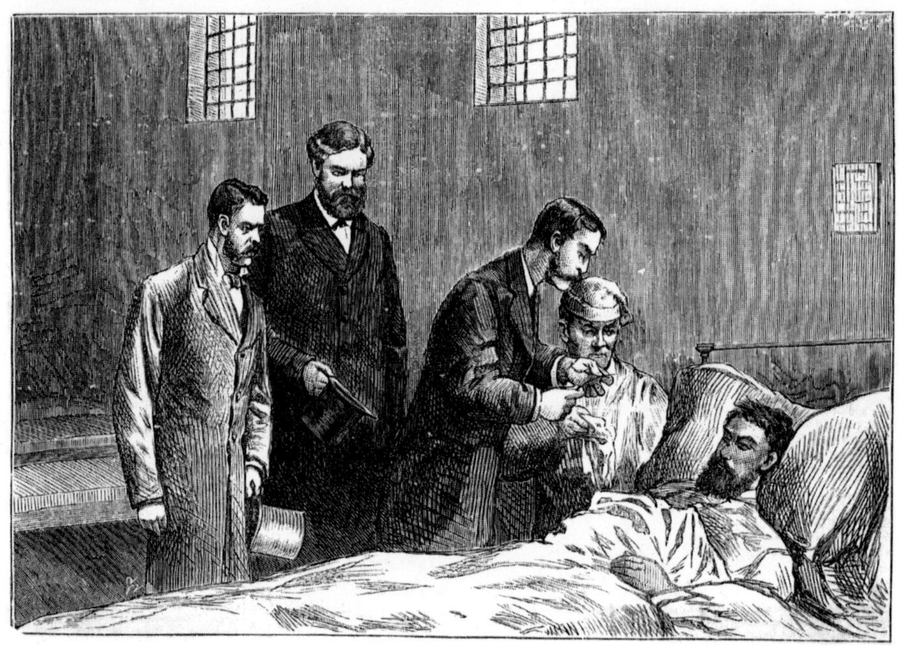

EDWARD KELLY IN THE HOSPITAL OF THE MELBOURNE GAOL.

A Strange Apparition Ned Kelly's Fight and Capture

The Illustrated Australian News, 17 July 1880

A STRANGE APPARITION—NED KELLY'S FIGHT AND CAPTURE.

"His head, chest and sides were all protected with heavy plates of quarter-inch iron. Many shots hit him, yet he always recovered himself, and tapping his breast laughed derisively, as he coolly returned their fire. It appeared as if he were a fiend with a charmed life."—*The Age* report.

The Kelly Hunters

The Illustrated Australian News, 17 July 1880

SENIOR CONSTABLE KELLY.

SERGEANT STEELE.

SUPERINTENDENT SADLEIR.

SUPERINTENDENT NICOLSON.

GUARD DOWSETT.

INSPECTOR O'CONNOR.

Ned Kelly's Boot!

The Kerang Times and *Swan Hill Gazette*, 23 July 1880

Ned Kelly's boot was obtained at the time of his capture by railway-guard Dowsett, who is now on the Queenscliff line, and whose plucky conduct in connection with the capture of the Kellys has been deservedly lauded. The boot is at present in the keeping of the police. It is a 'top' boot, and has evidently covered a shapely limb. At the place the big toe would occupy is the hole caused by the bullet which wounded the outlaw, and about an inch from the hole, nearer the heel, is a clot of blood. The upper portion of the boot is such as is worn by the mounted constables, and the greater part of the stiffening has been taken off. It is therefore more than probable that the upper, at least, is one of those worn by the unfortunate policemen who were so barbarously murdered by the Kellys at the King River.

Two brothers of the unfortunate man Sherritt, who was shot by Byrne, of the Kelly gang, have applied to be allowed to join the police force, and to be stationed at Greta.

Destruction of the Kelly Gang – Stopping the Special Train by Mr Curnow

The Australasian Sketcher with pen and pencil, 31 July 1880

THE AUSTRALASIAN SKETCHER

No. 103.—VOL. VIII. MELBOURNE, SATURDAY, JULY 31, 1880. PRICE 6d.

DESTRUCTION OF THE KELLY GANG: STOPPING THE SPECIAL TRAIN BY MR. CURNOW.

Ned Kelly the Bushranger

The Australasian Sketcher with pen and pencil, 31 July 1880

NED KELLY, THE BUSHRANGER.

Destruction of the Kelly Gang – Interior of the Press Carriage of the Police Special Train

The Australasian Sketcher with pen and pencil, 31 July 1880

Destruction of the Kelly Gang

The Australasian Sketcher with Pen and Pencil, 31 July 1880

Reports from Superintendent Hare and from Superintendent Sadlier on the operations of the police at Glenrowan have been received by the Chief Secretary and have been handed to the press for publication.

From Superintendent Hare's Report we make the following extract:

> From the date of my arrival at Benalla up to Sunday, the 27th June, I heard nothing positive concerning the movements of the outlaws, although their agents and sympathisers were particularly active and I was privately informed that the outlaws were about to commence some outrages which would not only astonish Australia, but the whole world. On the 24th I received a communication from you that Sub-Inspector O'Connor and his

blacktrackers were to be sent back to Queensland. I informed Sub-Inspector O'Connor accordingly. The next morning he started away from Benalla with his "boys". I had but one Queensland black of our own at Benalla and there was another at Mansfield. I telegraphed for the one at Mansfield to be sent down to Benalla at once, so that I might have two trackers in case anything happened before Mr Chomley, who had gone to Queensland for a fresh supply of trackers for our own force, returned, as I did not expect him back for eight or 10 days. On Sunday, the 27th, I was at the telegraph office at Benalla at 10 o'clock a.m. I received telegrams from all the stations in the district that all was quiet.

I made an appointment with the telegraph master to be at the office again at nine p.m. About half-past two o'clock that day I received a memo from the railway telegraph office to go to the general telegraph office as there was important information for me there and a memo to the same effect had been sent to the telegraph master. I lost no time in going there and received a message from Beechworth that Aaron Sherritt, in whose house I had a watch party, had been shot the previous evening at six o'clock. I immediately sent for Superintendent Sadlier and we consulted together as to the best course to adopt. First of all we decided to give you all the information in our possession and ask you to request Sub-Inspector O'Connor to return without loss of time to Benalla with his 'boys', as we considered they might have a good chance of tracking the outlaws from Sherritt's house. About eight o'clock that evening I received a telegram from you informing me that Sub-Inspector O'Connor would be sent up by special train, leaving town at 10 o'clock. I also telegraphed to you asking authority to send on a pilot engine in front of our train. Your reply to me was, "A good idea. There's no knowing what desperate deed the outlaws may now be guilty of. Have the pilot".

The whole afternoon Mr Sadlier and myself were engaged in the telegraph office warning all stations to be on the alert and at places where there were no telegraph offices private messengers were employed and sent out to convey the information of the outrage at Beechworth and to be on the alert also. I started off then for the railway station, having previously sent word to the stationmaster to have an engine ready to go to Beechworth as soon as possible, as it was my intention to take up my party and the two trackers in the event of Sub-Inspector O'Connor not consenting to return. I told Mr Stephens, stationmaster, that a special was to leave town at 10 o'clock and that I wished the engine that I had ordered to act as pilot to the train to Beechworth which would reach Benalla about two a.m. He informed me that he had no engine there which could run to Beechworth, that line requiring peculiar engines. I requested him to get the engine which was to come down to Wangaratta from Beechworth the following morning to get up steam at once, run down to Wangaratta and wait there till my arrival so that it could act as pilot thence to Beechworth. He consented to do this and also to have trucks ready to convey the horses and men from Benalla to Beechworth. I then returned to the telegraph office where Mr Sadlier had remained during my absence.

We made arrangements for horses and provisions to be ready for the trackers and had the following men accompany me to Beechworth, Senior Constable Kelly, Constables Arthur, Barry, Gascoigne, Canny, Kirkham and Phillips, leaving a party behind us all ready equipped with two blacktrackers for Mr Sadlier in case anything occurred while I was away. I remained in the telegraph office until 10 o'clock p.m. Having completed all arrangements, I went to lie down for two or three hours as I expected to reach Sherritt's house by daybreak the next morning to commence tracking from there. At one o'clock I went to the railway station, had the horses put in the trucks and waited the arrival of the special which reached Benalla, I think about half-past one. Mr Rawlins, a gentleman residing at Winton, asked me to allow him to travel in the special to Beechworth from Benalla as he had a pass on all the railways. I told him I had no objection to his doing so.

The engineer in charge of the Benalla station suggested that I should put a constable in front of the engine to keep a lookout along the line. I accordingly chose Constable Barry for this duty and saw him securely fastened on the engine. I afterwards ascertained that the engine that brought the train from town had become disabled on the way up and it was decided to send it as the pilot and send the Benalla engine to Wangaratta with the train. The engine-drivers refused to allow Barry to go on their engine, so I recalled him. The occupants of the train from Melbourne were as follows, Sub-Inspector O'Connor, his wife and sister, five Queensland trackers and six gentlemen connected with the press. My party already mentioned joined the train here. Previous to starting I asked the stationmaster to give me the key of the railway carriages, as the guard insisted on locking us in. He complied with my request.

The pilot engine started about five minutes before our train. We went along at a rapid pace without interruption until within two or three miles of Glenrowan station I heard our engine whistle. I put my head out of the carriage, looked ahead and saw the pilot pulled up within 300 yards of us. I immediately unlocked my carriage, jumped out of the train and walked towards the pilot. When about a few yards beyond our engine I met a man walking towards me from the pilot with a lamp. He came from the pilot engine and told me that he had been stopped by a red handkerchief being held up and lit by a match held behind it. When he pulled up he saw a man without coat or hat approaching who appeared greatly excited and told him that the line had been broken up either this side or the other of Glenrowan.

He said the man told him the Kellys had taken possession of everybody in Glenrowan and that they said they were going to attack the police on their arrival. I asked him where the man was. He said after giving the information he ran away into the bush as he had left his wife and family at home and that he was a schoolmaster at Glenrowan. He said, "I invited him to go on the engine, but he declined". I then ordered all the carriages to be unlocked, lights extinguished and gave the occupants the information that had been given to me and to be ready for any emergency. I at once walked towards the pilot, taking with me three men, leaving Sub-Inspector O'Connor and his men with Senior Constable Kelly and the remainder of my men. I walked along the line myself, and distributed the men on each side, telling them to separate and keep a sharp lookout. When I reached the pilot, the engine-driver repeated the story about the schoolmaster and I told the driver to go on quietly in front of the train. He declined doing so until I jumped on the engine myself and brought up the three men with me. I placed the men in the best position and told them to keep a sharp lookout and be ready for anything that might occur. I took up my position at the opening of the engine and then told the driver to go ahead cautiously and be ready to go ahead or backwards at any moment in the event of my directing him to do so. He said his engine was in a very disabled state, having lost its brake, and could not be depended on. He advised that he should shunt back to the train and that the two engines should be hitched on together, and so take on the train. I consented to this and we shunted back.

I then directed Senior Constable Kelly to jump on the other engine with three men and to put them in the most secure places, prepared for any emergency. I gave information to Sub-Inspector O'Connor of what I had ascertained and done, and we started off at a slow pace towards Glenrowan.

When we reached the station everything was in darkness, not a soul moving anywhere. I got off the engine and told every man to jump out of the train and keep a sharp lookout. I then started off in company with Mr Rawlins to the stationmaster's house, which was about 70 or 80 yards from the station, where I saw a light in the window. I knocked at the window and looking through saw a woman and children. She asked, "Who's there?" I answered, "Police, open the window". I asked her where her husband was. She replied, "They have taken him away into the bush". She was greatly excited and for some time could scarcely answer me. I begged her to be calm and tell me who had taken her husband away. She said, "The Kellys". I asked in which direction they had gone and she pointed in the direction of Warby Ranges. I immediately hastened back to the station with

Mr Rawlins who told me he was thoroughly acquainted with the country and would gladly render me all the assistance he could. He told me he was unarmed and asked me if I had any spare arms. I told him "No", but that I would give him my revolver and stick to the double-barrelled gun myself.

On reaching the station I told the men what I had been informed of by the stationmaster's wife and to lose no time in getting the horses out of the train and saddling them. Whilst the men were so engaged, Constable Bracken appeared on the platform in a very excited state. He said, "Superintendent Hare, I have just escaped from Jones's hotel where the Kellys have a large number of prisoners confined. For God's sake go as quickly as possible, otherwise they will escape". I called on the men to follow me with their arms as quickly as they could. Many of them were holding horses. I told them to let go the horses as the Kellys were in the house and follow me, running off towards Jones's hotel. Some six or seven men followed me. Amongst them were some of the blacktrackers, but I cannot say who any of them were.

When approaching the hotel the place was quite silent and dark and when within about 20 yards of the verandah I saw a flash of fire, but could not distinguish any figures. Instantly three persons also commenced firing from the verandah, which was in total darkness. The moonbeams at the back of the house caused our men to be plainly seen. A continuous fire was kept up on both sides. I was struck by the first shot and my left arm dropped helpless beside me. The firing was continued on both sides with great determination for about five minutes, when it ceased from the verandah and screams of men, women and children came from the inside of the house. I at once called on my men to cease firing, which they did. When the firing commenced I called upon the men to be steady and I cannot speak too highly of the conduct of the men on this occasion as they stood with firmness receiving volley after volley from the verandah and replying to it. The men were all on my right and the fire seemed to come in a line, as if the men were on parade. I kept using my gun with my right hand and I think I fired six shots. I had great difficulty in loading, having but the use of one arm. I had to put the stock of the gun between my legs in order to reload. I cannot remember any of the men who were with me during the firing except Senior Constable Kelly.

I told him I was badly wounded and directed him to take all the men and surround Jones's hotel, so as to prevent the escape of the outlaws, and saw this was being done. During the firing there were shouts from the outlaws calling on us to fire away, we could do them no harm. Feeling that I was losing large quantities of blood, I returned towards the railway platform. On my way thither I saw Sub-Inspector O'Connor running up a drain with some of his boys. As I passed him I called out to him I was hit. Senior Constable Kelly called out to me to send some more ammunition at once from the train. I did so directly I arrived at the platform and Mr Rawlins volunteered to take the ammunition round and distribute it amongst the men, which he did.

There were a number of gentlemen of the press on the platform when I arrived there and they very kindly took a handkerchief and bound up my arm. I then returned to the front, intending to go round the men posted, but after visiting two or three of them. I felt myself getting very weak and faint from loss of blood. When I again reached the platform I was staggering and the gentlemen of the press assisted me into a railway carriage. I intended to run down to Benalla to have my arm dressed and to return immediately it was done.

After getting into the carriage I was given a little sherry, which rallied me considerably, but the blood was still flowing from my arm. I started an engine away to inform Superintendent Sadlier of what had occurred, requesting him to come as soon as possible with every available man on the station and bring up a supply of ammunition, and shortly after that I followed another engine to Benalla. Owing to my great loss of blood I had great difficulty in keeping myself from fainting on my way down. We reached Benalla in about 10 minutes. On my arrival there I asked the stationmaster to telegraph to Wangaratta and direct

Sergeant Steele to bring every available man he had on the station by the pilot engine, which was waiting for me there to Glenrowan, as we had the Kellys surrounded in a house, but to be careful not to let the engine come within a mile and a half of Glenrowan as the rails had been torn up. I then started off to the Benalla telegraph office, which was about a mile and a quarter distant from the station. Being afraid to walk that distance by myself, feeling so faint, I asked a Mr Lewis, school inspector from Wangaratta, whom I met, to accompany me, which he did. On the way we called at Dr Nicholson's.

This was about four a.m. I told the doctor I was shot by the Kellys and I wished him to dress my arm, as the blood was still flowing freely. I told him I could not wait to have it done then, but to follow me to the telegraph office, as I wished him to return to Glenrowan with me and to lose no time about it. I then started off with Mr Lewis, leaving Dr Nicholson to dress. On reaching the telegraph office I could barely stagger in. I found the office open and dictated a telegram to the stationmaster to send to you. I also sent a telegram to the police at Beechworth and Violet Town, directing them to proceed with all available force to Glenrowan, as the Kellys were surrounded in a house and as I did not know how much assistance might be required to secure them.

I then laid down on a mattress and Superintendent Sadlier came into the office. I told him what had occurred and to hasten back as quickly as possible and I would follow him. His reply was "Don't be such a fool. You are a regular glutton. You have one bullet through you now and I suppose you want more". He then left the office and hastened away. Just then Dr Nicholson entered. He examined my wound and told me I had sustained a very bad fracture of the wrist and that it would be madness for me to return. He procured an impromptu splint and lint and with the assistance of Mr Lewis and the telegraph-master dressed the wound. During the dressing I fainted.

How long I remained in that state I do not know, but when I came to myself both the doctor and Mr Lewis had gone and the telegraph-master gave me some strong spirits and with his assistance and that of one of his clerks, I walked to my lodgings about a quarter of a mile away. I was unable to proceed and was confined to bed all day suffering great pain.

At about three o'clock Doctor Charles Ryan arrived from Melbourne and dressed my hand and Doctor Nicholson, returning just then, assisted in the operation. In conclusion, I wish to place on record the very great assistance rendered to me by Superintendent Sadlier from the time I arrived at Benalla up to the eventful day. He spared neither time nor trouble and I would desire strongly to urge upon you the necessity of suitably acknowledging his services. Whilst mentioning the assistance rendered to me by Superintendent Sadlier, I would also desire to place on record my high appreciation of the conduct and services of the police force, both of Queensland and Victoria, who by their steadiness and courage seconded my efforts and contributed to the successful termination of the duties they were especially called upon to perform.

The following is from Superintendent Sadlier's Report:

I was first made aware of the encounter with the gang by Superintendent Hare's return at about four a.m. and after exchanging a few words with him as to the position of affairs, proceeded to Glenrowan by train accompanied by the whole of the reserve on the Benalla station. Immediately on reaching Glenrowan and on dispersing to take up the best positions we could find around the building, numerous shots were fired from the direction of the house, striking the ground and fences close to us. After finding Sub-Inspector O'Connor and learning what I could from him of the positions of the men, I made myself assured that the buildings were surrounded by the police and in this I was greatly assisted by Constable Dwyer, who was always willing to run the gauntlet under fire from one post to another. It was not, however, until the capture of Ned Kelly and then only from his statements that there was any assurance that some of the gang had not passed through our lines, as the prisoner himself had done. We had occasional firing from the outlaws within the house and could hear them calling out and rapping on their armour, but after this arrest the remainder of the gang slackened their fire greatly and only a shot at intervals was heard. About 10 a.m. I called on the persons kept prisoners by the gang to make their escape and allowed 10 minutes grace before recommencing firing, and soon after the word was passed on by the posts nearest to the front of the building a general rush was made by these persons and no further shot was fired by the police until they had all been examined and passed out of the lines. We had ascertained from these prisoners that the two outlaws, Dan Kelly and Hart, were still alive, and that Byrne was dead.

These two survivors were called on several times to surrender and on failing to do so several of the police repeatedly appealed to me to let them rush the building. This I would not permit for various reasons, chiefly that the party rushing in could not be supported by those outside, that a long, narrow passage through the house had to be traversed before the outlaws, whose exact position in the buildings was not known, could be reached, that they could not be knocked over on account of the armour, until the police actually had their hands on them, that I knew they still had large supplies of ammunition, that there were yet several hours of daylight and that the final capture or destruction of the two outlaws was a matter of certainty. I therefore held to the determination, though under considerable difficulties, to sacrifice no life in this way if it could be avoided. I think it was about three p.m. when Senior Constable Johnson, volunteered to set fire to the building, and after a short consultation with Sub-Inspector O'Connor and some of the senior members of the force present, arrangements were made accordingly.

A strong firing party was placed under cover in front of the building and another at the end to be fired, and protected by their fire the senior constable was able to carry out his work and return in safety. This precaution was considered necessary as a few minutes before it was reported that the two outlaws were seen at one of the windows. It was known at this time that Martin Cherry was lying wounded in a detached building, shot by Ned Kelly early in the day, as it has since been ascertained, because he would not hold aside one of the window-blinds and arrangements were made to rescue him before the flames could approach him. This was subsequently done.

When the fire had taken, the Reverend Gibney, a clergyman of the Church of Rome, with great bravery passed towards the building, in spite of all remonstrance and the constables and myself, with a view of stopping him, rushed forward and this movement immediately changed into a general rush for the building, when, as I have stated, Cherry was removed, as well as the body of Byrne, the latter from the burning building. It was found impossible to reach where the other outlaws were and it is clear from the Reverend Gibney's statement that these were dead when the fire took place and it is impossible to say whether they had been killed by our last volley or had shortly before taken their own lives. Before proceeding briefly to refer to the conduct of the police under my command, I wish to call attention to that of Mr Jesse Dowsett, an employee on the railway, who, armed with a revolver only, stood manfully to his ground in the capture of Ned Kelly.

His conduct has been specially commended to me by the members of the force who witnessed it. I understand also that Mr Charles Rawlins, of Lake Winton, was also in Superintendent Hare's company at the first encounter, but that officer will be in a better position than I for describing what his conduct was. I have also to acknowledge the readiness with which Dr John Nicholson, of Benalla, accompanied my party to afford any professional assistance that might be necessary and his services were at once afforded to Ned Kelly when captured. The conduct of every member of the police force engaged was completely satisfactory. From Sub-Inspector O'Connor I had throughout the day continual assistance and advice, and with regard to the members of the Victorian force, my only difficulty was in restraining a few too eager spirits. I have already alluded to the conduct of Senior Constable Johnson. He did the special work I sought by him in the face of special danger, as all then supposed. I am assured, for I was not present on the spot, that the men who captured Ned Kelly had a difficult and dangerous business for the short time it lasted.

Mr Curnow's Statement:

The Chief Commissioner of Police has received the following report from Mr Curnow, late schoolmaster at Glenrowan, of his proceedings in connection with the Kelly gang:

On Sunday morning, 27th June, at about 11 o'clock, Mrs Curnow, my sister, brother-in-law and myself were out for a drive, when in passing through Stanistreet's railway gates we were bailed up by an armed man on horseback, who turned out to be Ned Kelly, the outlaw. Another armed man was behind him and I was told that he was Byrne. After a while Ned Kelly gave directions for the horse and buggy to be taken into Mrs Jones's yard. Mrs and Miss Curnow went into Mrs Stanistreet's and my brother-in-law and I stayed at the gates taking part in the conversation going on there.

We had not been bailed up many minutes before I was informed by Mr Stanistreet that the outlaws had caused part of the railway line to be torn up, with the purpose of wrecking a special train which they expected would pass through Glenrowan. Someone, I forget who, also told me that the gang had been at Beechworth during the night before and had shot several police. I doubted this, but afterwards ascertained from Dan Kelly that they had actually been in the vicinity of Beechworth and had done 'some shooting'. The gang afterwards told me, in fact, they made no secret of it, that they had caused a part of the line to be torn up at a dangerous part beyond the station in order to wreck a special train of inspectors, police and blacktrackers, which would pass through Glenrowan for Beechworth, to take up the 'Kelly' trail from there.

They stated that they would shoot down all those who escaped death from the wrecked train and that if any civilians were in the train they should share the same fate, as they had no business accompanying the police. The outlaws affirmed that they were justified in doing this. On hearing their intentions I determined that if I could by any means whatever baulk their designs and prevent such a sacrifice of human life I would do so. This purpose governed the whole of my sayings and doings while I was with the outlaws. On reflection I thought it best to inspire them with confidence in my sympathising heartily with them and if I could do this, I thought that they would allow me enough liberty to be able to do something to frustrate their intentions. In the early part of the afternoon the outlaws proposed a dance and came and asked me to join in it. I objected on the ground of having on nailed boots, when the thought flashed through my mind that if I could induce Ned Kelly to accompany me to the school for a pair of dancing boots, on the journey there in passing the police barracks, Bracken, the trooper stationed there, might see him and would be able to give an alarm.

I felt sure that as Bracken had been stationed at Greta he would know him. So I said to Ned Kelly, after being pressed to dance, that I would do so with pleasure if he would accompany me to my home for a pair of dancing boots. He agreed quite readily to go with me and we were getting ready when Dan Kelly interfered and said that Ned had better stay behind and let him or Byrne accompany me. Someone else also urged Ned Kelly to stay back and said that the house was near the police barracks. Ned turned and asked me if it was and I replied, "Yes, we shall have to pass the barracks. I had forgotten that". He then said that we would not go and I consented to dance with Dan. Shortly after Ned declared that he would go down and bring Bracken and Reynolds, the postmaster, up to Jones's.

I had ascertained from Mr Stanistreet that his revolver was still in his possession and to gain the consent of the outlaws to my going home and taking my wife, child and sister with me and thus being at liberty to make a dash for Benalla, I told the gang in strict confidence that Mr Stanistreet possessed a loaded revolver from the Railway Department and that though I knew he would not use it against them, someone else might get it and do them an injury. I advised them to demand it of him at once and I believe they did. With the same object in view and after hearing Ned Kelly solemnly assert to Mrs Jones and others that he would not shoot Constable Bracken, I told him that he had better take Dave Mortimer, my brother-in-law, with him to call Bracken out, as the trooper knew his voice well and would suspect nothing. I also kept warning them to keep a sharp lookout for enemies and did my utmost to ingratiate myself with them. On obtaining a suitable opportunity I asked Ned Kelly again would he allow me to take Mrs Curnow, the baby and my sister home when he went for Bracken and I assured him that he had no cause for fearing me, as I was with him heart and soul. He then said that he knew that and could see it and he acceded to my request. I think it was about 10 o'clock on Sunday night before the outlaws started for the police barracks taking with them a Mr Reynolds, Mr Gibbins, Mr Mortimer, myself, wife and sister.

We reached the barracks and Constable Bracken was taken by the outlaws without bloodshed. Ned Kelly then told me that I could go home and take the ladies with me. He directed us to "go quietly to bed and not to dream too loud" and intimated that if we acted otherwise we would get shot, as one of them would be down to our place during the night to see that we were all right. He had previously declared that they would wait at Glenrowan till a train came. When we reached home, which was about 200 yards from the police barracks, I put the horse in the stable with the ostensible purpose of feeding him well, as he had starved all day. While supper was being got ready I quietly prepared everything, including a red lama scarf, a candle and matches, to go to Benalla, intending to keep close to the railway line in case of a special coming before I reached there.

In overcoming Mrs Curnow's opposition to my going, for she was in a state of the utmost terror and dread and declared that both I and all belonging to me would get shot if I persisted in going and in securing the safety of my wife, child and sister while being away, time passed, and just as I was about to start I heard the train coming in the distance. I immediately caught up the scarf, candle and matches and ran down the line to meet the train. On reaching a straight part of the line, where those in the train would be able to see the danger signal for some distance,

I lit the candle and held it behind the red scarf. While I was holding up the danger signal I was in great fear of being shot before those in the train would be able to see the red light and of thus uselessly sacrificing my life.

The train, which proved to be a pilot engine, came on and stopped a little past me and I gave the alarm by informing those in it of the line being torn up just beyond the station and of the Kelly gang lying in wait at the station for the special train of police. On being told by the guard that he would go back and stop the special which was coming on and seeing him do it, I ran home to appease my wife's anxiety and terror and to protect them as far as I could. We had not the least hope of an escape from being shot dead, for we felt certain that the outlaws must have heard the whistling and stoppage of the pilot engine near our place and would divine that I was stopping the train, as we were the only ones liberated, to our knowledge. We therefore felt sure that at least one of them would ride down and take revenge for my betrayal of their trust in me. Though I represented myself to Edward Kelly as a sympathiser, my sole motive in doing so was to save life, to uphold justice and of course to secure as far as possible the safety of my family. Thomas Curnow, late of Glenrowan S.S., 1742.

The Kelly Tragedy

The Illustrated Sydney News and New South Wales Agriculturalist and Grazier, 5 August 1880

Burning of Jones hotel and preparing for the funeral

RUINS OF JONES HOTEL AFTER THE FIRE.

THE TOWNSPEOPLE "BAILED UP" BY THE KELLY GANG—THE THIRTY PRISONERS.

Horse ridden by Ned Kelly at Glenrowan.

Ned Kelly's Trial

The Kilmore Free Press, 12 August 1880

Considerable interest is manifested throughout the district and in the town in the proceedings which are being taken in connection with the prosecution of Edward Kelly, and the numerous arrivals and stealthy movements of the police tend to heighten the fast-increasing curiosity into excitement not unmixed with alarm. Captain Standish, Superintendent Sadlier, Sub-Inspector Kennedy and Mr Gurner, the Crown solicitor, arrived by the first train from Melbourne today, which also picked up Sergeant Steele, Senior Constable Kelly, and a number of other officers of police at Benalla and Wangaratta, and brought them on, several others being left to proceed hither during the night. Mr C.A. Smyth arrived yesterday, and is prepared to go on with the prosecution tomorrow, but there is great talk of a postponement being applied for by the defence, on the ground that sufficient time has not been afforded them to prepare an answer to the charges which have been preferred against the outlaw. A disagreement has already taken place between Ned Kelly and his solicitor, for what reason, however, it has not been made public, but it has been of such a nature that Mr Zincke has thrown up the case, and positively declined to have anything more to do with the matter. I believe the rupture occurred in consequence of the prisoner's friends having retained David Gaunson to appear with Mr Zincke without the latter's knowledge or consent, their reason for so doing being that it was thought the member for Ararat would be enabled to exercise some influence with the Government on Kelly's behalf, while Mr Zincke would be expected to act in a similar manner with the political party in the Assembly of which he is a member. Mr Zincke warmly resented such a proposal, I am told, and threw up the case.

Mr Gaunson is expected to arrive by the night train, and as he will not be able to see the prisoner to receive instructions till the morning, he will probably apply for a remand till Saturday. The Crown Prosecutor will insist upon the case being gone into, and from what I can learn there is a probability of the desired remand being granted till next day. I believe there are other and more serious reasons which have influenced Mr Zincke in throwing up the case, but at present it is impossible to ascertain them, as the parties concerned are most reticent.

The police are mustering in strong force. Great activity prevails, and every precaution is being taken to prevent an accident or a demonstration of the friends and sympathisers of the outlaw, who are arriving hourly and can be seen hanging about the town in a most uninviting manner. Kelly continues quiet and orderly in the gaol, but appears to grow impatient as the time for appearing in court arrives. Mrs Skillion made an attempt to communicate with her brother this afternoon through the police, by bringing a new hat to the camp, and requesting it might be conveyed to Ned in exchange for the one which he brought with him on Sunday, but it was feared that the hat was intended as a sign of some dangerous import, and it was detained by the police and not conveyed to the outlaw as requested. It is anticipated that Kelly's friends will create a disturbance tomorrow indeed. An indefinite something is talked of being done, but every precaution is being taken, and should anything occur the police will be prepared for the emergency. With respect to the murder of Aaron Sherritt, it appears that immediately prior to the tragedy, Sherritt was sitting in the hut telling Constable Duross that some short time before the murders on Stringybark Creek he and Byrne got into a row in which a Chinaman was nearly killed, and as it was feared the Chinaman would die, warrants were issued for their apprehension. Sherritt was arrested, but Byrne kept out of the way and eluded capture. While in the log watch-house awaiting his fate, he was visited by Byrne, who knocked at the wall about midnight and wanted him to escape, but Sherritt said that the Chinaman was getting better, and advised Byrne to give himself up, but the latter would not consent to do so, and disappeared in the bush as mysteriously as he came. Just as Sherritt had finished telling of this occurrence, a knock was heard at the door, and by going to see what was the matter the unfortunate man met his fate.

It has transpired that Byrne frequently slept at a well-known hut about two miles from Beechworth, and upon the news arriving of Byrne's death, the occupant of this hut was greatly distressed and quite inconsolable for days. The outlaws and their friends were experimenting as to how best to prepare bail-resisting armour for many months, and although the person who finally succeeded in producing the necessary article is not known, it has transpired that four whole months were expended in making the sets of armour which the gang used at Glenrowan. Circular saws were first tested, and as they failed to resist a rifle ball metal cut off a tank was tried with a like result, and, as a last resource, plough moulds were had recourse to, and with a success already well known.

I met young Reardon at Glenrowan this morning. He is improving slowly and is able to go about, but the slugs have not yet been extracted. Young Reardon was shot by Sergeant Steele while trying to escape by the back door, and had it not been for the top rail of the fence, there is no doubt whatever he would have been shot dead. Steele is not to blame, as if Reardon had thrown up his hands when called upon to do so, instead of attempting escape into the hotel again, he would never have been fired at.

Kate Kelly has not yet arrived, but it is believed she is riding across country, and will appear at the court in the morning.

Mr Gaunson, who brought with him a special permit to visit the outlaw was conveyed to the prisoner and a lengthened interview took place. It is stated that the cause of the rupture with Mr Zincke results from the inability of the latter, whether from political or private motives I cannot say, to obtain from the Government an order to enable the friends of the outlaw to visit him.

Ned Kelly is said to have planted a large amount of the spoil from the Euroa and Jerilderie bank robberies, and as he is the only survivor of the gang who knows anything about the whereabouts of the spoil, the friends of the outlaw desire to unearth it, and as Mr Zincke could not obtain from the Government the favours that have been given to Mr Gaunson, it was not difficult to bring about a change so desirable to the outlaw and his sympathisers. Mr Gaunson's interview with Ned Kelly extended till after 12 o'clock tonight. A remand is to be applied for a week, but if the bench will not grant this, the defence will be prepared to go on next day. Kelly will be moved from the gaol at eight o'clock, and the court will open at 10 o'clock.

Ned Kelly in the Dock – A Sketch from Life

The Illustrated Australian News, 28 August 1880

THE ILLUSTRATED AUSTRALIAN NEWS

No. 294 MELBOURNE, SATURDAY, AUGUST 28, 1880. PRICE SIXPENCE.

KELLY IN THE DOCK.—A SKETCH FROM LIFE.

The Beechworth Police Court During the Trial

The Illustrated Australian News, 28 August 1880

Our Illustrations

The Illustrated Australian News, 28 August 1880

To whatever motive attributable – whether morbid curiosity, misdirected sympathy, or the infection of a passing epidemic – there is no gainsaying the fact that notorious criminals invariably excite for the time being intense interest in the mind of the general public. Under all circumstances there is something peculiarly fascinating in the terrible and tragic. It is absurd to suppose that the feeling is confined to any particular class of people. It is common to all, to gentle and simple, to the daintiest of the fair sex no less than to those whose instincts are supposed to be the reverse of refined or elevated. When executions formerly took place in public the crowds that assembled to witness the majesty of the law vindicated were not composed, as many imagine, of the lowest and most degraded of the population. Even when cruel deaths were inflicted, when horrors now almost too dreadful to describe were enacted in the face of day, there were found in the multitude of eager spectators representatives not alone of the modern pit and gallery, but of the stalls and dress circle. It is not surprising, therefore, that the bushranger Ned Kelly and his doings should attract considerable attention, and that incidents and facts in themselves trifling should, when associated with his name, assume a certain degree of significance. The sketch of Ned Kelly in the dock is taken from an original watercolour, the only likeness that may be regarded as really authentic of the outlaw apart from photographs which date many years back. It is the work of Mr J. H. Ashton, an artist whose abilities have been recognised not alone in Victoria and other Australian colonies, but in the mother country also. It may be mentioned as an incident of this trial that the bushranger did not seem to relish the delicate attentions of the artist on the occasion. Under the impression that the gentle limner was somehow connected with the administration of the law and that the likeness was required for legal purposes, the prisoner, as soon as he discovered our artist in the act of taking him, immediately covered his head with a rug which he had carried with him into court. Not, however, before our artist had accomplished his purpose.

Ned Kelly is a man above the ordinary stature, being about 6 feet 2 inches in height. He is robust and strongly built. His head is not by any means of the criminal type, nor are his features unprepossessing. His forehead, though low, is broad and indicates intelligence. His eyes are dark, but furtive and restless. His cheekbones are prominent and give a triangularity to his face, the lower portion of which is covered with a straggling beard. The general expression of his face betrays a Celtic origin. He is well known to be of Irish extraction. His conduct in the dock was quiet and respectful, though there seemed a tendency at times to pose as a sentimental hero. With a curious perversion of that sense of generosity and fair play which Irishmen as a rule lay claim to, Ned Kelly appears to share in that notion common to many of his class in Ireland that under certain circumstances killing is not murder. He appears to take credit to himself that neither he nor his mates were wholesale and indiscriminate murderers. The vendetta which existed between him and the police has been at the bottom of the outrages with which his name will be associated in the records of crime. It would seem that he was animated by the spirit of the avenger of blood, such as is found amongst savage nations, and that on the principle of retaliation no less than that of self preservation, he considered himself justified in taking the lives of the constables at Mansfield. A doctrine more dangerous to the social well being of any civilised community it would be difficult to imagine. If for a moment tolerated, or supposed to be an element of extenuation in the consideration of his case, it would be destructive of all legal obligation or moral ties in all that concerns the social relations of a people removed from barbarism. Beside the bushranger in the dock stands Sergeant Steele, a valuable officer, who was more immediately connected with the capture of the outlaw.

Sketches During the Trial

The Illustrated Australian News, 28 August 1880

SKETCHES DURING THE TRIAL.

In this sketch Constable Thomas McIntyre is represented giving his evidence of the murder of Constables Lonigan and Scanlon near Mansfield in October 1878. The witness was one of the party sent out under Sergeant Kennedy in search of Kelly and his mates. He saw, as he alleges, the two constables shot down by the ruthless hand of the prisoner and only escaped a similar fate by leaping on Kennedy's horse and galloping into the bush.

Amongst the sympathisers in court we may refer to the following as amongst the more prominent: Mrs Skillion is the eldest sister of Ned Kelly. Her husband is at present undergoing a sentence of imprisonment for horse-stealing and for many years was known at Greta as a struggling cockatoo or small farmer. Mrs Skillion is a woman of considerable astuteness, force of character and determination. She is an excellent horsewoman, and although there is nothing to prove that to her attention the Kelly gang were indebted for the supply of the necessary provisions during their concealment, there exists a shrewd suspicion that she knew something about the matter. She is the mother of a large family and about 33 years of age, trials and hardships making her look older as her face presents a wizened, sharp, careworn aspect. Her movements from the first were closely watched by the police, but little information could be gleaned by them beyond the fact that she was constantly on the alert, that she was frequently observed flying about the country on horseback, that she was known to have purchased quantities of provisions largely in excess of her own requirements or those of her family, and that her periodical visits to Melbourne were calculated to raise serious doubts as to her objects being of an ordinary character. Kate Kelly is a younger sister of the bushranger, and is about 17 years old. She is supposed to have assisted Mrs Skillion in her labours on behalf of her outlawed brothers, but her conduct has never amounted to what could be construed into an overt act calculated to prejudice the course of justice and shield the bushrangers from the penalties of their crimes.

She appears to be of a lively temperament and to have often indulged in humorous chaff at the expense of the police, who were told off to keep her under surveillance. Many a weary and purposeless ride she has given the troopers over the roughest country and often has innocently inquired if they would like to know where the money stolen from the banks had been planted. It must be admitted that the authorities exhibited a great deal of leniency and consideration towards the young woman who, had she been in any other country, would probably be the inmate of a prison on the bare suspicion of being an accomplice after the fact. Tom Lloyd is well known as a personal sympathiser of Ned Kelly, though in saying so we do not for a moment imply that he in any way approved of the atrocious conduct of the gang. He is a near relative of the Kelly family. He is a farmer residing near Greta and was included in the prescription of those who, after the promulgation of the *Outlawry Act*, had been apprehended and imprisoned on suspicion of assisting the gang. Nothing of an illegal nature could be proved against him by the police and he soon regained his liberty. When Ned Kelly was arrested he interested himself in arranging for his defence and accompanied by Mrs Skillion, visited Melbourne and consulted several lawyers, the selection finally falling upon Mr David Gaunson. Dick Hart is a younger brother of the outlaw who was shot at Glenrowan. There is nothing against his character beyond the fact that on one occasion he was fined £4 for having rescued some cattle which had been impounded for trespass. He is known to be as a rule quiet and respectful and informed the police that so far was he from approving of the conduct of his brother, the bushranger, that he would have afforded assistance to the police if in his power to do so. The brother of Joseph Byrne has been also classed as a sympathiser, but there seems nothing to identify him with their criminal acts.

It has been clearly indicated that many of the Chinese at the Woolshed and other places in the north-eastern district were warm sympathisers with the Kelly gang, and it is believed often gave them very material assistance in evading the pursuit of the police.

The Trial of Edward Kelly

The Argus, 20 September 1880

An application was made to Mr Justice Barry in chambers on Saturday by Mr C.A. Smyth, Crown Prosecutor, for an order to transfer the trial of Edward Kelly from the Beechworth Circuit Court to the Central Criminal Court. The application was made under Section 33 of the *Judicature Act* No. 502, which provides that wherever any person shall have been committed for any felony or misdemeanour committed, or supposed to have been committed, at any place out of the jurisdiction of the Central Criminal Court and it shall appear to the Supreme Court in term time or to any judge thereof in vacation that it shall be expedient to the ends of justice that such person should be tried for such offence at the Central Criminal Court. It shall be lawful for the Court or judge to order that such person shall be tried for such offence at the Central Criminal Court and the trial shall be held there accordingly.

Mr Smyth, having referred to the Section of the Act, said that an affidavit was made by Mr Gurner, the Crown Solicitor, in support of the application, which showed that it was advisable that the trial should be held in the Central Criminal Court and not at Beechworth.

He read the affidavit, which was as follows:

1. That the above named Edward Kelly was at a court of petty sessions held at Beechworth on the 10th and 11th days of August, 1880. Committed for trial to the Assize Court to be held at Beechworth in the northern bailiwick, on the 14th October next, upon the respective charges of the murder of Constable Thomas Lonigan and Constable Michael Scanlon.

2. That the said offences for which the said Edward Kelly was so committed for trial were perpetrated at Stringybark Creek, Wombat Ranges, in the said northern bailiwick, on the 26th October, 1878.

3. That on the 4th day of November, 1878, the said Edward Kelly, charged with the said offences, was by an order under the provisions of the *Felons Apprehension Act* 1878 No.612, made by his Honour Sir William Foster Stawell, Chief Justice of the Supreme Court of the colony of Victoria, adjudged and declared to be an outlaw by a declaration to that effect under the hand of the said Sir William Foster Stawell, Chief Justice and filed of record in the aforesaid Supreme Court.

4. That on the said 4th November, 1878, Daniel Kelly (a brother of the said Edward Kelly), Joseph Byrne and Stephen Hart were also by an order of the said Sir William Foster Stawell, made under the provisions of the said statute, adjudged and declared an outlaw for the same offences as the said Edward Kelly.

5. That since the aforesaid declarations of outlawry, I am informed and believe the said Edward Kelly was at large until the 28th day of June, 1880, when he was apprehended at Glenrowan, in the said northern bailiwick.

6. That I am informed, and verily believe, that since the said outlawry and up to the arrest of the said Edward Kelly, Daniel Kelly, Joseph Byrne, and Stephen Hart formed an organized gang of armed highway robbers, under the leadership of the said Edward Kelly and during the said period were the cause of much terror to the law-abiding and peaceable inhabitants of the said northern bailiwick.

7. That I am informed and believe that in the said bailiwick and more especially in the neighbourhood of Beechworth aforesaid, the said Edward Kelly has numerous relations, friends, and sympathisers, amongst whom strong feelings exist in favour of the said Edward Kelly.

8. That from the lawless conduct and threatening demeanour of some of the relations friends and sympathisers of the said Edward Kelly. I believe efforts would be made to intimidate certain of the jurors on the jury panel of the said Assize Court, and that some of the said jurors might probably be thereby deterred and intimidated from finding a verdict in accordance with the evidence.

9. That should a jury find a verdict of guilty against the said Edward Kelly, I verily believe that those members of the said jury who live in the country districts of the said bailiwick would be liable to serious injuries in their persons, families and property at the hands of the said relations, friends and other sympathisers of the said Edward Kelly.

10. That for the foregoing reasons I verily believe a fair trial cannot be had at the said Assize Court to be held at Beechworth aforesaid.

11. That I am advised and believe it is expedient and essential to the ends of justice that the said Edward Kelly should be tried at the Central Criminal Court, Melbourne, within the central bailiwick, or any presentments that may be prepared against him upon the charges aforesaid.

Mr Smyth said that he relied more particularly upon the 8th and 9th paragraphs in the affidavit, stating that the jury would be liable to intimidation.

Mr Gaunson, who appeared for the prisoner, said he had to oppose the application and asked for an adjournment. There were certain statements in Mr Gurner's affidavit which required to be answered and he had no opportunity of communicating with Kelly. He was allowed by the gaol regulations to see him only on Mondays and Thursdays and it was after he had seen him last Thursday that he received notice of this application. Besides the authorities would not allow any of his friends and relations to see him. With regard to the paragraph in the affidavit in relation to the friends and sympathisers of the prisoner, he mentioned that the Crown had caused to be arrested in 1879 about 20 persons said to be sympathisers, and after detaining them in gaol for a long time without preferring any charge against them, let them go.

Mr Justice Barry said he could not go into that question.

Mr Gaunson said he only alluded to it for the purpose of showing that these men had been at large ever since and had committed no acts of lawlessness or violence. He also pointed out that he had no time to instruct counsel and that though reference was made to there being four outlaws, it was not stated that three of them were dead.

Mr Justice Barry asked what adjournment was wanted.

Mr Gaunson said till the 30th September, Mr Smyth objected to so long an adjournment, though he would have no objection to a reasonable adjournment. There were a great number of witnesses to be examined, and it was coming close to the time when the Assize Court would be held.

After some further discussion, it was agreed that the application should be adjourned till Wednesday next.

Trial and Conviction of Edward Kelly – Sentence of Death

The Argus, 30 October 1880

The trial of Edward Kelly on the charge of murdering Constable Lonigan was resumed in the Central Criminal Court yesterday, before his Honour Sir Redmond Barry. The Court reassembled at nine o'clock.

Mr C.A. Smyth and Mr Chomley prosecuted and Mr Bindon appeared for the defence.

Frank Beacroft, draper's assistant living at Longwood, said that he was with Mr Gloucester at the time the Faithfull's Creek station was stuck up. He gave evidence similar to that of Gloucester in reference to the statements made by the prisoner as to the manner in which Lonigan had been shot.

Robert Scott, manager of the National Bank at Euroa, gave evidence as to the prisoner sticking up the bank on the 10th December, 1878. He asked Kelly who shot Lonigan. Kelly said, "Oh I shot Lonigan".

Cross-examined by Mr Bindon:

The prisoner treated me and Mrs Scott well.

Henry Richards, police constable stationed at Jerilderie, New South Wales, said that in February, 1879, the police station there was stuck up by the prisoner and three other men. Prisoner said he had come to shoot him because he had tried to shoot him (Kelly) on the punt at Tocumwal two months before. He said he also intended to shoot Constable Devine as he was worse than a blacktracker and was always following him about. Constable Devine asked the prisoner about the shooting of the police in Victoria. The prisoner said that a reward of £100 had been offered for him for shooting Constable Fitzpatrick. He was not guilty of that, as he was 200 miles away at the time that Fitzpatrick was shot in this way. He had gone to arrest Dan Kelly. His mother asked him if he had a warrant and he said he had not and his mother then said that Fitzpatrick could not arrest Dan if Ned was there, that Dan tried to take the pistol from Fitzpatrick and in the scuffle the pistol went off. Prisoner also said that he had not gone out to shoot Kennedy, Scanlon, and Lonigan but was determined to get their arms. The reason he shot them was that they were persecuting him. He said he had Sergeant Kennedy's watch, and he intended to return it in due course of time.

Cross-examined:

Kelly told Mrs Devine that he would not shoot her husband. The remark about the shooting at Tocumwal referred to this. About two months before, while he and another constable were on patrol duty on the New South Wales side of the Murray, they saw four men in a punt and he called out that he would shoot them if they did not answer. The men proved to be Victorian police.

Edward M. Living, clerk in the bank of New South Wales, Jerilderie, said that after the bank was robbed, in the course of a conversation with him, prisoner said that he had shot the police with a gun he had. "It was an old one, but a good one and would shoot round a corner". Prisoner went to the newspaper office to give a written statement for publication. The proprietor was not in and his wife refused to take it. Prisoner gave him the statement and he afterwards handed it to the police.

The statement was tendered in evidence, but was not received.

John William Tarleton, clerk in New Zealand, was clerk at the Bank of New South Wales, Jerilderie, in February, 1879. Prisoner stated that people talked about their shooting the police, but they had done it in self-defense.

The police had been persecuting him ever since he was fourteen and he had been driven to become an outlaw. He had a revolver which he said was taken from Lonigan after he was shot. He said he shot Kennedy and Lonigan and that Hart and Byrne were miles away at the time. The prisoner left the impression that he had done all the shooting himself.

John Kelly, senior constable of police, gave evidence as to the Glenrowan affair, and produced the armour the prisoner had on when he was wounded. Prisoner said to Constable Bracken, "Save me, I saved you". He (witness) replied. "You showed little mercy to Sergeant Kennedy and Scanlon". Prisoner said, "I had to shoot them or they would have shot me". Asked him where Kennedy's watch was, and he said he didn't care to tell.

The witness corroborated Constable McIntyre's version of the conversation between him and the prisoner at the lockup. Between three and six o'clock the same morning had another conversation with prisoner in the presence of Constable Ryan. Gave him some milk and water. Asked him if Fitzpatrick's statement was correct.

Prisoner said, "Yes, I shot him".

Arthur Steele, sergeant in charge of the Wangaratta police station, gave evidence as to the arrest of the prisoner at Glenrowan. When he was captured he said, "Don't kill me, I never hurt any of you". Senior Constable Kelly said, "You did not show Scanlon and Kennedy much mercy". Prisoner said, "If I had not shot them they would have shot me". In reply to other questions, the prisoner said he had intended to shoot every one that escaped from the wreck of the train. Prisoner was asked if it was true about his shooting Fitzpatrick. He said, "Yes, it is true I shot him".

Cross-examined by Mr Bindon:

> I arrived at Glenrowan about five o'clock in the morning. First saw the prisoner about a quarter-past seven. There was some firing. There were about a dozen constables there in the morning, besides the blacktrackers. There were 53 in the evening. I fired at a young fellow named Reardon. I fired at

him because I thought it was one of the outlaws. The police fired into the hotel. I believe there were a number of people in the hotel, but I did not know of it at the time. After the boy was shot and I understood that there were people in the house, I called on them to come out. We fired in answer to firing from the house. Martin Cherry and a boy named Jones were shot. I was accused of shooting the boy. There was nothing but slugs in my gun. That boy was shot before I arrived. Never said to Mrs Jones that if she would say that Ned Kelly shot her son I would forward her application for a portion of the reward to the Government. Never heard of such a thing before today.

Re-examined:

The boy Reardon recovered. Can't say who shot Cherry.

Samuel Reynolds, medical practitioner, at Mansfield made a post-mortem examination on the body of Thomas Lonigan. There were two wounds, the one in the eye, the other on the temple, which was merely a graze. He had also a wound on the left arm and one on the left thigh. They were all gunshot wounds. The wound through the eye was the cause of death.

Cross-examined by Mr Bindon:

The ball that struck the eye must have come slightly slanting. Did not think the other wounds were inflicted after death. I should say that Kennedy was standing up when he was shot, as he had the wound right in the centre of the chest. I did not make a regular post-mortem examination of Kennedy's body. I extracted a bullet from Lonigan's thigh. It was an ordinary revolver bullet.

Re-examined:

If wounds were inflicted before the circulation had actually ceased, it would be impossible to state accurately whether they were before or after death.

This closed the evidence for the prosecution, and the Court adjourned for an hour to allow Mr Bindon an opportunity of considering whether he would call any witnesses. On the Court resuming, Mr Bindon stated that in the course of the case he had objected to certain evidence that had been tendered and he wished to know whether his Honour would reserve a special case on the points for the consideration of the full Court. He referred more particularly to the evidence given after Lonigan had been killed. He contended as the prisoner was not being tried for the murder of Kennedy or Scanlon, that therefore no evidence should have been given in regard to them.

His Honour said that if an act were doubtful or ambiguous, or capable of two meanings, the conduct of the person before at the time or after the time of doing the act was admissible to show the motive and reason for his conduct. This evidence was admissible to show whether the shooting of Constable Lonigan were accidental or justifiable.

Mr Smith then addressed the jury, reviewing the evidence on behalf of the Crown:

Mr Bindon then addressed the jury on behalf of the prisoner. The evidence, he said, was in one sense most elaborate, but the great bulk of it was quite extraneous matter. It would be the duty of the jury to exclude everything from their minds but what related to the death of Constable Lonigan. What occurred at Euroa, Jerilderie and Glenrowan was altogether irrelevant, and with regard to what occurred at Stringybark Creek, they had only the evidence of one witness. That one witness (Constable McIntyre), had given a very consecutive and well prepared narrative after the event, but he was in such a state of trepidation at the time of the affray, that he could not have made the minute observations he professed to have done, and could not possibly have picked out the prisoner from amongst the gang as the particular person who shot Lonigan. His statement was therefore to be received with discredit.

The prisoner and his three mates were following a lawful pursuit in the bush, when a party of men in disguise, fully armed policemen in plain clothes, as they afterwards turned out to be, came upon them and an unfortunate fracas occurred, in which Constable Lonigan lost his life. Who shot that man no one could tell. McIntyre said that he saw the prisoner fire at him, but there were shots fired by others at the same time and to tell which was the fatal bullet was a matter of impossibility. Only two men were alive who were in the fray and it was simply a question of believing the statement of the one or that of the other.

Unfortunately for the prisoner, his mouth was closed and they had only the statement of McIntyre before them. That statement, moreover, was not only that of a prejudiced witness, but the corroborative evidence given was of most peculiar and unreliable character being simply a variety of remarks made by the prisoner himself remarks made either ad captandum, for the purpose of screening others, or for keeping the persons he had in durance in subjection. Evidence of this character was of a most illusory nature, and ought to have no weight with the jury. The prisoner was not the bloodthirsty assassin the Crown Prosecutor had endeavoured to make out.

Both before and after the shooting of the police he showed that he had the greatest possible respect for human life, for he had many previous opportunities of assassinating policemen, if that was his desire, and at Euroa and Jerilderie he never harmed one of the persons who fell into his power. The jury had an important and serious duty to discharge, and he had to urge them not to take away the life of a man on the prejudiced evidence of a single man.

His Honour, in summing up, said that the prisoner Edward Kelly was presented against for that he, on the 26th October, 1878, at Stringybark Creek, in the northern bailiwick, feloniously, wilfully and with malice aforethought, did kill and murder Thomas Lonigan. Murder was the highest kind of homicide. It was the voluntarily killing of any person in the Queen's peace by another person of sound mind, with malice prepense and aforethought, either expressed or implied. Malice was twofold.

It might be proved by expressions made use of by the prisoner, which showed a malevolent disposition and that he had an intention to take away the life of another man without lawful cause. It might also be proved by the prisoner procuring materials to cause the death of another, such as purchasing a sword, or a knife, or poison, and if those weapons or the poison were used, it was evidence from which malice might be inferred, unless there was some justification for their use. As, for instance, if a man bought a pistol intending to shoot, and went out intending to shoot him and if on the way he was assailed and overpowered by another with whom he had no intention of quarrelling and should kill him, he would be justified in using the pistol in self defense.

If, however, having bought the pistol, he proceeded to carry out his original intention and did so, it would be murder. And if two or three or more persons went out together with an intention of an unlawful character, they were all principals in the first degree and each was liable to account for the acts of the others. So if four men went out armed intending to resist those in lawful pursuit of an object, and one of these four men interfered with those on their lawful business, and killed them the four would be equally guilty of murder, and might be executed. Here four constables went out to perform a duty. It was said they were in plain clothes. But with that they had nothing to do. Regard them as civilians, he used the word because it had been made use of in the course of the trial, although he thought it inappropriate, what right had four other men armed to stop them? They had the evidence of the surviving constable as to what had occurred, that two were left by their companions at the camp, what right had the prisoner and three other men to desire them to hold up their hands and surrender? But there was another state of things which was not to be disregarded.

These men were persons charged with a responsible and as it turned out a dangerous duty and they were aware of that before they started. They went in pursuit of two persons who had been gazetted as persons against whom warrants were issued, and they were in the lawful discharge of their duty when in pursuit of these two persons, therefore they had a double protection, that of the ordinary citizen and that of being ministers of the law, executive officers of the administration of the peace of the country. Whether they were in uniform or not, there was no privilege on the part of any person to molest them and still less was there power or authority to molest them as constables.

The jury had been invited to be extremely careful before relying upon the evidence of Constable McIntyre. He went further and told them to be careful in considering the evidence of all the witnesses. According to the law of this country, the principles of evidence were the same on all sides of the Court, at the common law, at the equity and at the criminal side with some few exceptions. As, for instance, in treason there must be two witnesses, although not necessarily to the same overt act. In perjury there must be generally two witnesses, or one witness sworn and certain circumstances deposed to on oath to corroborate him.

There must be two witnesses to a will. Some documents must be signed by an attorney, some documents must be attested by a notary public but with these and some other unimportant exceptions one witness was sufficient to prove a case on either side of the Supreme Court. McIntyre was the only survivor of this lamentable catastrophe. The jury would have to consider the manner in which he had given his evidence and say whether they thought from his demeanour or mode of giving his evidence that he was stating what was not true. It was not his province to land or to censure him, but if he had not escaped there would have been no survivor to give evidence today. The jury were properly told that the prisoner was not on his trial for the murder of either Scanlon or Kennedy, but he had admitted the evidence of what had occurred prior to the shooting of Lonigan, because the jury might infer from it what was the motive for shooting Lonigan or whether the shooting was accidental or in self defense. Besides the testimony of McIntyre, there were also the admissions made by the prisoner himself at different times, and at different places, to different persons.

Two classes of those admissions were made at Euroa and Jerilderie and the other at the time of his capture. On the first two occasions, the prisoner was not under any duress, and it was for the jury to say what motive he had in making the admissions. There was no compulsion upon him he answered questions which were put to him when he might have held his tongue. These admissions were spoken to by five different persons at one place, by three at the other and by three at the third and it was for the jury to say whether these witnesses had concocted the story or not.

The jury then retired and after deliberating about half-an-hour returned into Court with a verdict of guilty.

The prisoner having been asked in the usual way if he had any statement to make said:

> Well, it is rather too late for me to speak now. I thought of speaking this morning and all day, but there was little use and there is little use blaming any one now. Nobody knew about my case except myself and I wish I had insisted on being allowed to examine the witnesses myself. If I had examined them, I am confident I would have thrown a different light on the case. It is not that I fear death, I fear it as little as to drink a cup of tea.

On the evidence that has been given, no juryman could have given any other verdict. That is my opinion. But as I say, if I had examined the witnesses I would have shown matters in a different light, because no man understands the case as I do myself. I do not blame anybody, neither Mr Bindon nor Mr Gaunson, but Mr Bindon knew nothing about my case. I lay blame on myself that I did not get up yesterday and examine the witnesses, but I thought that if I did so it would look like bravado and flashness.

The court crier having called upon all to observe a strict silence whilst the judge pronounced the awful sentence of death.

His Honour:

Edward Kelly, the verdict pronounced by the jury is one which you must have fully expected.

The Prisoner:

Yes, under the circumstances.

His Honour:

No circumstances that I can conceive could have altered the result of your trial.

The Prisoner:

Perhaps not from what you can now conceive, but if you had heard me examine the witnesses it would have been different.

His Honour:

I will give you credit for all the skill you appear to desire to assume.

The Prisoner:

No, I don't wish to assume anything. There is no flashness or bravado about me. It is not that I want to save my life, because I know I would have been capable of clearing myself of the charge and I could have saved my life in spite of all against me.

His Honour:

The facts are so numerous and so convincing, not only as regards the original offence with which you are charged, but with respect to a long series of transactions covering a period of eighteen months, that no rational person would hesitate to arrive at any other conclusion but that the verdict of the jury is irresistible and that it is right. I have no desire whatever to inflict upon you any personal remarks. It is not becoming that I should endeavour to aggravate the suffering with which your mind must be sincerely agitated.

The Prisoner:

No, I don't think that. My mind is as easy as the mind of any man in this world as I am prepared to show before God and man.

His Honour:

It is blasphemous for you to say that. You appear to revel in the idea of having put men to death.

The Prisoner:

More men than me have put men to death, but I am the last man in the world that would take a man's life. Two years ago, even if my own life was at stake and I am confident if I thought a man would shoot me, I would give him a chance of keeping his life and would part rather with my own. But if I knew that through him innocent persons, lives were at stake I certainly would have to shoot him if he forced me to do so, but I would want to know that he was really going to take innocent life.

His Honour:

Your statement involves a cruelly wicked charge of perjury against a phalanx of witnesses.

The Prisoner:

I daresay, but a day will come at a bigger court than this when we shall see which is right and which is wrong. No matter how long a man lives, he is bound to come to judgment somewhere and as well here as anywhere. It will be different the next time they have a Kelly trial, for they are not all killed. It would have been for the good of the Crown had I examined the witnesses and I would have stopped a lot of the reward, I can assure you and I do not know, but I will do it yet, if allowed.

His Honour:

"An offence of this kind is of no ordinary character. Murders have been discovered which had been committed under circumstances of great atrocity. They proceeded from motives other than that which actuated you. They have had their origin in many sources. Some have been committed from a sordid desire to take from others the property they had acquired, some from jealousy, some from a desire for revenge, but yours is a more aggravated crime, and one of larger proportions, for with a party of men you took up arms against society, organized as it is for mutual protection, and for respect of law".

The Prisoner:

That is the way the evidence came out here. It appeared that I deliberately took up arms of my own accord, and induced the other three men to join me for the purpose of doing nothing but shooting down the police.

His Honour:

In new communities, where the bonds of society are not so well linked together as in older countries there is unfortunately a class which disregards the evil consequences of crime. Foolish, inconsiderate, ill-conducted, unprincipled youths unfortunately abound, and unless they are made to consider the consequences of crime they are led to imitate notorious felons, whom they regard as self made heroes. It is right therefore that they should be asked to consider and reflect upon what the life of a felon is. A felon who has cut himself off from all decencies, all the affections, charities, and all the obligations of society is as helpless and degraded as a wild beast of the field. He has nowhere to lay his head, he has no one to prepare for him the comforts of life, he suspects his friends, he dreads his enemies, he is in constant alarm lest his pursuers should reach him, and his only hope is that he might use his life in what he considers a glorious struggle for existence. That is the life of the outlaw or felon and it would be well for those young men who are so foolish as to consider that it is brave of a man to sacrifice the lives of his fellow creatures in carrying out his own wild ideas, to see that it is a life to be avoided by every possible means, and to reflect that the unfortunate termination of your life is a miserable death. New South Wales joined with Victoria in providing ample inducement to persons to assist in having you and your companions apprehended, but by some spell which I cannot understand, a spell which exists in all lawless communities more or less, which may be attributed either to a sympathy for the outlaws, or a dread of the consequences which would result from the performance of their duty, no persons were found who would be tempted by the reward. The love of country, the love of order, the love of obedience to law, have been set aside for reasons difficult to explain, and there is something extremely wrong in a country where a lawless band of men are able to live for 18 months disturbing society. During your short life you have stolen, according to your own statements, over 200 horses.

THE PRISONER:

Who proves that?

HIS HONOUR:

More than one witness has testified that you made the statement on several occasions.

THE PRISONER:

That charge has never been proved against me and it is held in English law that a man is innocent until he is found guilty.

HIS HONOUR:

You are self-accused. The statement was made voluntarily by yourself. Then you and your companions committed attacks on two banks and appropriated there from large sums of money, amounting to several thousands of pounds. Further, I cannot conceal from myself the fact that an expenditure of £50000 has been rendered necessary in consequence of the acts with which you and your party have been connected. We have had samples of felons and such as those of Bradley and O'Connor, Clark, Gardiner, Melville, Morgan, Scott, and Smith, all of whom have come to ignominious deaths, still the effect expected from their punishment has not been produced. This is much to be deplored. When such examples as these are so often repeated society must be reorganized, or it must soon be seriously affected. Your unfortunate and miserable companions have died a death which probably you might rather envy, but you are not afforded the opportunity".

THE PRISONER:

I don't think there is much proof that they did die that death.

HIS HONOUR:

In your case the law will be carried out by its officers. The gentlemen of the jury have done their duty. My duty will be to forward to the proper quarter the notes of your trial and to lay, as I am required to do, before the Executive any circumstances connected with your trial that may be required. I can hold out to you no hope. I do not see that I can entertain the slightest reason for saying you can expect anything. I desire to spare you any more pain, and I absolve myself from anything said willingly in any of my utterances that may have unnecessarily increased the agitation of your mind. I have now to pronounce your sentence.

His Honour then sentenced the prisoner to death in the usual form, ending with the usual words, "May the Lord have mercy on you soul".

THE PRISONER:

I will go a little further than that and say I will see you there where I go.

The court was cleared, and the prisoner was removed to the Melbourne Gaol.

The Kelly Trial – The Scene in Court

The Illustrated Australian News, 6 November 1880

It would be difficult to define the class of criminals to which this notorious bushranger can be said to belong. That he is out of the ordinary run of those who constitute the 'devil's regiment', there can be little doubt. Kelly is not necessarily a man of bloodthirstiness. He did not commit murder wantonly, as Morgan, Sullivan and other wretches are known to have done. He acted in accordance with the wild dictates of the savage who kills from a motive of revenge. He thought himself shamefully used. He believed that he and his family were ruthlessly hunted by the police. His lax notions on the subject of horse-stealing had led him into trouble, and made him a marked man. The police did no more perhaps than their duty in keeping the Kelly family under surveillance, but he considered that this was in order to goad him to desperation that the authorities might take advantage of his retaliatory acts and consign him to prison.

Probably the Kellys were no worse than the generality of the folks who had settled in Greta and the neighbourhood, but they had rendered themselves notorious for their ill-deeds and lawless character. It was therefore the bounden duty of the police to keep them in check, even to the extent of harassing them. There is nothing to show that Fitzpatrick, when he sought to arrest one of the brothers, had allowed his zeal to outstrip his discretion, and so far as can be gleaned he is in no way responsible for the outrage which led to the murders of the Wombat Ranges and the death of so many innocent people. Ned Kelly thought otherwise. He considered that he was the victim of an official vendetta, and he took measures accordingly. He took to the bush, shot the police sent in pursuit of him, robbed banks, and lived the life of an outlaw until finally brought to book. In no sense could he be regarded as a hero. That he did not die with his companions is difficult to explain, unless that at one period of the fatal night at Glenrowan he contemplated clearing away and subsequently altered his mind.

Again, he certainly robbed the corpse of poor Sergeant Kennedy, an act worthy only of the vilest sneak. At the same time he had never insulted or ill-used a woman. He was directly responsible for no murders except those of the unfortunate police and a supposed informer, whom he seemed to regard as fair game. And thus it was that he displayed so much coolness and indifference in the dock, although on trial for his life. He had long made up his mind to his fate, and trial by jury was a mere formality. Unlike Scott (Captain Moonlite), he preferred allowing counsel to conduct his case rather than appear inflated with a conceited notion of his ability to defend himself.

As he told the judge, he felt free from the consciousness of having been guilty of any crime except such as that arising from a desire to protect his own life. This, while it showed how utterly demoralised and depraved in mind he had become, explained the absence of all compunctious visitings during the recital of the evidence given by the witnesses. Owing to his early training in vice he had lost all notions of right and wrong, he was guided merely by the wild justice of revenge. It is, therefore, impossible to sympathise with him on any ground. He was nurtured in lawlessness and reared in crime, and as a fitting sequence he ends his career upon the gallows. He received all the consideration possible at the hands of the Crown, and those employed to conduct the prosecution.

No judge could hold the scales of justice more evenly, and with so much impartiality, as his Honour Mr Justice Barry, before whom the case was heard. Mr C. A. Smyth and Mr Chomley, who prosecuted, pushed no point beyond its natural bearing and Mr Bindon, the prisoner's counsel, and Mr Gaunson, his solicitor, exerted themselves on his behalf to the utmost. Under such circumstances Edward Kelly must indeed be a hardened ruffian if at the supreme moment he feels otherwise than convinced that he himself is alone responsible for the violent and ignominious death to which he has been condemned.

Death of Ned Kelly

The Argus, 8 November 1880

We regret, as will all right-thinking colonists, that His Excellency the Governor had to pass through the painful scene which was enacted at Government house on Saturday morning, and which, it seems, is to be repeated today, in connection with the condemned man Edward Kelly. For these proceedings we have to thank that gentleman whom the Legislative Assembly has lately chosen to honour with its confidence, for without Mr David Gaunson they would have been impossible. In every community great criminals elicit a curious and morbid sympathy. Morgan and Gilbert and the Clarkes, and the other members of the original Gardiner gang found a wretched mob in Sydney to throw up caps in their behalf. Jack Sheppard, the burglar, and Dick Turpin, the footpad, are heroes to audiences of the Little Bourke Street type to this day. What is generally wanting when an agitation on behalf of criminals is afoot, however, is some public man who will so far debase himself as to take the lead and give the ugly movement shape and form, and this office the Chairman of Committees has kindly consented to perform on the present occasion.

The public has been carefully led to believe that Mr Gaunson has obtained no fee so far. It is to be presumed that he was willing enough, when he undertook the work, to handle the bank notes of the culprit, how obtained, it is needless to particularise, but as the money has not been forthcoming, Mr Gaunson is now securing recompense for work and labour done in the shape of notoriety. It may be a capital advertisement to him in his future practice if it is understood that his functions begin where the task of other solicitors ends. Respectable members of the profession who have to defend a criminal are satisfied when they have obtained for their client a fair trial, but business may be pressed upon the man who lets it be known that he will head a mob agitation afterwards, and who, moreover, has a political position which he can prostitute for the purpose.

It is, no doubt, a misfortune that Mr Gaunson should have a position to abuse. The Kelly feeling had practically died out, and the wretched murderer might have gone quietly to the grave, and his history might have been speedily forgotten, if the Chairman of Committees had not worked up the demonstrations which have disgraced the city, and the direct effect of which must be to further confuse the Kelly class in their ideas of right and wrong. If other outrages occur a very serious responsibility will lie at the door of the agitator and as it is, there is a difficulty in pronouncing which is the worst enemy of society, the man who committed the murders or he who excuses them. Vanity and unscrupulousness are said to be the leading characteristics of the criminal who has been condemned by law, and certainly these would seem to be the leading features of the offender whose conduct has now to be pronounced upon by society.

Under ordinary circumstances petitioners for the reprieve of a prisoner are entitled to have every statement weighed, and the members of the Executive in such cases may naturally feel a doubt as to their duty. In the present case, however, hesitation on the part of Ministers would be unseemly. Kelly's life had been forfeited by law long before he was captured, for notorious crimes which admit of no justification. He was a thief, and when the police went to apprehend him on a serious charge, he laid in ambush for them and shot them down. The gang he headed afterwards trapped and murdered a man who was giving information to the officers of the law.

Kelly was captured in an attempt to decoy a large body of the police to sudden death. He tore up the rails in order to upset a train, and then he, being protected by armour, could with ease have shot any survivors. The bald recital of such crimes to which others can be added, is sufficient to excite a thrill of horror, and to prove that if Kelly is not hanged capital punishment must be abandoned once and for all. The Executive, however, has no authority to abrogate law in this manner. It can advise His Excellency to exercise the prerogative of mercy when reasons for mercy exist, but that is all, and in this case there is everything to aggravate and nothing to extenuate the crime. The murder of the police for revenge was accompanied by the plunder of the dead, and to this day the watch which the widow of Sergeant Kennedy desired as a memento of a brave and good man has been withheld. If a Government could reprieve Kelly it would naturally go on to disband the police, for it would have said that any criminal against whom a warrant is issued is at liberty to shoot his would-be apprehenders, and the state could hardly put its own officers into a position of that kind.

But the situation does not admit of serious discussion. The officers of justice are the servants of society they incur peril on our behalf, and they must be protected at all hazards. We cannot therefore but believe that the Ministry will today emulate the firmness of His Excellency the Governor, and will allow the petitioners to know at once that their request is not so much as to be listened to. The appearance of wavering would be a cause for regret. The agitation casts a stigma upon the population of Victoria, and the only way to remove the blot is for our rulers to rebuke the promoters, and, in so doing, to represent the whole community.

Some 200 persons of both sexes gathered on Saturday morning at the Town Hall for the purpose of accompanying the brothers Gaunson to Government House on behalf of the murderer, Edward Kelly. The crowd was, however, of a very nondescript character, and being apparently ashamed to travel in such company, the Gaunsons, along with Mr Hamilton, young Caulfield, and Kate Kelly, secretly left in a cab, and proceeded by themselves to Government House. His Excellency said that the resolution they had presented would be laid before the Executive at a meeting to be held today, but told them it would be deception on his part to hold out the faintest hope of a reprieve. In reply to Gaunson he also pointed out that it was no case for petitions. The Executive had come to their decision after due deliberation and care, and the law had to be carried out, otherwise the responsible authorities would have to answer to the country. In spite of this very plain speaking, the Gaunsons are still agitating. At the instance of Gaunsons' petitions were hawked about the town and suburbs yesterday, and their emissaries even intruded into church grounds, canvassing for signatures. At St. Patrick's Cathedral some of them were found obtaining signatures from a number of boys, and were ordered off. It is stated that this morning a deputation of 'ladies' will wait on His Excellency, and plead for Kelly's life.

IN HIS SPEECH AT THE MEETING HELD ON FRIDAY NIGHT IN CONNECTION WITH THE CONVICT KELLY, MR DAVID GAUNSON SAID:

> As to the pulling up of the rails at Glenrowan, the fact was that the prisoner had no intention of destroying the special train and its occupants, but actually arranged with Curnow to stop the train, with the view of capturing the police party.

UPON THIS THE *BALLARAT STAR* OF SATURDAY REMARKS:

> We yesterday spoke to Mr Curnow on the subject, and that gentleman informed us that the story of Kelly he narrated is a deliberate falsehood, and that there was no mention of the foolish idea of asking a train full of police to stop at the bidding of the scoundrel. On the contrary, Curnow was told to go home, and that if he said or did anything he would be shot, so that when he did stop the train he was in fear of a bullet at any moment from one or other of the outlaws, who, he believed, were watching him. The object of the convicts lying statement appears to be to discredit Curnow for the sake of revenge, and to minister to his own vanity in leading silly fools to believe that he (Kelly) was so much a power in the locality as to be in a

position by merely sending a messenger to stop a train full of constables. In reading any statement put forward by Kelly it should be remembered that he has lied notoriously on various occasions, and repeatedly contradicted his own tales. This last lie about Curnow in no way tallies with his previous narratives as to allowing the latter to go on the memorable night in question.

The Execution

The Argus, 12 November 1880

Immediately after sentence of death was passed on Kelly, additional precautions were taken to ensure his safe custody in the Melbourne Gaol. He was placed in one of the cells in the old wing, and irons were riveted upon his legs, leather pads being placed round his ankles to prevent chafing. The cell had two doors, an outer one of solid iron, and an inner one of iron bars. The outer door was always kept open, a lamp was kept burning overhead, and a warder was continually sitting outside watching the prisoner. During the day he was allowed to walk in the adjoining yard for exercise, and on these occasions two warders had him under surveillance. He continued to maintain his indifferent demeanour for a day or two, professing to look forward to his execution without fear but he was then evidently cherishing a hope of reprieve. When he could get anyone to speak to, he indulged in brag, recounting his exploits and boasting of what he could have done when at liberty had he pleased. Latterly, however, his talkativeness ceased, and he became morose and silent.

Within the last few days he dictated a number of letters for the Chief Secretary, in most of which he simply repeated his now well-known garbled version of his career and the spurious reasons he assigned for his crimes. He never however, expressed any sorrow for his crimes on the contrary, he always attempted to justify them. In his last communication he made a request that his body might be handed over to his friends an application that was necessarily in vain.

On Wednesday he was visited by his relatives and bade them farewell. At his own request his portrait was also taken for circulation amongst his friends. He went to bed at half-past one o'clock yesterday morning, and was very restless up to half-past two, when he fell asleep. At five o'clock he awoke and arose, and falling on his knees prayed for 20 minutes, and then lay down again. He rose finally at about eight o'clock, and at a quarter-to nine a blacksmith was called in to remove his irons.

The rivets having been knocked out, and his legs liberated, he was attended by Father Donaghy, the Roman Catholic clergyman of the gaol. Immediately afterwards, he was conducted from his cell in the old wing to the condemned cell alongside the gallows in the new or main building. In being thus removed, he had to walk through the garden which surrounds the hospital ward, and to pass the handcart in which his body was in another hour to be carried back to the dead-house. Making only a single remark about the pretty flowers in the garden, he passed in a jaunty manner from the brilliant sunshine into the sombre walls of the prison.

In the condemned cell the last rites of the Roman Catholic Church were administered to him by Father Donaghy and Dean O'Hea. In the meantime a large crowd of persons had commenced to gather in front of the gaol, and the persons who had received cards of admission assembled in the gaol yard. A few minutes before 10 o'clock, the hour fixed for the execution, Colonel Rede, the sheriff, and Mr Castieau, the Governor of the gaol, proceeded to the condenmed cell, followed by the persons who had been admitted. The latter numbered about 30, and included Superintendent Winch, Sub-Inspector Larner, several constables and detectives, three or four medical men, a number of justices of the peace, and the representatives of the press. The gallows is situated in the centre of the new wing, and consists simply of a beam of timber running across the transept over the first gallery, with rope attached and a trap-door in the gallery floor. Warders were arranged on the side galleries, and the onlookers stood on the basement floor in front of the drop. The convict had yet two minutes to live, but they soon flew away. The sheriff, preceded by the governor of the gaol, then ascended to the cell on the left hand side of the gallows, in which the condemned man had been placed, and demanded the body of Edward Kelly.

The governor asked for his warrant, and having received it, in due form bowed in acquiescence. The new hangman, an elderly grey-headed, well-conditioned looking man, named Upjohn, who is at present incarcerated for larceny, made his appearance at this juncture from the cell on the opposite side of the gallows, entered the doomed man's cell with the governor, and proceeded to pinion Kelly. At first Kelly objected to this operation, saying, "There is no need for tying me", but he had to submit, and his arms were pinioned behind by a strap above the elbows. He was then led out with a white cap on his head. He walked steadily on to the drop, but his face was livid, his jaunty air gone, and there was a frightened look in his eyes as he glanced down on the spectators.

It was his intention to make a speech, but his courage evidently failed him, and he merely said, "Ah, well, I suppose it has come to this", as the rope was being placed round his neck. He appeared as in court, with beard and whiskers, never having been shaved. The priests in their robes followed him out of the cell repeating prayers, and another official of the church stood in front of him with a crucifix. The noose having been adjusted, the white cap was pulled over his face, and the hangman stepping to the side quickly drew the bolt, and the wretched man had ceased to live. He had a drop of 8 feet, and hung suspended about 4 feet, from the basement floor. His neck was dislocated and death was instantaneous for although muscular twitching continued for a few minutes, he never made a struggle. It was all over by five minutes past 10 o'clock, and was one of the most expeditious executions ever performed in the Melbourne gaol.

Half an hour afterwards the body was lowered into the hospital cart, and taken to the dead-house. On removing the cap the face was found to be placid, and without any discolouration, and only a slight mark was left by the rope under the left ear. The eyes were wide open. The outside crowd had increased by 10 o'clock to about 4000 men, women and children, but a large proportion of them were larrikin-looking youths, and nearly all were of the lower orders. When the clock struck 10 the concourse raised their eyes simultaneously to the roof of the gaol expecting to see a black flag displayed but they looked in vain, for no intimation of the execution having taken place was given. One woman, as the hour struck, fell on her knees in front of the entrance, and prayed for the condemned man. As the visitors left the prison the crowd dispersed also, and no disturbance occurred.

An inquest was subsequently held upon the body, and the jury returned a verdict that deceased had been judicially hanged, and that the provisions of the act for the private execution of criminals had been properly carried out. The remains will be interred in the gaol yard this morning.

Death of Sir Redmond Barry

The Australian Town and Country Journal and *The Telegraph*, 27 November 1880

Sir Redmond Barry, Judge of the Victorian Supreme Court, died this morning at six o'clock. Although he had been unwell for a few days, still his death was quite unexpected. Sir Redmond Barry first became ill with a carbuncle in the neck on November 2nd, four days after sentencing Kelly to death. It will be recollected that when the late judge sentenced Kelly to death the latter said, "I will see you there where I go".

At first it was not thought serious, although painful, and the judge was confined to his house nearly ever since. He attended court on the 11th and 13th instant and also attended a meeting of the Council of the University on the 15th. The carbuncle after this assumed immense proportions and the case became serious.

Yesterday, however, deceased appeared much better and the latest bulletins last night were favourable. During the night, however, he collapsed, and died at six o'clock this morning.

News of his Honour's decease took the city by surprise. On every hand deep regret is expressed. The courts are not sitting today, as it is a public holiday. The city corporation flag and flags all over the city are being flown at half-mast.

Harbouring an Outlaw – The Court Case of Mrs Ann Jones

The Illustrated Australian News, 4 December 1880

Mrs Ann Jones, recently the proprietress of the Glenrowan Inn, where the desperate encounter with the police and the Kelly gang took place, was brought up at the Wangaratta police court on November 25th, before Mr Foster, P. M., on a charge of harbouring Edward Kelly. She knowing that at the time he had been guilty of the murder of Constable Lonigan. Mr Chomley, instructed by Mr Normoyle, of the Crown Solicitor's office, conducted the case for the Crown and the accused was defended by Mr J. Dwyer. The Crown Prosecuter, in opening the case, said "the prisoner was charged with being an accessory after the fact and he would prove first the prisoner's knowledge of the murders of the police and secondly, the fact of her harbouring Kelly and his companions, as well as expressing acquiescence in what Kelly did on the day previous to the encounter with the police at Glenrowan".

Evidence was then called and Constable McIntyre proved the murders and Detective Ward the fact of a conversation between himself and the prisoner subsequent to them, in which she referred to their commission and offered to give any information that she might obtain. James Reardon, the man who was compelled to pull up the railway line by the Kellys, stated that after going back to the stationmaster's house on the Sunday morning the prisoner invited Ned Kelly up to her house to have breakfast, and when someone remarked there was no room in the house, she replied there was plenty. During the night Dan Kelly offered to let Reardon's wife and other people leave, but Mrs Jones put a stop to it and said, "No one goes out of here until Ned Kelly gives them a lecture". She produced two keys, one of the front door she gave to Dan Kelly and the other of the back door she kept herself. After her remark about the people not being allowed to leave, she spoke to Ned Kelly and he cautioned Reardon and others against trying to leave.

When the police came in the morning and the firing commenced, she told the Kellys to leave and not to skulk inside when they had promised her to fight them hand to hand. Sullivan, the man who assisted Reardon in pulling up the rails, corroborated this evidence in its main points and further deposed that the prisoner and Byrne seemed to be on intimate terms, as she was trying to get a ring off his finger in a playful manner. After she gave Dan Kelly the key of the front door he locked it and she locked up the bar. Mrs Stanistreet, the wife of the then stationmaster at Glenrowan, detailed the circumstances of the place being stuck up by the Kellys and further stated that the prisoner had invited the Kellys to her place to breakfast and had told her daughter to go over and prepare it. Margaret Reardon, one of the incarcerated prisoners at Glenrowan, was examined as to the demeanour of the prisoner and was explicit in her statement that Mrs Jones had prevented the people leaving through her representations to Edward Kelly. She also stated to Byrne, when there was a remark made as to the scarcity of bread in the house, "I have plenty of bread, but I am keeping it for you".

John Delany, a resident of Greta, who was also a prisoner at the hotel, was examined. He had incurred the displeasure of the gang in someway and when he asked to be allowed to go home Mrs Jones said, "No, revenge is sweet and I would give 5s a head for some more Greta –". She was in and out with the gang all day and seemed to be on the most friendly terms with them, ordering her son to sing a poetical effusion in praise of the outlaws. She also told Delaney she would be glad if the gang stayed a week at her place, and when the police came up and began to fire she exclaimed, "This is that – Fitzpatrick's work". Edward Reynolds, another of those imprisoned by the gang, gave similar evidence and further stated that when he went out at the back door in the afternoon she told Ned Kelly to look out as he was going to escape. This last witness closed the evidence for the prosecution, and Mr Chomley asked that the prisoner should be committed. Mr Dwyer contended that no prima facie case had been made out, but that it was apparent Mrs Jones had been actuated by the same motives as the others and had done what she did in the hope of placating the outlaws. The bench decided to send the case to a higher court and committed the prisoner to take her trial at the next court of assize to be held at Beechworth. Bail was allowed, the prisoner in £100 and one surety of £100, the police authorities consenting to accept the prisoner's son as surety.

The Story of My Fight with Ned Kelly

The Euroa Advertiser, 21 January 1910

THE STORY OF MY FIGHT WITH NED KELLY BY SERGEANT STEELE:

On Sunday, 27th June 1880, I was informed of the shooting of Aaron Sherritt at Woolshed Creek, and on that night I posted the men in my charge at various bridges and crossings in the neighborhood of Wangaratta. I received orders from Superintendent Sadlier on Sunday night to report the state of things in my district, and it was for the purpose of sending a telegram to that officer that I went to Wangaratta telegraph office shortly after midnight. Different stations were then reporting, and I sent my telegram at two a.m., stating that all was quiet. As I was about to leave, the postmaster told me to wait, as a telegram was arriving for me, but it transpired that it was for Superintendent Hare, who was expected by special train on his way to Beechworth with a party of police and blacktrackers. The telegram was given to the operator to deliver to Superintendent Hare at the railway station, but as we heard a train arriving just then, I accompanied him to the station, where we found that it was not the police train, but an engine that had come from Beechworth to take the train from Wangaratta. At my instance the stationmaster asked Benalla what time the police train had left, and as it was discovered that it was due. I became somewhat anxious, and the stationmaster and I walked a quarter of a mile or so along the line towards Glenrowan.

The night was beautifully clear and frosty, and by listening intently I could hear the volley firing in the direction of Glenrowan, though the stationmaster was sceptical for a time. Further firing shortly afterwards convinced us, and I hurried back to the railway station and sent a telegram to Superintendent Sadlier, telling him that there was heavy firing at Glenrowan and that I was starting from Wangaratta with all available men, and advising him to reinforce from Benalla, and await news at the telegraph office. As I was leaving the railway station the driver of the Beechworth engine called to me that he heard a horseman galloping along the line, but I could not hear it until, at the driver's request, I got on to the footplate. The noise of the horse's feet clattering along the sleepers some miles along the line towards Glenrowan could be then heard distinctly, and I immediately hurried to meet him. I had walked nearly a mile before we met, and then I discovered that the horseman was Constable Bracken, who told me in a few excited sentences that the Kellys had stuck up the police train, had wounded Superintendent Hare in the wrist, torn up the rails on a curve near Glenrowan, and that the outlaws were wearing tin cans on their head. Asking Bracken to dismount I got into his saddle and galloped back to the township, and, after telegraphing to Superintendent Sadlier what Bracken told me, received a reply "Superintendent Hare just arrived, not seriously injured". I got my men together, and we started for Glenrowan at a gallop.

There were six of us in the party, and we did not draw rein for the 10 miles until we arrived at a railway crossing half a mile from Glenrowan township. Here we hung up our horses to saplings, and proceeded on foot towards Mrs Jones's hotel. The moon was then within an hour or so of setting, but in the long shadows cast by the hills, etc, surrounding the town we could see the outline of the building while still some distance away. There was no light in the house, and everything was calm, no sound being heard save a whispered remark or our own footsteps, as we stealthily marched in single file. We were approaching the hotel when a voice challenged us and replying "Wangaratta police", Senior Constable Kelly, who it was had spoken, ejaculated "Good boys!" Senior Constable Kelly, with Constables Phillips and Arthur, were three of Superintendent Hare's party, and were keeping sentry, with the protection of a log, until daylight. In reply to my questions Kelly told me that there was no one nearer to the hotel than he and his companions were, and I suggested getting closer to prevent a possible escape of the outlaws, but he thought there was a sure chance of someone being shot, and he showed me a rifle with blood on it, indicating that someone had already been wounded.

The moon had got very low by this time, and, as it was a bad light, I said I would take up a position behind a tree that stood about 10 yards from the back door of the hotel premises. I reached the tree safely, by making a zigzag course, but everything was quiet inside the hotel for 25 or 30 minutes. I then heard a train approaching from the direction of Benalla, and at the same time there began a great commotion in the house, a rattling of iron plates, and a lot of talking. The train contained Superintendent Sadlier's party, and as the men were leaving the carriages the outlaws came on to the front verandah of the hotel and fired frequently at them. I could not see the figures owing to an obstructing chimney at the side of the house, but the flashes of the rifles were visible. There were answering shots from the police in various directions.

About this time a woman came to the back door of the hotel and cried out, "For God's sake, don't shoot me! Let me go!"

I told her to come towards me and she would not be molested, and she returned to the house for a minute or less. When she reappeared, she said, "For God's sake, don't shoot me and my child!" and ran towards the tree which was sheltering me. I showed her the direction in which to go, and she walked away towards the railway station. Just as she passed me I noticed the figure of what appeared to be a man crawling along a water channel at the back door of the hotel, and I called to him to throw up his hands or I would shoot. I repeated this two or three times, but the figure continued to crawl away as if attempting to flank me behind the tree, and as no notice was taken of my warnings, I fired. The man did not speak even then, but he returned to the door, and as he was approaching it, still on his hands and knees, I fired again. It was in this way that the civilian, Mr Reardon, received his wound, but it can be understood how, through suspicious movements in the darkness, and by neglect of oft-repeated warnings to declare his inoffensiveness, he was injured. When Reardon regained the house I heard Dan Kelly call out, "You dogs!" for I knew his voice well, and I replied to him that he and his mates might as well surrender, as it was all over with them. There was a quiet spell for a while, but shooting was resumed by the police with much more vigour than before, and several bullets hit the tree behind which I was standing, the position becoming so dangerous that I lay down for a time. The shooting once more slackened, however, and there was only an odd shot fired until daybreak.

Some time after daybreak, and before the sun appeared, I heard some disturbance behind me, and in the dim light I could see the figure of a man approaching. I heard someone call to him, "Don't come down here, you fool, or you'll be shot!", but he came walking quietly along. Then a constable cried out, "Look out! It is one of the beggars, and he is covered with iron", and then there were several shots at once fired at him. He was then 150 yards or so from me, and in the dull light I was at first convinced that the man was Tommy Reid, a well known district blackfellow. The figure was exactly like his at the distance in that half-light, a tall man, with a blanket round his shoulders, and thin, black legs. I called out, therefore, to men in my vicinity to be careful with their shooting, but the deception became apparent as the outlaw, for it was Ned Kelly, came closer, and what I had thought was the blackfellow's blanket was a fawn-coloured cape or cloak, and black strappings on a pair of grey trousers had given the appearance of the thin, black legs.

How We Captured Ned Kelly

The Euroa Advertiser, 11 March 1910

BY EX-SERGEANT JAMES O'DWYER:

It was a remark made by Aaron Sherritt to a mounted constable, on Thursday night, between eight and nine o'clock, June 24th, 1880, which led to the capture and destruction of the Kelly gang at Glenrowan four days after. Sherritt lived with his mother in a small weatherboard house at the Sebastopol Creek, near Beechworth; and, though in the pay of the Government (receiving 10/- per day from Captain Standish to find out the haunts of the Kelly gang) was doing more to baffle the police in the interests of the Kelly gang. The mounted constable referred to was sure that Sherritt knew where the gang were hiding, if he could only get him to open his mouth and for this purpose visited several hotels, treating Sherritt to drinks. It was about nine p.m. both entered a certain hotel on the Chiltern road, in the suburb of Beechworth, and as they entered, the barmaid, for whom Sherritt had an affectionate regard, was leaning on her elbows on the counter, talking to a miner, their heads close together. Sherritt, stung by jealousy, remarked to the constable as they took their seats at the other end of the counter. "That girl often sees Joe Byrne", "When?" "Every Saturday night". "Are you sure?" "Well, I heard so". He said nothing more when Maggie came to them and asked what they would have. After the constable left Sherritt, he went back again and questioned Maggie about her seeing Joe Byrne. To this she answered "The devil a man could have told you that but Sherritt. I suppose he told you that a while ago here". "No, he did not", the constable replied. "Oh, yes, I know he must have, and somebody else will know soon, too." So that when Joe Byrne met her on the Saturday night, at the usual meeting place, Maggie, who regularly brought all the daily papers, told him of the incident in the hotel, and how Sherritt had betrayed him. This led to the attack on Sherritt and his murder.

The hiding place of the gang was an old mining shaft, 25 feet deep, from which ran a drive 30 feet long by 12 feet eight inches wide. It was 100 yards from a junction of three roads to Chiltern, Yackandandah and Kiewa, 11 miles from Beechworth. This was the hiding place of the gang for the year and 10 months that they were bushranging. It was when on his trial, sitting on a seat beside the dock in the old Supreme Court, waiting for Sir Redmond Barry, the Chief Justice, at the lunch hour, that Ned told me of this hiding place and other incidents. I said, "Why didn't you tell me of all this at Glenrowan?" "Because there was as much provision there as would do 10 men, and I did not want you to have it", Ned answered. On Saturday night, and at about the very time Aaron Sherritt was shot, I was in company with Sergeant Steele at the Wangaratta railway station, attending to the arrival and departure of trains. Sergeant Steele pointed out a good many of the Kelly sympathisers who were on the station, telling me who they were and what they had done. That night, while in bed, I was dreaming of the Kelly gang. I dreamt of Ned and the very clothes he wore, which I subsequently found to be correct. It was at 1.25 p.m., when Mr John Hall, telegraph operator, received a wire from Beechworth. "Information Kelly gang. Get Sergeant Steele". I met him hurrying out, and he exclaimed "O'Dwyer, your dream has come true". We got Sergeant Steele, and Hall wired, "Sergeant Steele is here". Detective Ward, who was at the Beechworth end, replied. "Watch party at Aaron Sherritt's house stuck up last night. One man shot".

It was 1.40 p.m. when Sergeant Steele sent the message to Captain Standish, and arrangements were made for a special train to leave Melbourne that night. Steele also wired to Superintendent Sadlier at Benalla, after which he sent every constable on the station out to guard all the different crossings over the Ovens River. My place of guard was the railway bridge over the river at the Wangaratta railway station. I remained thereon all night, and at 3.40 a.m. Mounted Constable Moore rode down to me, telling me of Bracken's escape, and that the Kellys were at Glenrowan. Even at that distance, Moore and myself could hear firing going on. I hurried up to the police station, and there saw all the others in bustle and excitement, saddling up and getting ready. Steele came into my room with Bracken, and said that Bracken should have my horse to ride back with them to Glenrowan, as the one he brought with him was completely done up. "And how am I to go", said I, "You will go in the pilot engine brought down from Beechworth for Superintendent Hare's train. Mr Marsden (Clerk of Petty Sessions, and Constable Walsh will be with you. Constable Kane will have to remain to look after the station". "I'll make that engine-driver drive quickly, to be there before you", I said, and so we were, though it took Steele and the men only 35 minutes to go the 11 miles from Wangaratta to Glenrowan.

As Mr Morgan, engine-driver, and his fireman, Dowsett, Marsden, Walsh and myself, on the engine, approached at a rapid pace, we saw in the distance of half a mile a red light, and approaching towards us on the line. Morgan slowed down. The person who held the light was found to be Mr Rawlings, an auctioneer, of Benalla, who volunteered with Superintendent Hare's party. All of us then, but Morgan, who remained with his engine, walked down the line to the station, where we were met by the reporters who had come up from Melbourne. It was at this very moment 5.10 a.m. that the whistle of another train sounded. We looked down the line and saw the train coming slowly into the station. "Here is Superintendent Sadlier and his reinforcement", said one of the reporters. Turning round to his men who had clustered round us, Superintendent Sadlier said, "Now, men, I want you to spread yourself round the hotel, and be sure to let no person pass you. And when you are walking up to it, walk three yards apart from each other, so as that you will not be a target for the Kellys to fire at you. Come, you, O'Dwyer, with me".

As we got round to the east side of the hotel we were challenged by Constable John Milne. He was one of Superintendent Hare's party and was walking alongside Superintendent Hare when he was shot. "It's all right, Milne," said Superintendent Sadlier, and just then he got sight of Sub-Inspector O'Connor and his men in the trench. As both of us walked towards Sub-Inspector O'Connor the bullets from two of the gang standing at the front window of the hotel whizzed over our heads. O'Connor said, "Jump down, Sadlier". Superintendent Sadlier commenced to question O'Connor as to what was done up to that time. "Let us give them a volley", he then said, placing his rifle on the bank, and fired at one of the gang standing at the window inside. The trackers, Kirkham and myself did the same, as also all the men surrounding the hotel, about 27 men all told. The hills around echoed back the sound of the volley firing, and as the women in the hotel commenced to scream. "Oh, there are women inside", Superintendent Sadlier said. "I believe it is full of them", was the answer. "Then, if it is, we must cease firing", and he ordered me to pass the word round. As I went along to the men I heard Superintendent Sadlier calling out in a loud tone, "All you innocent people come out at once and you will not be molested". As I went round I found that a good many of the men had only from three to four rounds of ammunition, and asked me to bring them some.

When we got back again to Superintendent Sadlier, I told him of the shortness of the ammunition with some of the men, and taking his book out, he scribbled a message for me to take to the station and wire to Benalla for the ammunition to be sent at once and also refreshments for the men. As I got up on the bank, the whizz of a bullet knocked my hat off. The officers both shot at the man who fired from the hotel at me. It was at that time Byrne, one of the outlaws, was shot. Two hours after, I was informed by Mr Reynolds, the Glenrowan postmaster, who was one of the prisoners in the hotel, that Byrne, standing at the window, saw me leave the trench and fired at me, after which he turned to the bar, and filled a glass up with brandy, and was just reseating with his back to the counter, "Here is to many happy more days in the bush with the Kelly gang". While the glass was to his lips, the bullet struck him, and the blood ran from him and fell on the shoulder and body of Mr Reynolds and Mr Reardon, a plate-layer on the line, as they lay on the floor, under a sofa close to the window from which Byrne fired his last shot at me. At this time it was not clear daylight. Ned Kelly stole away from the hotel by the back, and in doing so dropped his Winchester rifle that he took from Constable Scanlon at the time of the murder of the police. Ned walked a couple of hundred yards away from the hotel, and lay down under a large fallen log. Just then, some constables of the Wangaratta contingent, were walking up to the back of the hotel from the railway line.

Ned's armour, which he had on, rattled, which caused the police to stand, one of the constables asked, "What noise was that?" "Oh, it must be the noise of the horse's hobbles", replied another. Ned Kelly, in relating this incident to Superintendent Sadlier and myself as he lay on the couch in Mr Stanistreet's office afterwards, laughed, saying that he could have pinched on of the constables legs at the time.

When I returned to the platform after sending the telegram, one of the reporters pointed to Ned Kelly as he stood, firing at the constables around him. I hurried across the line and over the railway fence. A constable was behind a large tree close to the fence, and said, as I got over, "There is Ned Kelly". As I ran towards Ned, who was about 60 yards in front of me, I heard someone say, "Boys, let us rush him". Someone behind me cried "Look out, O'Dwyer he has you covered", and, looking, I saw Ned Kelly with revolver pointed straight at my face. I turned my head to the left shoulder as the bullet whizzed by my right ear. While Ned Kelly turned to fire at me I was running upon him. Sergeant Steele, who was only 15 yards from Ned, shot him in the thigh with a charge of small duck-shot, and Ned Kelly was just falling to the ground, wounded, as Steele, Senior Constable Kelly, Montford and myself and Dowsett were on him. As Kelly was falling he tried to turn his revolver on Sergeant Steele. Steele seized his wrist and took the revolver from him. It was that moment that Dowsett, the fireman on Mr Morgan's engine, came up and took possession of Ned Kelly's revolver. While Steele was struggling with Ned Kelly for the revolver, I took the iron helmet off his head. Steele said, "Well, Kelly, I have got you at last". "Yes, Steele", Ned replied. "Don't let them kill me. I never shot or injured one of you". "You tried hard to do so, just now your last shot whizzed by my ear", I answered.

I was, at the time, on one knee, undoing the leather straps holding the armour on, as Doctor Nicholson, Rawlings and one of the reporters came up. Ned smiled when the doctor stooped down to examine his wounds, "This is the first time you had me a patient, doctor", he said. "Why don't the police use bullets instead of duck-shot? It was your shot, Steele, that done me". As Ned was carried down to the station, I returned to Superintendent Sadlier, and reported Ned Kelly's capture. "Are you sure?" "Yes, and I have reason to know as it was his last shot that whizzed by my ear. And there, too, sir, is the mark of his blood on my trousers".

When I went into the stationmaster's office, where Ned Kelly was, I said, "Will you have a nip of brandy, Ned?". "Yes, please, if you'll give it to me". "Certainly, why shouldn't I?". I answered. "Put it to my lips, I cannot take it in my hand". As I was taking the glass from his lips, some of the brandy fell on his long, brown-coloured beard and, looking up, he said, "Give me a bit of bread I am very hungry". Superintendent Sadlier, sitting on a chair at the foot of the couch, said, "Yes, Ned, you shall have every care and attention, and get anything you want".

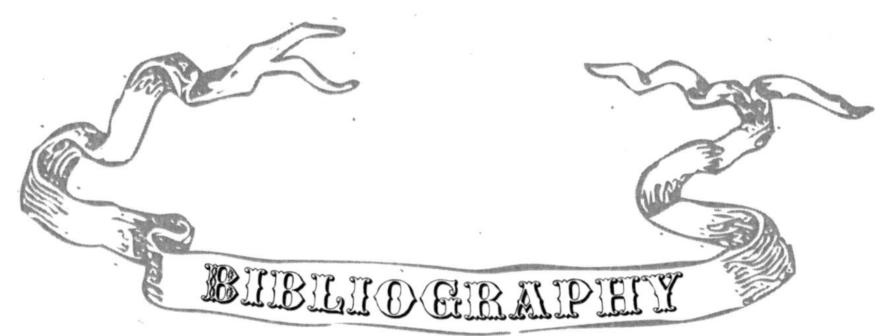

All of the newspaper articles included in this book have been compiled and edited from The National Library of Australia Trove Website.

A Juvenile Bushranger, *The Argus*, 22 October 1869, p. 2

Another Cold-Blooded Murder – The Killing of Aaron Sherritt, *The Australasian Sketcher with Pen and Pencil*, 3 July 1880, p. 150

A Search Party in the Wombat Ranges, *The Illustrated Australian News*, 21 February 1879, p. 21. State Library of Victoria.

A Search Party in the Wombat Ranges, *The Illustrated Australian News*, 21 February 1879, p. 26

A Strange Apparition Ned Kelly's Fight and Capture, *The Illustrated Australian News*, 17 July 1880, p. 120. State Library of Victoria.

Atrocious Murders by Bushrangers, *The Argus*, 29 October 1878, p. 5

Benalla Police Court, *The Benalla Ensign and Farmer's and Squatter's Journal*, 22 October 1869, p. 3

Benalla Police Court, *The Benalla Ensign and Farmer's and Squatter's Journal*, 29 October 1869, p. 2

Benalla Police Court Crowded, *The Benalla Ensign and Farmer's and Squatter's Journal*, 13 May 1870, p.2

Bird's Eye View of Glenrowan, *The Illustrated Australian News*, 17 July 1880, p. 116. State Library of Victoria.

Bushranging in Victoria Two Constables Shot and a Sergeant Missing, *The Argus*, p. 5

Country News, *The Argus*, 6 June 1870, p. 1

Current Topics, *The Geelong Advertiser*, 5 May 1870, p. 2

Daring Outrage by the Kelly Gang of Bushrangers, *The Australasian Sketcher with Pen and Pencil,* 21 December 1878, p. 155

Death of Ned Kelly, *The Argus*, 8 November 1880, p. 4.

Death of Sir Redmond Barry, *The Australian Town and Country Journal,* 27 November 1880, p. 10; *The Telegraph*, 23 November 1880, p. 2

Destruction of the Kelly, *The Illustrated Australian News*, 3 July 1880, p. 103–06

Destruction of the Kelly Gang, *The Argus*, 29 June 1880, p. 5

Destruction of the Kelly Gang, *The Argus*, 2 July 1880, p. 7

Destruction of the Kelly Gang, *The Argus*, 30 June 1880, p. 6

Destruction of the Kelly Gang, *The Australasian Sketcher with Pen and Pencil*, 31 July 1880, p. 183

Destruction of the Kelly Gang, *The Australasian Sketcher with Pen and Pencil,* 3 July 1880, p. 152. State Library of Victoria.

Destruction of the Kelly Gang – Interior of the Press Carriage of the Police Special Train, *The Australasian Sketcher with Pen and Pencil*, 31 July 1880, p. 189

Destruction of the Kelly Gang – Stopping the Special Train, *The Australasian Sketcher with Pen and Pencil,* 31 July 1880, p. 177. State Library of Victoria.

Edward Kelly in the Hospital of the Melbourne Gaol, *The Illustrated Australian News*, 17 July 1880, p. 117. State Library of Victoria.

Edward Kelly on Remand, *The Benalla Ensign and Farmer's and Squatter's Journal*, p. 3

Extermination of the Kelly Gang, *The Illustrated Australian News*, 17 July 1880, p. 113. State Library of Victoria.

Finding Byrne's Body and the Capture of Ned Kelly, *The Illustrated Australian News*, 3 July 1880, p. 105

Further Outrages by the Kelly Gang, *The Geelong Advertiser*, 12 December 1878, p. 3

Harbouring an Outlaw – The Court Case of Mrs Ann Jones, *The Illustrated Australian News*, 4 December 1880, p. 231

Horse Stealing Charge, *The Benalla Ensign and Farmer's and Squatter's Journal*, 29 April 1871, p. 2

How We Captured Ned Kelly, *The Euroa Advertiser*, 11 March 1910, p. 6

Incidents Sketched at Glenrowan & Ned Kelly's Arrival in Melbourne, *The Illustrated Australian News*, 3 July 1880, p. 100. State Library of Victoria.

Kelly on Remand, *The Benalla Ensign and Farmer's and Squatter's Journal,* 19 October 1869, p. 3

Latest Telegrams, *The Geelong Advertiser*, 6 May 1870, p. 2

Law Notices, *The Argus*, 30 May 1870, p. 5

Murderous Attack on a Constable, *The Argus*, 22 April 1878, p. 3

Ned Kelly at Bay, *The Australasian Sketcher with Pen and Pencil,* 3 July 1880, p. 145. State Library of Victoria.

Ned Kelly in the Dock - A Sketch from Life, *The Illustrated Australian News*, 28 August 1880, p. 1. State Library of Victoria.

Ned Kelly the Bushranger, *The Australasian Sketcher with Pen and Pencil*, 31 July 1880, p. 184. State Library of Victoria.

Ned Kelly's Boot!, *The Kerang Times and Swan Hill Gazette*, 23 July 1880, p. 4

Ned Kelly's Trial, *The Kilmore Free Press*, 12 August 1880, p. 4

Never Taken Alive, *The Argus*, 30 October 1878, p. 6

Night Attack on the Glenrown Hotel, *The Australasian Sketcher with Pen and Pencil*, 3 July 1880, p. 153. State Library of Victoria.

Our Illustrations, *The Illustrated Australian News*, 28 August 1880, p. 154

Outlaws in Camp, *The Australasian Sketcher with Pen and Pencil*, 21 December 1878, p. 145

Portraits, *The Illustrated Australian News*, 3 July 1880, p. 101. State Library of Victoria.

Power Recruiting Bushrangers, *The Argus*, 5 May 1870, p. 4

Reward for Constable Hall, *The Benalla Ensign and Farmer's and Squatter's Journal*, 19 August 1871, p. 2

Reward for the Apprehension of Edward Kelly, *The Argus*, 4 May 1878, p. 8

Robbery, *The Argus*, 7 May 1878, p. 5

Sketches During the Trial, *The Illustrated Australian News*, 28 August 1880, p. 153. State Library of Victoria.

The Beechworth Police Court During the Trial, *The Illustrated Australian News*, 28 August 1880, p. 152. State Library of Victoria.

The Bushranging Tragedy Scenes and Incidents, *The Australasian Sketcher with Pen and Pencil*, 21 December 1878, p. 149. State Library of Victoria.

The Chronicle, *Williamstown Chronicle*, 2 November 1878, p. 2

The Destruction of the Kelly Gang, *The Argus*, 5 July 1880, p. 6

The Execution, *The Argus*, 12 November 1880, p. 6.

The Fight Between Constable Hall and Kelly, *The Argus*, 2 May 1871, p. 7

The Greta Outrage, *The Argus*, 22 May 1878, p. 10

The Kelly Bushrangers at Jerilderie, *The Illustrated Australian News*, 21 February 1879, p. 26

The Kelly Hunters, *The Illustrated Australian News*, 17 July 1880, p. 121. State Library of Victoria.

The Kelly Outrages at Euroa – Bank Robbery at Euroa, *The Illustrated Australian News*, 27 December 1878, p. 219

The Kellys at Euroa, *The Illustrated Australian News*, 27 December 1878, p. 216. State Libray of Victoria

The Kelly Tragedy, *The Illustrated Sydney News and New South Wales Agriculturalist and Grazier*, 5 August 1880, p. 1 Supplement. State Library of Victoria.

The Kelly Trial – The Scene in Court, *The Illustrated Australian News*, 6 November 1880, p. 202

The Kelly's Visit to the Police Station Jerilderie N.S.W., *The Illustrated Australian News*, 21 February 1879, p. 17. State Library of Victoria.

The Mansfield Bushrangers, *The Bendigo Advertiser*, 2 November 1878, p. 3

The Mansfield Bushrangers, *The Bendigo Advertiser*, 4 November 1878, p. 3

The Mansfield Murderers, *The Argus*, 17 December 1878, p. 6

The Mansfield Murderers, *The Argus*, 18 December 1878, p. 6

The Mansfield Murderers, *The Bendigo Advertiser*, 30 October 1878, p. 2

The Murder of Sherritt, *The Illustrated Australian News*, 3 July 1880, p. 97. State Library of Victoria.

The Murders, *The Gippsland Times*, 1 November 1878, p. 3

The Outlaws at Bay – Scene of the Attack on Jones's Hotel at Glenrowan, *The Illustrated Australian News*, 3 July 1880, p. 104. State Library of Victoria

The Police Murders, *The Argus*, 12 November 1878, p. 5

The Police Murders, *The Argus*, 15 November 1878, p. 6

The Police Murders, *The Argus*, 18 November 1878, p. 5

The Police Murders, *The Argus*, 30 October 1878, p. 6

The Police Murders, *The Argus*, 4 November 1878, p. 6

The Police Murders, *The Argus*, 5 November 1878, p. 6

The Police Murders - Supposed Traces of The Kelly Gang, *The Argus*, 2 November 1878, p. 8

The Police Murders Finding of Sergeant Kennedy's Body, *The Argus*, 1 November 1878, p. 6

The Police Tragedy, *The Geelong Advertiser*, 30 October 1878, p. 4

The Story of my Fight with Ned Kelly, *The Euroa Advertiser*, 21 January 1910, p. 6

The Trial of Edward Kelly, *The Argus*, 20 September 1880, p. 7.

Trial and Conviction of Edward Kelly – Sentence of Death, *The Argus*, 30 October 1880, p. 8

Wangaratta Despatch Country News, *The Argus*, 8 May 1871, p. 6

Wangaratta Police Court, *The Argus*, 14 November 1870, p. 7